Allow Me to Live My Grief ...

and Heal from the Inside Out

———— Ligia M. Houben ————

Allow Me to Live my Grief... and Heal from the Inside out.
© Ligia M. Houben
   info@ligiahouben.com
ISBN: 978-0-9857589-6-7
Total or partial reproduction by any means or method is prohibited without the written authorization of the copyright holders..
All rights reserved.

My Meaningful Life, LLC

Text proofreading and editing:
   Abby Hale

Cover design and realization:
   Andrej Semnic
   semnitz@gmail.com

Interior formatting and composition:
   Daiana Morales

Validations

I had the privilege of meeting Ligia Houben in 2012 at one of the ADEC conferences[1]. It was one of those divine meetings that came to bless your life! Since then, we have had many opportunities to share our experiences as thanatologists or educate our Hispanic community in the United States on the topic of grief.

Ligia is diaphanous and genuine, and that is reflected in this new book where, once again, she opens her heart to us and shares with us her personal experiences of grief to help us understand our own. In addition, her vast knowledge of the subject allows her to provide us with valuable and useful information for those of us who daily cope with the physical absence of our loved ones.

Allow Me to Live My Grief is a book every griever, counselor, student, teacher, and religious leader needs to read. Acquiring it will be an invaluable investment!

Mateo Gómez
Certified Thanatologist Grief Counselor at Forest Lawn Cemeteries

---

[1] Association for Death Education and Counseling.

Allow Me to Live My Grief by Ligia M. Houben is a loving narrative based on her personal experiences of loss. As a thanatologist and counselor, she presents her personal experiences in combination with her professional experiences with her clients, thus creating a vital companion guide for anyone experiencing grief and needing support in their life journey. This book is so valuable for the bereaved because it is accompanied by guidelines, questions, and recommendations from the author, thus helping the bereaved transform their grief into personal and spiritual growth. I highly recommend this book not only to those who find themselves experiencing a loss but also to counselors looking for more information and inspiration in the field of loss and grief. Excellent work, Ligia!

ANA P. BENDAÑA, Thanatologist
and Registered Nurse with a specialty
in hospice and palliative care

You have in your hands a book that will make you feel accompanied in your grieving process in a sweet, honest, and compassionate way, just as the author knows how to do. Ligia lovingly guides you to face your pain head-on, to accept it, and embrace it. Here, you will clearly understand the natural process of a great loss and obtain valuable and reflective tools to face it. Her story touched my heart because, like her, I lost my mother and reconfirmed that when they are gone, their legacy flourishes among us.

NADIA VADO,
Author and Speaker

Dear Ligia:

Reading your writings on profound transformation, I have felt a surprising peace and inner openness. It could be said that you have the gift, virtue, and wisdom to transmit what you feel. The way of reaching, of accepting, of living, you teach it as if you had been a companion during that process.

Your teaching abilities and your sweetness of expression have made your book my favorite. It is a work that should be known to many of us who work in health, as well as to all who cultivate the culture of life and the loss of yesterday, today, and tomorrow.

I can only wish that the light of success and teaching continues to shine on your path.

A double hug to you and your mom in Heaven. Thanks for having put you on our path.

Dr. María Berenguel Cook, Founder and President of the Peruvian Society of Palliative Care. Former President of the Latin American Association of Palliative Care

As a beautiful tribute to the memory of her dear mother, Ligia Houben gives us in this opportunity the experiences of her grieving process, by opening the windows of her heart and sharing from the depths of her being and, in a personal way, her testimony of grief. At the same time, she interweaves her vast professional knowledge in the field as a thanatologist and specialist in life transition issues, which makes this book also a work of support for bereaved people. The life testimonials and personal stories of grief and transformation seal this delivery to readers with valuable resources and tools for coping with and transforming their grief.

ORALÍ FLORES, Founding Member of the PUDE[2] Association. Certified Facilitator in Ligia Houben's 11 Principles of Transformation® and ICC Certified Coach

Years ago, I lost my parents in a period of little more than a month. It was then that Ligia Houben unexpectedly appeared in my life.

Ligia came to me on recommended by someone who had mentioned my recent loss to her. She had me start writing without me realizing that she was guiding me to transform my loss with her 11 Principles interwoven in the form of questions that I, in turn, developed through tears. Not only did I express my pain in writing but also through tears... I embraced my sorrow; I lived my grief.

Embracing grief, sorrows, and losses—whatever they may be—has taught me to recognize and grow.

Years later, Ligia, the professional on the subject, the one who knows how to make us live and face our grief, finds herself facing an immense loss, and, of course, she not only has to transform it but also see beyond that—something she perfected after the loss of her father and many years of study and work as a professional—to grow even more at this age and accept that we are never really prepared for loss. This book will help the reader to see it and understand it, in the same way it helped Ligia with her own healing.

---

2 People United in Pain and Hope.

I could see Ligia's love for her beloved mother and could see the sorrow that was approaching her. Her mother was already 100 years old, and that, just like in my case, when I lost my mom at the age of ninety-seven, gave her more time to love and enjoy her. Even though they always told us, "Do not cry. Think of the many years you had her." Yes, many years to learn to love her more and better. The common thread, the common denominator between Ligia and me, is, and always will be, our beloved mothers.

The questions, stories, and testimonies you will read here will help you face, process, live, accept, and see that we are not alone in the face of such great sorrows. With my heart in my hand, I recommend this book, which, among other elements, also helps to identify primary and secondary loss, as Ligia clearly explains here. You will identify, in the same way, other losses and grief that we are not even aware we are living, as well as the elaboration, the importance, and the different stages of them. This book helps to recognize, process, and let go of grief.

To conclude, I tell you that for me "signs" do exist (you will read about this, too). In this case, this is one of those indisputable signs why Ligia asked me to write something here... Thank you, Ligia, for the privilege.

I recommend that you immerse yourself in this book, which, in turn, will make you immerse yourself in your own self.

Marily A. Reyes,
President and CEO,
The Cove/Rincón

This book is dedicated to the memory of my mother,
Alicia Gallegos de Martínez,
and to all the people who have suffered the loss of a
loved one, who will continue to live forever in
our hearts, for love is eternal.

I thank God for the mother He gave me, for the love I feel for her inspired me to write this book. My gratitude is extended to my family, whom I love so much and who have witnessed my healing as I have lived through my grief. I want to thank my husband Mario for his support with the cover design, my daughter Diana for her help, and my sister Marielena for her constant support when working on this book.

I feel infinite gratitude for each person who, with their heart in their hand, shared their story of loss. The value of their contribution is immeasurable and touches the fibers of our hearts.

I thank Abby Hale and Daiana Morales for their guidance and help in proofreading, editing, and creating this book. I also want to thank the editors of my original book in Spanish because they are very special to me, as they have worked on my last four books. It began with Alfredo Sainz Blanco, who was the editor of my book *Transforma tu pérdida. Una antología de fortaleza y esperanza*. Later, he and Magaly Perez worked together on the biographies of my parents. I am infinitely grateful to them for having carried out my dream once again with the Spanish version of this book.

Finally, I thank you, dear reader, because you are allowing me to enter your heart and accompany you in these moments. Writing a book is a process in which we bear our soul, and with my soul in my hand, I thank you.

Important Notice

The information contained in this book is based on my personal and professional experience. At no time does it replace the help of a professional. If you feel that your grief is stronger than you are, seek help as soon as possible.

The stories shared here are real. With the exception of some cases, the names have been changed to protect the confidentiality of my clients.

A Gift for the Reader

You can access your free *Companion Workbook* through the following link: ligiahouben.com/workbook

Index

Foreword ... 19

Preface ... 23

Introduction ... 25

Live Your Grief ... 31

Sharing My Wounded Heart ... 35

It Takes Just a Moment ... 41

Are We "Really" Prepared? ... 45

The Morning After ... 53

In the Early Days, I Was in Another Dimension ... 63

Welcoming Peace into My heart ... 69

What Will Your Change Look Like? ... 75

Loss of Identity ... 83

Accepting the Loss ... 87

A Period of Transition ... 91

"Death": The Word We Do Not Want to Say ... 95

Grief: Our New Companion Whom We Do Not Welcome ... 99

One Moment at a Time ... 113

Exploring the Feeling of Guilt ... 185

Connecting with Your Spirituality ... 205

Accompaniment ... 223

Where Are We Focusing on Our Grief? ... 237

Self-Care ... 259

The Relationship Does Not End, It Transforms: Continuous Bonds ... 271

Healing, Honoring, and Transforming ... 281

Healing From the Inside Out ... 291

Stories from the Soul ... 321

Final Reflection ... 373

Final Words ... 375

Bibliography ... 377

About the Author ... 387

Annex ... 389

Foreword

Ligia Houben has been my "go-to" expert on cultural expressions of mourning. For many years, Ligia helped me teach workshops that trained facilitators of grief support groups in faith communities. More recently, (before COVID shut down in-person workshops, we conducted grief support workshops in Miami-area Catholic Churches and Morningstar Renewal Center. We share a passion for equipping people who feel the calling to comfort those who mourn. Ligia's knowledge, experience, and wisdom are now written as a gift to you in the book you have in your hands.

When Ligia asked me to write a prologue for her latest book, *"Allow Me to Live My Grief..."* I felt honored to consent. Here are my comments to the readers of this treasure chest of wisdom as you begin your journey through the pages of this book and on your sojourn through grief.

An experienced thanatologist, Ligia examines her personal experience after her mother's death as an example of a loss lived. She invites the reader, who has also lost a loved one, to walk together through the grief journey by sharing her personal story. While the loss of her mother is the most recent, the author shares her earlier loss—the death of her father when she was 12—a loss that transformed her life and led her to the spiritual calling to study Thanatology and serve those who are caught in the grip of grief. The reader will feel her passion and compassion as she takes us through her personal history of losses and uses her story as a teaching tool to address the multiple issues and concerns related to coping with loss. As Ligia tells the story of living with grief, her emotions pulsate through the words. As she opens her heart, the reader will appreciate her genuine transparency.

The book's theme song is that everyone has a right to grieve, and each person's grief is unique. While using the example of her mother's death, she describes the multiple facets of living with grief. She experienced what the grief expert Kenneth Doka calls *"disenfranchised grief."* By authentically sharing her personal story, she shows us how important it is to give ourselves the space to lament the loss of a loved one.

Although she is a certified expert in the field of grief counseling, she admits that after the death of her mother, she discovered a new identity, that of "the wounded healer"[1].

Here are some of the gems in this treasure chest of knowledge about the grieving process.

Ligia's non-judgmental encouragement invites the reader to live your Grief. She says, "Remember that what we ignore does not cease to exist, it is simply repressed. We must face it to live it to the fullest."

---

1 *The Wounded Healer* by Henri Nouwen.

The reader will learn:
- The multiple manifestations of grief.
- Many tools and strategies for processing grief.
- Clarification of common misunderstandings about grief.
- The difference between "mourning and grieving."
- The statements of advice that are commonly thought to be helpful but are not.
- How to accompany those who are grieving.
- The principles of living with mourn.
- How to unpack the myths of the grieving experience.
- Practical techniques for coping with loss.
- How to transfer your pain by creating a legacy to honor the one you lost.

The author draws from her experience as a professional grief counselor to teach the principles of living with grief. If I were a university professor teaching a class on grief and mourning, I would list this book as required reading. This comprehensive textbook discusses and enlightens the multiple dimensions of the grief experience.

The author has documented and supported her points with references to a wide variety of influencers in the area of grief. At the end of each section, the reader will find practical suggestions for processing grief as well as questions that invite self-reflection. This is a must-read for anyone who desires to comfort those in grief and for those who are still navigating their own grief journey. She covers it all; from the first grief reactions to the final task of reconstructing your world after a loss.

Finally, I sincerely appreciate Ligia's positive and hopeful worldview. It is evident that she associates grief with eternal love and invites the reader to a non-judgmental space where there is freedom to express your pain without getting trapped in grief. By transparently opening her heart to the reader, Ligia offers this book to the world as an offering of love.

Rev. Dr. Dale Alan Young, Author of
How to Take Your Spiritual Temperature
and *Comforting Those Who Mourn*

Preface

Dear reader, if you are holding these pages in your hands, you have probably lost a loved one. If so, I want you to know that I offer you this book with all my love as a source of help for those moments when you may feel lost, hopeless, and confused in the face of so much pain. I know how much it hurts to lose a loved one who meant so much to us. Here, I share with you what has helped me in my own process of losing my beloved mother, as well as what has helped thousands of people in their own grief work. In a special way, I want to tell you that people—like you and me—who have suffered a loss have opened their hearts and shared their stories with us. My soul is filled with emotion as I introduce them to you. They have been clients I have accompanied in their grief and members of my bereavement support. Throughout these pages, you will find their thoughts and, at the end, all their stories in their original format.

Please keep in mind that I am not imposing my ideas on you because grief is something personal and fluid.

I share with you what I know through the training I have received as a thanatologist on the subject of grief. Take what helps you and put the rest aside. At the same time, I accompany you by telling you my own story. From my heart, I hope you will take most of these ideas and open your mind and soul as you find points of connection. We are united in pain. We are united in love.

From my heart to yours,
Ligia M. Houben

Introduction

> Many grievers do not give themselves permission or receive permission from others to mourn. We live in a society that often encourages people to prematurely move away from their grief instead of toward it
>
> ALAN D. WOLFELT

We live in a society where we are expected to be well, to be productive, to be successful. Messages are repeated such as *keep a positive mind, learn to be happy,* and *be grateful.* All of this is wonderful. I am a great believer in the value of being positive and embracing gratitude and joy in the spirit. However, what happens when we lose a loved one and we feel pain in our heart? What do we do with grief? What do we do with death? Do we talk about these issues? These are topics that we prefer to avoid and talk about something else... until they happen to us; then, they become valuable.

The grim and inconceivable experience of the COVID-19 pandemic shook the foundations of our assumptive world in 2020. You may ask what I mean by "assumptive world." It is about our world as we assume it to be. Jeffrey Kaufman describes it clearly and precisely:

The assumptive world refers to the assumptions or beliefs that ground, secure, or orient people, that give a sense of reality, meaning, or purpose to life... Or it may be that an assumption is such a familiar aspect of one's sense of reality that its disruption is hard to conceive (2002, p. 1).

In a way, the coronavirus has brought the issue of grief into our consciousness. Thus, there has been a proliferation of articles and programs aimed at alleviating the effects of the losses produced by this pandemic. However, their purpose is more to find solutions than to find a space for grief.

I remember when I was teaching the seminars "Transforming Grief and Loss: Strategies for Helping your Clients through Life Transitions" for mental health professionals through the U.S. company PESI[1], I always emphasized the need to acknowledge grief. Those seminars were based on my *11 Principles of Transformation*®, a methodology aimed at transforming grief into an opportunity for personal growth I introduced in my self-help book: *Transform Your Loss. Your Guide to Strength and Hope.*

The *11 Principles of Transformation*® are as follows and constitute a model of grief transformation[2]:

- First principle: Accept your loss
- Second principle: Live your grief
- Third principle: Develop your spiritual dimension
- Fourth principle: Express your feelings
- Fifth principle: Share with others

---

[1] Professional Education Systems Institute.
[2] At the end of the book, you will find more information about the 11 Principles of Transformation® program.

- Sixth principle: Take care of yourself
- Seventh principle: Using rituals
- Eighth principle: Live the present
- Ninth principle: Modify your thoughts
- Tenth principle: Rebuild your world
- Eleventh Principle: Visualize the life you want

Because I consider it important for you to know what the principles consist of, I will share them with you briefly so that you have an idea of what this methodology consists of and it can serve as a reference since, throughout the book, you will find some of these elements of healing. It is an evolutionary process that is intended to help you transform your loss and transform your life.

The *11 Principles of Transformation*® methodology can be succinctly described as follows:

First principle: *Accept your loss.* This is the first step in our grief journey. I understand that it is not easy to accept the reality of what has happened to us; however, the opposite is denial, which causes us to remain stuck. If we remain in that space, it will be very difficult for us to continue on our path with peace in our hearts.

Second principle: *Live your grief.* This principle is basically the purpose of this book: to be able to confront the pain that grips your heart and validate the emotions you are experiencing. Instead of ignoring it, process it. As we recognize it and make it our own, we will be able to free ourselves from it or, at least, lessen it.

Third principle: *Develop your spiritual dimension.* As human beings, we all have a spiritual aspect that helps us connect with our essence through tools that I will talk about later in this book.

Fourth principle: *Express your feelings.* I consider it very important to express how we really feel because we want to connect with our hearts. All emotions have a place in our lives; what is most important is how to manage them.

Fifth principle: *Share with others.* We all have a story, and this principle invites us to share it with others. We are social beings, and it is beautiful to make meaningful connections even through pain. It is said that a shared burden feels lighter.

Sixth principle: *Take care of yourself.* Taking care of ourselves is not selfish; it is a responsibility. It is something that is under our control and can make a big difference in living through a loss. We can take care of ourselves in different ways and in all areas of our lives.

Seventh principle: *Use rituals.* If you like rituals, we integrate them into this book as well. Creating a meaningful action can give a special meaning to what we are commemorating when we suffer a loss as it helps us connect with our inner selves in a special and unique way.

Eighth principle: *Live the present.* The present moment is all we have. Many times, we get stuck in the past or fill ourselves with fear and worry for the future, which is uncertain. The only sure thing is today. Let us live it with our hearts.

Ninth principle: *Modify your thoughts.* Our thoughts are a powerful tool if we know how to use them to our advantage. When confronted with a loss, it can make a difference in how we will experience and eventually transform it.

Tenth Principle: *Rebuild your world.* After suffering a loss, our world can crumble. It is up to us to stay in the ruins or to gradually build the foundation for an existence with meaning and purpose.

Eleventh principle: *Visualize the life you want.* This is the last link in the transformation process. After we have reconstructed our world and integrated the loss into it, we will have the ability to visualize how we wish to continue living.

Live Your Grief

> We have the right to feel and express
> our pain. Grief, as much as love,
> is part of our reality.
>
> ALAN D. WOLFELT

As you can see, the second principle is "Live your grief" since I consider it an essential element for the transformation of our loss. I never suggest that we ignore it; on the contrary, I insist on the need to validate and process it. However, usually, if you are grieving, you often receive the message that you have to move on, that you should not feel the pain after a certain time, that you have to be strong... How do those messages make you feel when the unspeakable has happened? You have lost a loved one and your heart has broken into a thousand pieces. Precisely, it is because of what we go through when experiencing grief that I have written *Allow Me to Live My Grief... and Heal from the Inside Out*.

This book is based on my own experience of losing my mother and was born out of my need to let you know that you are not alone. I want to accompany you in your own process so that you can identify yourself by finding similarities with experiences that have happened to me. I have written it from the bottom of my soul, and I want you to feel as if we are together and I am talking to you. Many people have told me that this is how they felt when they read *Transform Your Loss: Your Guide to Strength and Hope*. That is how I want you to take on this book, for it is for you, the bereaved. If you are facing the loss of a loved one and do not feel understood by your friends, your family, society, or even yourself, this book will help you. I hope you will find understanding, support, help, and hope on these pages. Yes, it is possible to find hope in the midst of pain if we open our hearts and minds because what motivates us is *love*. Always keep in mind that this feeling does not end with death—that love is eternal. And when we lose a loved one, the relationship does not end; it is transformed.

In some parts of the book, I invite you to reflect on certain questions to help you process your own grief. Do this with me. Feel that I am by your side, understanding you, offering you my hand, and opening my heart to you. As I share my experience with you, I want you to keep in mind that each story is unique: my grief is unique, and your grief is unique. However, if there is one thing that unites us, it is the need to feel validated, supported, and accepted.

It is our right to grieve

Grieving is a right. You have it, just as I do. In my case, it matters little if my mom was 100 years old or if she had been 120. She was my mother. As Earl A. Grollman says, "The worst loss is the one that happens to you." I am not comparing my grief to that of a mother who lost her infant son or a wife who lost her husband of thirty-five years. No. I am not comparing, for each loss is unique and painful. I am only asking that they recognize mine and, at the same time, do the same with yours. Just as I have a right to grieve, *you also have a right to grieve.*

Allow Me to Live My Grief is also inspired by the stories of many of my clients, the challenges they have encountered in their grief process, and how they have handled them. You will find, woven throughout the text, comments that some of my clients shared with me. For reasons of confidentiality, I have used other names, as only in the case of a couple of the stories did the individuals wish to keep their identity.

As we embark on this process together, I also want to help you understand the difference between recognizing grief, living through it, and remaining stuck in that space of pain.

It is up to us to remain imprisoned in the darkness or to learn to incorporate the loss into our lives by realizing that our loved ones will live forever in our hearts.

In this space, I share with you my story with the desire to help you with yours.

Sharing My Wounded Heart

> This is not like anything I have felt before. It is different. Your mother… has died.
>
> RICHARD B. GILBERT

My mother died a few months ago, and I am experiencing a very profound grief. That should not be a surprise, right? The thing is that many people, knowing what I do, expected that, with my experience, the pain would not be so intense. They had certain expectations about how I would handle my grief, and one of them was that I would not live it so openly.

At this point, let me tell you about my profession: I am a grief specialist and thanatologist. I have written other books on dealing with loss. I have taught courses on death at the university level and over 100 seminars to mental health professionals throughout the United States on dealing with grief and loss. I am a life transitions and grief consultant and coach. In short, I have dedicated my life to helping others deal with grief and death. Actually, more than *dealing with it*, I wish with my soul that you could *transform it*: from grief to personal and spiritual growth.

What inspired me to help those grieving?

The reason I decided to enter the world of grief was not because of those decisions we make when we are children and people ask us: "What do you want to be when you grow up?" In those cases, we are most likely to say we want to be psychologists, architects, or teachers, but... thanatologists, dealing with death? Not really. It escapes our reality, although I will cover this topic in another chapter. I was saying that being a grief specialist is not an option that comes to mind when we are asked what we want to be when we grow up. I remember when I was a child, my father would ask me, "What do you want to be when you grow up?" and I would say, "I want to be a business administrator." I would say that because my father was an entrepreneur, and I wanted to be like him, although life had other plans for me—it threw me a curve ball very early on.

Below, I share with you the event that pivoted my life 180 degrees when I was only twelve years old. I wrote it in the form of an essay when I was in college while taking a course on thanatology.

The story of my father's death

The event of my father's death happened too fast. The mother superior of my school gave me the bad news: "Good people always leave this world earlier... You have to be strong... Your father is dead." Strong? What is the meaning of that word for a twelve-year-old girl who thinks of her father as her world? Strong... when you suddenly realize that your world has been shattered?

In the first few moments, my mind did not grasp the true meaning of those terrible words. "What do you mean he is dead?" I asked. I had spoken to him the day before. Then, reality embraced me with its dark shadows: I had become an orphan. Within my young girl's heart, a variety of feelings began to rise: anger, fear, despair. I had only an impetuous desire to ask God why He had taken my father from me. In the agony of my despair, I even doubted my faith. Screaming like a wounded animal, I fell to the floor, demanding my father to be back. The pain had begun to set in. In the end, after resisting the idea of going home for some time, I agreed to go with the mother superior. My house was chaos, as I had imagined. People were on every corner. Sorrowful comments such as "Poor thing, so young and without a father" were darts aimed at my heart. I remember, beside myself, yelling at everyone and telling them that they were hypocrites, that they had no idea of the pain I was going through, and to get out of my house immediately. My older sister tried to calm me down, but it was useless. I was angry and in despair. At the wake, I went from crying to laughing hysterically. The day after my father's death, he was transferred from Miami, where he died, to Nicaragua, and the wake was held in our house. He was placed in the center of the living room to say his last goodbye. I was shocked to see his inert body and feel his pale, cold face. His soul was no longer there. At that moment, a question came to my mind: what are we, a physical body or an immaterial soul? I did not understand the fact that I could feel my father's presence even though his body was lifeless. It was at that moment that my numbness began.

I lived the following weeks as if in a dream. I was like a robot with no sense of anything. Everywhere I looked, I saw sadness and desolation. My mother was taking care of her sick mother, my grandmother, who also passed away a month later. My sisters could not stop crying. People were dealing with the situation in their own way. Suddenly, it was just me and my loss, me and my own feelings of loneliness and despair. I did not know what to do with them. I was greatly helped by my childhood friend Lucrecia Díaz, who, being my neighbor, accompanied me throughout that first year of mourning. As I faced that grief, I felt inside me that I was no longer the spoiled child; I grew up all at once. I needed to get on with my life and learn to handle the situation I was forced to face, but the dreams of my father calling me kept coming and tormenting me. I would wake up restless in the middle of the night, wanting to see my father by my side. But of course, they were just dreams.

Time passed, and I had to learn to live without my father's presence and his warm embrace. I discovered that the more emotional you are, the more vulnerable you become. But it did not matter anymore. I could not fight my nature. My feelings wanted to come out again; I wanted to show them, to laugh and cry, to be part of the world again. Throughout our lives, we encounter many struggles, and the emotional ones are especially difficult to handle, but it is important to have hope and faith. I realized that even though I could never hug my father again, he would always be by my side, guiding me. The strength of his love is still as fresh as it was twenty-six years ago. The memories of him I hold in my heart will always be a part of my life.

My father's death was a profound loss, and it was what inspired me to help others process their own grief. I now find myself facing the loss of my centenarian mother, a process I will share with you in the next section. As I face this reality, I ask myself: Who am I?

Am I the professional, or am I the daughter? Well, actually, I am both. In this book, on these pages, I will talk with you about my grief and what has helped me. I will offer you insights that will help you process your own grief.

My main intention is to emphasize the need to validate our grief so that we can process and transform it. Only then can we welcome life anew and give ourselves the opportunity to find meaning and purpose.

It Takes Just a Moment

> Life changes in the instant.
> The ordinary instant.
>
> JOAN DIDION

"Life changes fast, life changes in the instant," says the American writer Joan Didion in *The Year of Magical Thinking* (2005), the book she wrote after her husband died of a heart attack. This feeling of experiencing an instantaneous change when we lose our loved one is reiterated by Venezuelan journalist Albor Rodríguez in her book *Duelo. Cómo me cambió la vida* en un instante ((2015, p. 45), where she shares the tragic loss of her infant and only son, Juan Sebastian, who drowned at the age of one year and four months.

We may think that these words apply when we have a sudden death, when we have a sudden loss, and when life changes us in an instant. However, they apply even when we are faced with the imminent loss of a loved one, when we are witnessing the prolonged death of someone very dear to us, someone whom we love with all our heart and who is part of our existence, of our daily routine. When that person dies, even if their death is expected, life changes immediately, as Edward Myers points out about what happened when his mother died after being ill for fourteen months: "I felt as if I had wakened into someone else's life, rather than my own. The place and the faces were familiar, but everything else had changed literally overnight" (1986, p. VII).

THE DAY THEY TURNED OFF THE LIGHT FOR ME

The day they turned off the light for me was June 7, 2020. My mother, Alicia Gallegos de Martínez, *mi madrecita amada* (my beloved mother), as I called her, passed away. On that day, my world collapsed.

How is it possible that from one moment to the next, my world can change in this way?

How is it possible that from one moment to the next, everything else ceases to make sense?

How is it possible that what was important has ceased to be important, for the source of my joy, the source of my meaning, the center of my life, ceased to exist?

That is what I felt on June 7, 2020, at 2:50 in the afternoon. A feeling of emptiness swept over me from head to toe, and I became an automaton; I became someone who suddenly could only think that her mother had passed away. Although I accepted it at the time it happened, the pain was immense. In fact, to this day, I have never really asked why. The intellectual part of me had understood that my mother was very frail and fought as hard as she could since she loved life; however, only two months shy of her 101st birthday, her body was too fragile, and she gave up. She had already lived what she had to live. Her frail body asked or rest, and that day, she rested. She rested in God's hands. She rested in eternal sleep. In what she believed so much and in what I also believe. However, as she entered that eternal sleep, the darkness in my life set in, and I simply entered a journey I have spoken much about, taught much about, and helped others navigate: the journey of grief.

I am no stranger to that journey because, as I told you before, I experienced it early in my life, at the age of twelve, when I suddenly lost my father. Now, at this stage of my life, losing my mother when I was sixty, the process was different. She was my mother and father for forty-eight years; she was my companion, friend, confidant, source of joy, inspiration, and life example... all of that was my mother and more. I lost her, and my assumptive world changed, and oh, how that world changes when we lose a loved one! That is what I felt that Sunday afternoon.

Knowing my strong attachment to my mother, my family was very attentive to me, including my two sisters. They were worried that I might fall into a very deep and painful hole. I shared with them how I was feeling and that I was slowly processing my grief and living my pain with intensity. I reminded them that this was my field, my specialty, and that I was processing my grief with my heart in my hand.

PROCESSING YOUR GRIEF

What type of loss are you experiencing?

_____

_____

How did your world change as you experienced this loss?

_____
_____

How did your family/close ones respond to your reaction?

_____
_____

Are We "Really" Prepared?

> Even when it is expected,
> death or loss still comes as a surprise.
>
> MEGAN DEVINE

For several years, I taught courses on death and dying at the university. I am a thanatologist and a member of ADEC (The Association for Death Education and Counseling), and I conduct seminars on death. However, nothing can truly prepare us for how we will feel when we lose a loved one; that happens after the fact.

Although I was aware that my mother's death was approaching, I did not envision the tremendous *shock* I would feel inside me when it happened. Seeing her lifeless body was surreal to me. That specific feeling was discussed in the program "Transforming Your Grief," presented in *Conversando con Tito Lagos-Basset*, where I was part of a panel of commentators on the losses we would have experienced and how we were processing grief while mourning. Clinical psychologist Rodolfo Muñoz pointed out precisely that nothing prepares us: that is a fallacy, since one thing is our understanding, our cognition, what we know, of reality. And another thing is what we feel when that happens.

My mother died after eight months under hospice care. The last two weeks of her life were quite delicate due to her fragile situation; therefore, the fact that she passed away was not a surprise. However, there is no use in knowing that it will happen. It is always painful to lose a loved one.

When we have to do things we do not want to do
I remember having to make decisions, doing the things we were supposed to do after someone passes away, and taking care of the logistics. Even though my mother had her funeral arrangements ready, there were last-minute decisions that had to be made. I remember having the paperwork from the funeral home available to make the call the moment my mother passed away. I dreaded that moment because I knew how painful it would be. However, I wanted to have things planned in advance so I could be in charge. The day my mother died, making that call to the funeral home was extremely painful and difficult, as I knew it would be the beginning of a process I did not want to be part of. They told me they would come to pick up her body in a couple of hours. I stayed by her side, wanting to make those last moments eternal. When the funeral home employees arrived at my home, and a family member came to the room to tell me they were already there, I could not believe it: "What, they are going to take her away so fast?

I asked for a few more minutes to be with her. I told them, "A little more, let me be with her a little longer," for I knew that taking her away would mean the end. I wanted to hold her a little more, to feel the warmth of her body, which was still lingering. I wanted to make that moment longer, to extend it just to feel her close to me. I thought, "Maybe if I hold her tight, they will not be able to take her away." I was in a surreal space between the reality and the feeling.

As the men from the funeral home came in, they asked me to leave the room while they moved my mother to the stretcher. As I watched them leave carrying her body, mine froze. If words can describe the pain I felt, it was as if someone had come with a knife and cut my heart into two pieces. The pain was so deep, mixed with the disbelief that she was being taken away from me, that this would be the last time I would have her in my home. The moment they took her out the door, I accompanied them along with some family members. I went to the funeral home's van, which was parked next to my car.

When I saw my mom's body between the two vehicles, I thought, "This is such a contrast!" as my car symbolized fun, remembering the endless times my mom would get in it to go for rides with me and, as she said, "To have fun." She loved to go out and enjoy life. From the moment we would get in, she used to look at the trees and say, "How beautiful those trees are!" or look up at the sky and say, "What a beautiful day." Then, my car represented happy times. Now, the van parked right next to it gave me a deep sadness, for in it, she would be taken away forever. No more happy rides. That van symbolized the final departure.

By the time she was taken away, I was beside myself. I felt my world stop there, and I started to walk away, alone, around the block in front of my house. For some reason, when I feel great pain, I tend to walk. I think at that moment, I could have walked the Camino de Santiago de Compostela and not stopped. I just wanted to walk and walk. I did the same thing when I lost my father. It has been said that we have a pattern for grief. I think that is mine: I need to walk. A family member offered to go it with me, but I refused. I realized that, as I cried so intensely, I did not want people around me. I did not want to be held. I wanted to be with my pain, and I was given the space. I did not want anyone to try to comfort me. I needed to be present with my grief and be still.

PROCESSING YOUR GRIEF

Has it ever happened to you that you want to be with your pain and they try to remove you from that space? How have you acted?

_____

_____

What helped you?

_____

_____

After walking, I returned home, where my family was waiting for me. The moment I entered, I felt the house, even with so many people in it, was very empty. It felt huge and desolate. My mother was no longer there to fill each and every space with her presence. I felt like dozing off and crying. I hugged my older sister, Alicia, and we stood still. I cried so hard my eyes looked like two fountains. I talked to my sister Marielena, who was in Kansas and could not travel because of the COVID-19 pandemic. Despite the distance, the three of us sisters were united by the pain of losing our mother. I spoke with my daughter, Diana, who lives in Finland; we talked and cried together. I also communicated with my best friend, Lucrecia Díaz, whom I mentioned earlier in my father's story. She accompanied me then and was also present at my mother's death. Lucrecia lives in Nicaragua, and even so, she accompanied me constantly during the whole process.

Other people called, but I just wanted to be alone. That night, I developed the biggest headache I have ever suffered. I am not prone to headaches, but this one was very intense. Most likely, it was from all the crying I had done. I could not eat. I felt that if I ate, I might vomit. I did not care whether I ate; I just wanted to go to bed, think, and pray. Amid this severe headache, I suddenly thought, "Mom, you had two severe headaches just before you died. This is like being connected to you." Within my great pain, it was like a way of identification, almost like magical thinking, which means believing that something that happened could have been caused by something I was not related to.

In the *Encyclopaedia Britannica,* we find this definition:

> Magical thinking, the belief that one's ideas, thoughts, actions, words, or use of symbols can influence the course of events in the material world. Magical thinking—the belief that wishes can impose their own order on the material world—is a form of primary process thought. Magical thinking presumes a causal link between one's inner, personal experience and the external physical world.

This is what Didion (2005) refers to as the constant succession of such thoughts she experienced when she suddenly lost her husband. The title of the book, *The Year of Magical Thinking*, caught my attention because what does the author mean by magical thinking? That way of thinking, as grief expert David Kessler says in his book *Finding Meaning. The Sixth Stage of Grief* (2019), is a common occurrence in bereavement. Didion, thinking about the first night without her husband, realizes why she wanted to be alone that first night: "I needed to be alone so that he could come back" (p. 33). That was the beginning for her of the year of magical thinking, and she was aware of that kind of thinking as she wondered if she was thinking like children, who can change the narrative. Does it happen to us then that we imagine that they will come back at some point? Could it be that because of our magical thinking, we think that we could erase what happened? Albor Rodriguez (2015) comments on what was happening to Didion as follows: "where she recounts episodes in which, dragged by a "superstitious source," her disturbed mind took for granted that her husband was still alive... According to science [magical thinking] enclose desires and fulfill a positive role of stability for the psyche, as if it were a defense mechanism" (p. 21). Rodriguez identifies with this type of thinking as she recounts the loss of her infant son, Juan Sebastian, in a frank and open manner. She shares her heartbreaking grief and, at the same time, amazes us with the resilience she demonstrates as she continues to move forward due to the support of her parents, as she says in the dedication: "To my parents who, with their love and concern, have kept me on the side of life."

In reality, our mind works in a way that we do not understand when facing a very deep grief. That first night, like Didion, I wanted to be alone. Little by little, my headache went away, and I cried silently, waiting for sleep to come.

PROCESSING YOUR GRIEF

Have you experienced magical thinking when losing your loved one?

_____
_____

What did that thought consist of?

_____
_____

Did you get to release it or are you still experiencing it?

_____
_____

SHARING THE LOSS OF MY MOTHER ON FACEBOOK

Before I went to bed, someone had asked me if I was going to announce my mother's death on Facebook because my relationship with my mom had been very public on this social network. I loved sharing pictures of her and the things we used to do. However, at the time, I did not feel like posting anything. About an hour later, after trying to sleep, I suddenly opened my eyes and felt the desire to express it. This is the post I shared:

With great pain in my soul and great love in my heart, I share with you that my beloved mother, Alicia Gallegos de Martinez, passed away this afternoon.

God gave us the great joy of enjoying her for 100 years and almost ten months. Our family feels a huge void for not having her physically with us anymore. However, her fighting spirit, her joy for life, and her faith toward God and the Virgin, will always live among us.

People were very present, and I actually felt very supported as I read each of the almost 500 comments they left me. I felt comforted through their words so full of love and support.

The Morning After

> There is no way to fill the void left by the person we loved. If our loved one was the center of our universe, now that center is removed.
>
> CHRISTINE A. ADAMS

The feeling I woke up with the next morning was indescribable. I experienced an effect of inner emptiness and distress. When I opened my eyes, I wondered: "What happened?" I always wake up with joy and, ever since my mom lived in my house, I would wake up with the hope of going to see her, to say good morning to her, to get into bed with her, and to pray with her. Suddenly, a feeling of uneasiness shook me that morning, and it was the first of many days in which I woke up with the impression that something was not right because I did not feel complete. And it was then that reality turned into a nightmare. My world had changed in an instant. The world I knew, and of which my mother was the center, had changed in a second. For some reason, I remembered Mircea Eliade's book, *The Sacred and the Profane*, which I had read during my master's degree in religious studies. That was the feeling I had: that I had left a sacred world and found myself in a profane one. How was I to find meaning in that profane world without that person who was my reason for being, my why when I woke up? That is how I found myself in those first days in which I was walking in a haze. It was hard for me to see the light because I felt I was in the middle of darkness.

Preparing the last rites

That day, June 8, 2020, I knew I had things to do, but my mind was overwhelmed, and I asked myself, "What do I need to do?" I knew I had to go to the funeral home with my mother's papers, which I already had ready since she had chosen their services many years before. She was very practical and organized; she even wanted to choose her casket. Her funeral arrangements were ready. She liked to have control over what would happen to her. When she chose to be buried in the Miami cemetery instead of being sent to Nicaragua to be buried in the family mausoleum, I asked her what made her want to stay in Miami, to which she replied: "I want to stay here so you can come visit me and pray for me."

After my mother passed away, I could not locate the contract I had been holding in my hands for the last few days without realizing that I had it right on my dresser. It was as if my mind was on something else, and it was impossible for me to concentrate. Has it happened to you that you find it hard to concentrate? This is a natural part of grieving; do not worry if it happens to you. We will explore this topic later.

Other actions to be taken

During the first few days after my mother's death, I was extremely busy, calling Social Security, calling Medicare, calling the pharmacy where she had her prescriptions to cancel the account, calling hospice to have the oxygen tank and nebulizer picked up... I kept going back and forth, asking myself, "What are the things that need to be done now?" What helped me get organized was to make a to-do list and check them off as I went along. That process can be mentally and emotionally intense. For example, something that had a big impact on me—and I know it happens to my clients as well—was picking up the death certificate. That day was extremely painful.

PROCESSING YOUR GRIEF

What things did you have to take care of that you wished you did not have to do?

_____

_____

What was the most difficult call?

_____

_____

Was someone with you?

_____

_____

WHAT WOULD THE FUNERAL BE LIKE?

I had always imagined my mother's funeral as something very big since I know the great value it has as a ritual. I had always wished to have a mass open to the public, the same as with the wake, but it was not possible, as it happened during the time of the coronavirus pandemic. In the COVID-19 section, I reflect on the value of this symbolic ritual that is the funeral.

My husband accompanied me to the funeral home, and we finalized the details of the arrangements that my mother had prepared many years ago. I finalized the last details. Because of the pandemic, we had to coordinate the church, the wake, and the funeral; everything had to be synchronized, and we decided what the wake would be like because of the times we were living in. Then I realized how much these rituals had changed from before and after the coronavirus. Before, you did not think about how many people would or would not come.

I wanted to have a wake and mass when it was possible to celebrate it, but not many spaces were available. It was Monday. Finally, it was decided that we would have the wake on Thursday night and the mass on Friday. I also ordered the flowers and the wreath that went on top of the casket. I remember looking at the catalog and thinking, "I am not getting a bouquet of flowers for her birthday. These are the flowers for her wake." However, I also wanted to order something special from me to her, so I ordered a huge heart made of red roses. That heart symbolized my eternal love for her. Death would not put an end to that immense love between us since death is not what defines a relationship, but love.

Just as with my father, my mother would be in my heart forever, for love does not die; love is eternal. As I was getting ready to go to the wake, I felt like I was in a haze again; I was actually living in a suspended space.

I was very present with my grief, crying, and, at times, in silence. I remember when I was in the car with my husband on our way to the funeral home, I could not say a single word. I was in a space that felt surreal. I was wearing all black because I wanted to show the world how I felt inside with my clothes.

As I entered the room where the casket was placed, I felt like I was transported to another dimension. I noticed the beautiful flowers sent by people accompanying me in the distance, and I approached to see my mother for the last time. When I saw her inside the casket, I thought she looked like a little doll, all in pink. Then, I practiced a sacred ritual between her and me. I put on her jacket the heart magnet that always united us. It was a symbol that we would be together forever. I gave it to her when I started traveling to give seminars. I have a magnet heart, and I gave one to her to wear all the time. She never stopped wearing it until her last day. By performing that ritual, I fulfilled what I promised her: we would always be together wherever we were.

I was next to her, but everything felt so different! I saw my mother, and it was as if it was not her; she looked different from the way she looked at the time she died, and I think that helped me in some way. It helped me to keep my composure during the wake because I imagined I was going to be inconsolable, and yet the opposite happened. Being as I am, a person who expresses herself a lot through tears, I found myself in a space of unreality. I missed my sisters, as they were not with me. One was for health reasons, and the other was because, living outside of Miami due to the pandemic, it was impossible for her to travel. That situation made everything different because, on the one hand, people who were in Miami could not go for fear of contagion, and, on the other hand, there were restrictions at the funeral home.

Just hug me

The few people who accompanied me to the wake and funeral came with masks, and we kept our social distance as best we could. Because of that, I was deprived of the hugs, those hugs that I wanted so much. Only a very dear friend who had just had a COVID-19 test came up to me and said: "I am fine. I want to give you a hug." It was a beautiful shared feeling. With everyone else, however, it was distant, as expected, so I missed the hugs.

I remembered that I had always thought that, upon my mother's death, I would want to carry a sign on my chest reading: "Just hug me." That idea came about because many of my clients had shared with me comments that people make after losing a loved one, along the lines of: "She is in a better place" or "She would not like to see you like this," which, instead of helping them, made them feel sadder or even angry. Because this topic is of great significance, I have set aside a specific chapter to elaborate on what does and does not help in times of grief.

Based on these comments from my clients, I used to say to my family and close friends in a humorous way that if my mother predeceased me at the funeral, I would hang a sign on my chest that said, "Just hold me. The irony, however, was precisely that I could not receive the desired hugs. I wondered, "Is this really happening?" From the bottom of my heart, I would ask, silently: "I want to be hugged. I want to be hugged..."

That showed me that in life, we have no control over anything. We think we have absolute control, and we do not. In reality, what do hugs mean? They mean support, they mean presence, they mean affection.

If you are facing a loss and did not receive the hug you have longed for, I want to tell you that, even though we are not physically close, I am sending you one with all my strength. Just feel my arms around you and hear my words: I am with you, from my heart to yours. That is all I can say. If you need that hug, just close your eyes and receive it in your heart.

The last goodbye

The next day, we had the funeral mass at Epiphany Church in South Miami, a very special church for me, as my mom and I used to attend mass there every Sunday. The ceremony was both beautiful and heartfelt. Even though I could not offer the public service I had longed for to honor my mother, I felt blessed to have been able to celebrate her and have that beautiful group of people, family, and close friends by my side.

At the end of the ceremony, I told Father Alex Rivera, who was my mother's spiritual guide and celebrated the mass, that I wanted to say a few words.

With much emotion in my heart, I addressed the people who were with me at that moment with the following words:

Dear friends, dear family:
As the Father said—as she used to say to him: "*padrecito*" (dear Father), she always told him—my mother loved this very special priestI love him so much, Father Alex! Every time we came to mass on Sundays, it was something very special for her, and, as Father Alex said, my mom lived a life as a testimony of faith, a testimony of love. That is what remains for us; that is what remains deeply for me.

It is an occasion in which I feel—and I am speaking for myself—a great pain because I will not have her physically. She was my companion; she was so much for me, and it is hard because it hurts us, and the absence hurts me…

The physical departure hurts my soul. However, I thank God for giving us such a beautiful mother and giving us the joy of a woman for 100 years.

Every day—she lived with Mario and me for two and a half years—when I went to open her curtains every morning, she would turn around and say: "What a radiant sun!" That is how she would wake up.

She was such a joyful woman! For everything, she was: "What a joy!" If you fed her, she would say, "How delicious!" A woman who lived joyfully. Now that I am looking at all the photos in the collage and I see all her expressions, they are all joyful! That was and will continue to be her. My mom will continue to live on in my heart as my dad lives on in my heart. My mom will also live on, and we will always honor her, as I discussed with my niece Alicia, her first granddaughter, whom she loved so much. She was so beautiful with her!

As my mom used to say, with her arms up like this, "*Arriba Corazones*" (Hearts Up!"). That is what we are left with: her life motto.

My mom followed my father's legacy for so many years, and now she leaves us this legacy, this example of faith, this example of love, this example of being there for everyone.

So I leave it also as an example of fortitude: ¡Arriba Corazones!

Then we left for the cemetery in the limousine behind the hearse. It seemed unbelievable to be in a car behind my mother in that way. It was a totally unreal experience. However, when we arrived at the cemetery, I was able to give a farewell ritual. It was my last goodbye to my beloved mother. Do not ask me where I got the strength. I can only think that my immense love for her and my faith made it possible.

In the Early Days, I Was in Another Dimension

> Sadness slows us down and, by doing so,
> seems to slow the world down.
> Sometimes bereaved people even say
> that living with the sadness of loss is
> like living in slow motion.
>
> GEORGE A. BONANNO

The first few days, I felt like I was in a haze. It seemed to me that everything had stopped around me, and I walked slowly in a formless space. I lost track of dates or whether I had eaten. The only thing I wanted was to be alone. Even being such a social person and knowing how much company helps, those first days, I preferred to be alone or with my immediate family. It is common to want to be alone when we are in deep grief. Sometimes, the phone overwhelmed me, and I wanted to avoid repeating the same story over and over again. It was a mixed feeling because, while I was grateful for the support, I wanted to be allowed to be in my solitude, even if it was only for a few hours. Sometimes, I did not want another person to call me. I did not want to have to answer; when I could, I answered. Sometimes, I would get so many texts or voicemails that it was impossible for me to keep up; however, in my soul, I was grateful for every gesture of support, of companionship, of affection.

I wrote a lot, dictated a lot on my cell phone (this greatly helped me in releasing the pain); I liked to talk with my sisters and my childhood friend Lucrecia. That was something constant because I cried and talked and cried again. It was cathartic; it was necessary for my soul.

I felt irritable and impatient

I found myself suddenly becoming impatient and irritable. I am a calm and collected person, but I suddenly noticed that I was losing my patience easily or that I was irritated by things like washing the dishes... Something so routine, yet I was angry that I had to do it. When we are grieving, we experience many emotions, not just sadness, as I will discuss later, so do not push yourself too hard or be surprised by your reactions.

Time in silence

In times of grief, we often say that silence is our companion, and indeed, it is. It helps us to enter into our thoughts and to feel our emotions. Many times, we welcome it; other times, it scares us. When my mother died, there was a great silence in my house. For the past two and a half years, that house had been filled with so many people: family, friends, and close ones who came or went to visit my mom. There were strangers, too: her caregivers, hospice people when she was under palliative care, nurses, doctors... What was happening was that the dynamics of my house were revolving around my mother, too, and suddenly the laughter, the noises, the TV, the people cooking, the people cleaning... all that stopped. My in-and-outs, my running, going to Walgreens drugstore, going to Publix grocery store, going to Winn Dixie's grocery store, and back to Walgreens.

Anything and everything for her and only for her. Going to work, coming home from work, having a late lunch to eat with her, then coming back; all those intense moments... having the phone by my side and explaining to my clients: "My mom has become more frail, so I am keeping an eye out in case something happens to her." I was blessed to work within a five-minute drive from home. That allowed me to know that if an emergency arose I would simply jump in the car and get there in a flash, as I did on a couple of occasions during the last stage of her life. That was my life. The life I had built around my mother. It was many sleepless nights, just listening, waiting, and paying attention to whether she would be okay. Jumping into her bed if she was restless, as she would only calm down with my presence by her side, by holding her. It touched my soul to help her feel safe. All those moments gave me meaning, purpose, and joy.

PROCESSING YOUR GRIEF

Have you noticed that you find yourself getting impatient or irritable?

_____

_____

What are the things that make you react unexpectedly?

_____

_____

How do you handle these situations?

_____

_____

EMOTIONAL NEED TO MAINTAIN CONNECTION WITH MY MOTHER

For the first month, it was almost obsessive to read the *chats*, watch videos, and listen to her recorded messages where she recited her favorite poem "Garrick" or sang songs of yesteryear full of joy. It was as if I was feeding on her, as if she was the water I needed to drink in the desert to quench my thirst. I was absorbing as much as I could until the last drop, the last drop of her memory, of her essence, of her gaze. I was looking at the photos again and reading the texts of the lady who helped me with her and the nurse; I wanted to recreate the story of each *chat*. Since my mother had several people who took care of her—angels in her life and in mine—then I recreated the story from different perspectives, wanting to absorb as much as possible her last months of life, the last words, the last gestures on her face, the last experiences, the last cute expressions... I recreated it all, recreated it, and recreated it again.

Something that also helped me process my grief was talking about my mother. When they asked me about her or told me something from the past, I would listen with so much joy because I felt this great desire to talk about her constantly. It was an inner need. All I wanted was to remember and relive in my mind the moments I had with my mother. It was like wanting to keep the connection in any way possible, something that also happens to many of my clients. It seems to be a very natural thing in bereavement. In a later section, I will elaborate on the issue of connection. Some people, with good intentions, tell you to stop talking about your loved one because you need to "let them rest."

However, talking helps us process grief and share the story.

In fact, each time we tell it, the story may change as you add details or let go of others. I remember a trauma training I took many years ago. The process was precisely to hold the space for the person who had suffered the trauma to tell the story over and over again. It was amazing how this helped to heal and see the things left out or magnified in each retelling.

PROCESSING YOUR GRIEF

How did you react the first few days after losing your loved one?

_____
_____

What helped you in the early days?

_____
_____

Have you felt the emotional need to maintain connection with your loved one?

_____
_____

Do you like to talk about your loved one?

_____
_____

Do you like to look at photos or do you prefer not to?

_____
_____

What memories does it evoke for you?

_____
_____

The place of netflix and youtube in my grief

It is interesting because after my mother died, I only wanted to watch movies, series, or documentaries about death, about grief, or about life after death.

Keep in mind that, being my field, I have always been fascinated by these topics; however, this was different. It was practically a need to know what was being talked about, what happens at death, what happens afterward, and how one feels when one loses a loved one.

Welcoming Peace into My heart

> Solitude is not something you must hope for in the future. Rather, it is a deepening of the present, and unless you look for it in the present, you will never find it.
>
> THOMAS MERTON

During the following months, although I continued to see the *chats*, that compelling need gradually diminished, and over time, more moments of peace emerged despite also experiencing moments of intense pain, the kind that reaches the marrow of your bones and the bottom of your heart.

I remember that in my prayers in those early days, when the weight of absence crushed me, what I asked God was: "Dear God, I ask you with my soul, give me peace when I think of my mother."

Between tears and smiles when remembering beautiful moments, I have been processing and experiencing my grief in a very connected way with myself. I continue to live it because the process is like that: it remains latent, almost imperceptible at times. I have integrated it into my daily life, as I have had to learn to live without her physical presence; however, my mother continues to live in my heart.

Finding meaning. Meetings by zoom

I mentioned earlier that my mom died on June 7, 2020. On May 7, a month before, I received an email from the person in charge of education projects at the Alliance for Aging, INC, in Miami, Florida—which is the city where I reside—proposing I facilitate Zoom meetings to support the community. The intention was to help people cope with what the coronavirus pandemic that had just started two months earlier represented. With great enthusiasm, I agreed, and we planned this wonderful initiative, which would be free of charge to the community. A month later, my mother died, and I was faced with this commitment, doubting my ability to carry it out immediately.

I reflected deeply on this opportunity, seeing it as one that would allow me to help and connect with others. Indeed, it was a blessing as I put my soul into the preparation of each of these presentations and moved out of my space of pain. By planning the different topics to help others, I helped myself. I believe very much in the principle that by helping others, you help yourself because you get out of your own movie.

PROCESSING YOUR GRIEF

Has it happened to you that in the midst of your grief you have had the opportunity to help others?

_____
_____

How have you felt about it?

_____
_____

> **Do you feel that it has helped you or, on the contrary, increased your pain?**
>
> _____
> _____

DEFINING THE LOSS

Most of the time, when people ask me what I do for a living, and I tell them that I help others deal with their losses, they think I am only talking about the death of a loved one. This is not the case. We suffer a loss when someone very important to us is no longer by our side, either by death, divorce, or distance. There are also other types, such as loss of health, accidents, and the new types of loss due to the COVID-19 that we have had to live through. In the book I mentioned to you, *Transform Your Loss: Your Guide to Strength and Hope*, I elaborate on the concept of loss and include others beyond the death of a loved one, such as divorce or the loss of a job. In the context of *Allow Me to Grieve and Heal from the Inside Out*, I have focused on the death of a loved one, as it is inspired by my story.

However, many of the comments and suggestions presented here for processing grief can also be applied to other types of losses.

LET US STOP COMPARING

When facing a loss, for some reason, many people tend to make comparisons about how they feel about it. Even people who often have the intention of helping may say,

"Look at how she is doing-who lost her dad-how well she is handling it." Or someone may think in a support group: "What he is going through cannot compare to what I am feeling." In reality, we cannot know how the other person feels because the loss is personal and related to what it represents for each of us. What happens when you lose the meaning in your life? What kind of loss is that? Are all losses the same?

Variables when experiencing the death of your loved one

Differences in the expression, duration, and intensity of the grief feelings experienced by the bereaved are directly related to some variables, such as the type of death, the level of attachment, the personality of the bereaved, and their loss history. As indicated in the article "El inventario de historias de pérdidas (IHP): Presentation and Clinical Utility" by Chaurand, Feixes, and Neimeyer:

> But there are always great individual differences depending on when the loss occurred, how it happened (violent *vs.* natural, sudden *vs.* anticipated), the ways of coping with such situations by the person (secure *vs.* insecure), etc. These are relevant factors in determining the level of depressive symptomatology or the level of these two forms of suffering are different from each other (2010, p. 4).

Among the variables that, to a greater extent, determine our grief is the type of death, especially if we feel that, in some way, it is sanctioned by society, as in the case of suicide.

Change and attachment

When we suffer a loss, there are two words that are closely related to it: "change" and "attachment." When we face the death of a loved one, there is always a change. Sometimes people say to you, "I want to be the same as I was before"; however, that is not possible. When there has been a loss, there is always a change.

On the other hand, we may think with sadness that we will never be the same again, as Patricia told me after experiencing the death of her husband: "I will never be the same as I was before." I explained to her that there is always a transformation and shared with her that I am not the same after the loss of my mother because there has been a change; however, that does not mean that I cannot make that change positive. It is very much up to us whether we allow ourselves to evolve inspired by the loss of our loved one. In my case, one change that has happened logically is that without having my mother as a recipient of so much love, I am giving more of it to other people. The flow of love we have is immense, and if we are used to expressing it, it simply gushes out.

That is what I feel in my heart because something I also try to do is to continue to keep the family together, as when my mother, who was the matriarch, was with us. A niece was telling me that I am continuing with the family the way my mother used to do, so there is a change there, a change that I embrace with all my heart.

What Will Your Change Look Like?

> Your journey will never end. People do not "get over" grief. Reconciliation is a term I find more appropriate for what occurs as the mourner works to integrate the new reality of moving forward in life without the physical presence of the person who died.
>
> Dr. Alan Wolfelt

Dear griever: you and I face a challenge in this particular matter. People want us to be the same as we were before we lost our loved one, and, as we said, this is not possible. After losing a loved one, a transformation has taken place within us. By this, remember that I do not mean it is a negative change, only a change. It is really up to us how it will be, whether we will become better people because of that loss or whether we will become bitter, angry, and unwilling to find some way to honor our loved one. Depending on how we handle the loss we are experiencing, the change that will occur in us can be very meaningful. In fact, we can become a better version of ourselves. So that is what we need to keep in mind: that it can be a positive change. We will explore how to handle that loss, which you may even transform into something bigger than yourself, in the last section of the book. For the time being, we will focus on opening the heart to validate your feelings and process grief for the purpose of healing from the inside out.

Attachment

The other word is "attachment." The closer we are to our loved ones, the greater the sense of loss when they are no longer with us.

This helps us understand how to deal with things and what happens to us. You may see it in your family: how different people handle the loss. Some may experience more grief than others; the reason is because of the bond they feel with the deceased. Let us understand this in order to understand ourselves and others. In that sense, change does not have to be a negative thing; depending on you, it can be a significant change. Keep in mind that when you lose your loved one, they will always be in your heart since the relationship does not end because love is eternal. I lost my father as a child, and he lives in my heart. I know that this will also happen with my mother because what changes and what gets transformed is the type of relationship, but the loving bond remains forever[1].

Additionally, I want to emphasize the effect that attachment has on us when we suffer a loss and share with you this text by psychiatrist and psychologist John Bowlby, who pioneered attachment theory and the study of child development:

Which for convenience I term "attachment theory" deals with the same phenomena that hitherto have been dealt with in terms of 'dependency needs' or of 'object relations'…

---

1 Taken from a video from my YouTube channel.

In contrast...During the course of healthy development attachment behavior leads to the development of affectional bonds or attachments initially between child and parent and later between adult and adult. The forms of behavior and the bonds to which they lead are present and active throughout the life cycle (and by no means confined to childhood as other theories assume) (1980, p. 39).

PROCESSING YOUR GRIEF

What change has been brought about in you by losing your loved one?

_____
_____

Has it been negative or have you been surprised by what you have learned about yourself?

_____
_____

How can you open your heart so that this change can help you honor your loved one?

_____
_____

YOUR HISTORY OF LOSS

One exercise I do with most of my clients is their loss history. I discovered this incredible tool when I was in my graduate program on loss and healing at St. Thomas University in Miami, Florida. I remember the professor telling us to go through the exercise and mentioning that we should include all types of losses, and it came to mind when I lost my bunny rabbit at the age of eight. At that moment, all the grief that I had never processed suddenly came pouring out unexpectedly, and I was able to release, in tears, the great pain that I had kept in my soul for many years. I was not even aware that I was still carrying the pain of that loss since I had never had the opportunity to process it. Therefore, doing that exercise was very cathartic and healing. It sometimes happens that, when facing a new loss, past griefs that were never processed come to light. Let us keep in mind that, throughout our lives, we face different types of losses and often keep them in the deepest recesses of our being. I suggest you do this exercise because something similar to what happened to me may happen to you: a loss that you have kept bottled up in your soul comes to the surface, and you can then process it to let it go. Because it has the potential to be very cathartic, I suggest you set aside a couple of hours and dedicate them to this exercise. Turn off your cell phone, have a box of tissues next to you, and, with your heart open, connect with your inner self.

Keep in mind that if other losses come to light, they have the potential to intensify the grieving of the current loss. We would call that "bereavement overload." This reminds me of Carla, who had lost her mother and was very upset because, in the midst of her grief, she remembered her ex-boyfriend Carlos, who had left her a couple of years earlier just before they were going to get married. She learned to suppress the pain at that time and used the mask of indifference. Because she did not get to process it, as she was experiencing deep grief for her mother years later, that unprocessed loss became present.

Another story that I have shared in seminars and with my clients because of how much it impressed me, as it showed me how suppressed losses affect us at an unconscious level, took place on an occasion when I was giving a workshop on grief and a lady came in who had recently lost her husband. She was looking for help because, in spite of having great pain in her heart, she was unable to cry. It was when I explained the history of losses and suggested that they think of the first loss they had experienced that she began to cry inconsolably. We kept silent and accompanied her until she gradually calmed down. Then I asked her if she would like to share with us what had caused her so much pain. She told us that, when asked to think of her first loss, she remembered when, at the age of four, she lost the little doll she slept with. Devastated, she went to tell her mother, who told her to go to the closet to get another doll since she had several, to which she replied: "No, Mom, this one is special; I sleep with it," to which the mother argued: "You do not cry for that, it is just a doll." The mother probably wanted to lessen her pain; however, that message stayed with her, and that is how she behaved all her life. In doing the loss exercise, she had the opportunity to visit that incident and give vent to all those pent-up tears.

This exercise is very valuable because it helps us know our patterns since we all have internal patterns, as Rev. Richard tells us in his book *Find Your Way After the Death of a Parent*. Reverend Gilbert, as I like to call him, was beloved by many and highly regarded as an author and educator in the Association for Death Education and Counseling (ADEC) to which I belong. This organization is also known as the Association of Thanatology.

How to develop a loss history

You can do the exercise in the following way: draw a timeline and start elaborating your story with the most recent loss (in this case, the death of your loved one), and then go back to the first one you remember. Keep in mind that a loss is any life transition that has caused you pain. Identify it in this way: the type of loss, how old you were, how you reacted to it, and how those close to you responded to your reaction.

Elaborating on a history of losses is so valuable that psychologists Chaurand, Guillem, and Neimeyer (2011) created the "Inventario de história de pérdidas (IHP)" (Loss History Inventory), which, in addition to asking about the type of loss and how it happened, asks whether the griever believes that the symptoms they are currently experiencing were caused by a loss in the past[2].

PROCESSING YOUR GRIEF

Example for developing your loss history

As you do this exercise, go back in time to the first loss you remember (not just the death of a loved one, but any situation that has caused you grief and felt like a loss) and continue to the present moment. The purpose is to get in touch with that side of us, process it, heal it and let it go.

---

[2] https://www.researchgate.net/publication/220015722_El_Inventario_de_historia_de_perdidas_IHP_Presentacion_y_utilidad_clinica

---

TIMELINE

FIRST LOSS _____ ACTUAL LOSS

This is an example of how you can elaborate it:

My first loss was _____

I was _____ years old. My reaction was _____

My family's reaction to my reaction was _____

PRIMARY LOSS AND SECONDARY LOSSES

I would like to talk to you about the concept of primary and secondary losses because it is to be expected that when a primary loss occurs, there will be other collateral losses. The loss of a loved one is the primary loss, which originates the secondary losses, which also need to be recognized and elaborated on. Because we suffer this loss, we may also be confronting other secondary losses from the first. Examples of this are loss of status, loss of the life you hoped to have in the future, loss of the realization of your plans together, financial loss, loss of security, loss of your partner, loss of support, purpose, or meaning (if you were the caregiver of your loved one). As you reflect on your primary loss, elaborate on secondary losses so you can process them as well.

Loss of Identity

A type of secondary loss you may be experiencing is that of identity. Being my mother's caregiver, that happened to me at the beginning of my process. Although I had a lady who took care of my mom and helped me by accompanying her, I was the person in charge of her physical, emotional, and spiritual well-being. I took care of everything around her. It was those other roles that are gone and gave meaning to my life that was building my own identity as her daughter, as her caregiver, as someone who made decisions for her, that gave me a very special and meaningful reason to wake up every day.

So, when my mom died, I asked myself: who am I now? As I reflected on that question, I came to realize that I had other very important roles in my life that also filled my soul, and that is where I focused. After deeply processing the loss of identity, I connected with my essence, with that person who loves to help and who has a mission in life to carry out: to continue helping the grieving in their darkest moments and guiding them to find their own light through their loss.

What fills my heart the most is that my mother's light illuminates my path and inspires me to continue my mission in an even deeper, more spiritual, more soulful way, if that is conceivable.

On the other hand, there is the possibility of continuing the invisible ties that arise due to attachment. In the case of widows and widowers, maintaining attachment to the deceased spouse has been shown to help them retain a sense of identity:

> It seems likely that, for many widows and widowers it is precisely because they are willing for their feelings of attachment to the dead spouse to persist that their sense of identity is preserved and they become able to reorganize their lives along lines they find meaningful (Bowlby, 1982, p. 98).

I can attest to what is contained in this quote, as that is what happened to my mom when my dad died. She was fifty-two years old, and I believe that the attachment she always felt toward him was what helped her to maintain her identity as his wife, as well as to acquire a new identity for the future, as she became a businesswoman following in his footsteps. I think that what she kept repeating with great determination, "I carry on your daddy's legacy," was what inspired her to develop this new identity to honor his memory.

One exercise I have done on identity loss with almost all my clients and highly recommend is to write down on a piece of paper, "Who am I?" because sometimes after a loss, due to the changes that arise, and especially if we have played roles that become non-existent, we may feel a sense of loss of identity. This can cause us to feel a great deal of confusion, leading us to not recognize who we are.

In doing this exercise of "Who am I?" you can add: "Who was I before my loss? Who am I now?" Something interesting can happen to us in this regard, as Welshons points out: "We honor loss when we recognize its ability to peel away the layers of who we think we are. Then we can experience who we really are" (2003, p. 194).

PROCESSING YOUR GRIEF

Who was I before I lost my loved one?

_____
_____

Who am I now?

_____
_____

Am I surprised to find out who I am?

_____
_____

Multiple losses

When we suffer different types of losses at the same time, we call them "multiple losses." They can cause in us what we call "*bereavement overload*"—a term introduced by the psychologist and gerontologist Robert Kastenbaum (1969)—which occurs when the burden of losses occurring successively or simultaneously becomes too much for the bereaved because they represent the challenge to be able to process one before the other happens.

These losses can occur as a result of primary loss, as mentioned above.

PROCESSING YOUR GRIEF

The primary loss I am experiencing is:

_____
_____

Secondary losses that have arisen due to the primary loss are:

_____
_____

How have secondary losses affected my grieving process?

_____
_____

Accepting the Loss

> I would say that ACCEPTANCE is the key to healthy grieving: acceptance of what happened and acceptance of what is felt..
>
> María, bereaved mother

In the case of the death of a loved one, we may continue waiting for the person, calling them, or simply refusing the possibility of their death.

Acceptance can be a challenge when we lose a loved one as we miss their physical presence. I understand this wholeheartedly. However, by not accepting the reality of what has happened to us, we stay in denial. Does this help us? Do you want to stay in that space? Regarding the 11 Principles of Transformation® system, you may have noticed that the first of these is "Accept your loss." This is perhaps the most difficult thing to achieve and the most necessary since it is the first step. Although it is not easy, it was what I did when my mother died. I accepted, with pain in my heart, that she had gone to be next to The Lord.

Please keep in mind that acceptance consists of not resisting the reality that you are living. It implies not staying in denial since resisting what has happened to us can do us more harm because it stagnates us. Remember the saying, "What you resist, persists." Additionally, we understand that acceptance itself can be a process, depending on the type of loss you have suffered. I explored this with John, a psychologist I met during the presentations I conducted for PESI. John, in his seventies, had vast experience of the subject of grief and recognized how important it was to come to terms with the loss itself. However, he also knew that this principle of acceptance could be a process depending on the type of loss. John found so much value in the model of the 11 Principles of Transformation® that he attended the seminar on three different occasions, each time I presented it in the state in which he resided.

What I suggest to you with all my heart is that you give yourself the opportunity to process it little by little since accepting it does not mean assuming the attitude of: "This happened to me, and I move on as if nothing happened." On the contrary, it implies opening the door to make room for the grieving process. That is precisely why I named my second principle: "Live your grief." We will talk about it extensively in the next section of the book. I have always said to my clients: "Live your grief, do not deny it, do not ignore it." And if I have said it over and over again, how can I not do it myself? I am living my grief.

The main complaint I have heard over the years in helping my clients through this process is that they are not allowed to grieve. I do not feel free to grieve, either. Since I am experiencing the same challenge, I wanted to take this opportunity to open my heart and help you open yours. I also want to touch the souls of all those people who do not allow others to express their grief openly because they do not know what to say, do not to hear about it, or it reminds them of their own losses. One thing I have noticed is how uncomfortable it makes people feel to see us cry. That reminds me of what psychologist Hugo Castelblanco tells us, who, upon losing his son, noted:

"Pain bothers, tears bother. When we see a person crying, we are tempted to say, 'Do not cry, it hurts you,' but the truth is that it is us who are being bothered!" (2021, p. 6).

Below, you will find the chapter dedicated to the one who accompanies you, as I wish to help you provide the best help to others in times of grief.

My mother: my meaning and my purpose

After writing these pages—which was in August 2020—I did not take up this book again, as I had the purpose of finishing it in March 2021. It was not for lack of desire but because my soul was crying out to write a book about my mother, immerse myself in her story, absorb every photo, and recreate every anecdote, and I decided to put this book on pause and dedicate myself wholeheartedly to my mother's biography. That is how *¡Arriba Corazones! Celebrando la vida de mi madre centenaria* was born, which was released right on her anniversary, as I had intended since I knew I would experience that first anniversary in a different way.

I wanted to dedicate myself fully to that project, sensing that it would be an essential element in my healing process. It gave meaning to my life because with my mother being the center of my existence—as I was her caregiver—my mother was also my purpose, the center of my existence, and my mother was also my purpose. No longer having her with me, the feeling of emptiness was tremendous, almost impossible to bear. That is why I decided to commit myself to finding meaning and filling my soul with elation since every time I turned on the computer and opened the document "My Mother's Book," my heart jumped with joy.

A Period of Transition

> I know why we try to keep the
> dead alive: we try to keep them
> alive to keep them with us.
>
> JOAN DIDION

I think that is what prompted me to write the book about my mother so soon. Seeing each photograph and writing down each anecdote was like keeping my mother alive, like having her with me. Moreover, after it was published, I came to understand that writing it had served as a transition since, after having had her physical presence every day, the separation had not been so abrupt but gradual. As I looked at each photograph and reconstructed each anecdote, it was as if I was still maintaining her presence by weaving her story together. And that was and is my purpose: that through that book, her memory, her teachings, her joy of life, her love for others, and her faith in God and Our Lady will not die. Thus, she will continue to live among all of us.

In the midst of so much pain, that was the best decision I could have made. In fact, writing a book about our loved ones is something I have suggested to many of my clients, as I feel it is both cathartic and sublime. In a later section, we will elaborate on the theme of how finding meaning in our loss helps us in the healing process.

Having lost my mother, I want to share with you the challenges I have faced in this process, as well as what has helped me, what has impacted me, and what has not helped me. I want to share it with you so that, through my experience, I can help you live your own process.

Unprecedented losses
due to the coronavirus pandemic

Having written this book between 2020-2021, I could not fail to mention the terrible pandemic of the coronavirus or COVID-19. This has happened globally and has resulted in multiple losses, which can add even more pain to the physical absence of a loved one, especially in these times when we do not have the same freedom to be distracted due to so many restrictions. Many people avoid going to the movies, shopping, and staying home alone. On top of that, they do not want to be bothering their family or friends. What is more, there are almost no face-to-face support groups; most are virtual, and many people feel it is not the same. These challenges today prevent people from being able to be with others, enjoy time together, hug, and be comforted by their loved ones in the face of loss. In particular, I have missed giving a hug to my clients who are also grieving because it is a silent way of showing that you are present and that you are with them in what they are feeling.

In addition, we have also lost track of the world we know, of what is familiar to us. We have lost our lifestyle, and the fear of an uncertain future has been discovered.

With the pandemic, accompaniment is almost non-existent. Relatives dying alone in a hospital, children unable to visit their parents in nursing homes, grandparents unable to see their grandchildren because of physical distance... All this has also brought with it feelings that we must be careful not to fall into isolation, fear, or anxiety. Thoughts such as: "What if I catch COVID-19?" all of this can add layers to our grieving process as, with the distancing, there can be a lack of that support that helps us so much to process it.

All of the above circumstances have increased the sense of loss that we may have within us. This is a classic example of secondary losses that can complicate the natural grieving process if left unattended. The coronavirus pandemic, also known as COVID-19, as we have said, has represented multiple losses because not only did a loved one die, but we have experienced other losses that sometimes we cannot elaborate on in the first instance. We have lost the assumptive world, the world we knew, many customs, the company of family and friends, the possibility of accompanying our loved one in the hospital or being by their side at the time of death, support groups, traditions, and rituals that confer a lot of meaning, such as the funeral.

There are other types of rituals that can also be of great significance and that, suddenly, you could not carry on, as happened to me. For a long time, I had thought that, after my mother died, I would travel to India as part of my grieving process. I dreamed of isolating myself in an *ashram* and spending time meditating and connecting intensely with my inner self. I imagined it would have to be a highly spiritual experience of great value. However, due to the COVID-19, it was not possible for me to do so, which made me very emotional. The opportunity will come to me at the right time if it is meant for me.

What has been a big challenge with the pandemic issue is that we do not see an end to it yet. It is now 2022, and new variants are still being developed. This continues to influence the way we deal with grief because, although there is no longer the confinement that took place at the beginning, many people—for fear of contagion—are not able to accompany the bereaved by attending the funeral, visiting them or expressing their condolences through an embrace.

PROCESSING YOUR GRIEF

Did you suffer any loss due to covid-19?

_____

_____

What emotions did you experience?

_____

_____

How did you handle the changes caused by the pandemic?

_____

_____

How did living through the covid-19 pandemic affect you in your own process?

_____

_____

"Death": The Word We Do Not Want to Say

> Humans do not know what to do with death.
>
> Rosa Montero

> Until it strikes someone with whom we have a close, vital relationship, we tend to think of death as something that happens to other people.
>
> Rick Taylor

> Dying permeates living, and yet. much of the public response to death and dying remains polarized between sensationalism and silence.
>
> Iona Heath

Dr. Iona Heath, in her book *Matters of Life and Death*, emphasizes that death has an indissoluble link with life since it is an integral part of it. Therefore, we wonder how it is possible that there is so much denial about it in our western society.

I remember when I took my first class on death. I was studying Psychology at the University of Miami, and after taking an elective on world religions, I decided to take another degree in Religious Studies because they offered a course that captivated me: *Death and Dying*. I was thrilled to take it, and I am not surprised as it became a catharsis for me. Every day I attended class was an opportunity to process the grief I carried in my heart for the loss of my father, something I had never consciously realized.

To demonstrate how this denial of death is represented, I wish to share with you the synopsis of Richard A. Kalish's "The Horse at the Dinner Table," a text that serves as a prologue to the book *Death and Dying, Life and Living* (2018).

The prologue tells us about a person who went to a dinner party where everyone was having a good time until they were invited into the dining room, where a horse was on the table. Nobody alluded to it and pretended not to see it. This is precisely the attitude that prevails in our society and interferes with our ability to share with others how we really feel when we have lost our loved ones. This is a great challenge that we, the bereaved, face.

Lingering death or sudden death

Which one hurts more? I have been asked this question repeatedly when presenting seminars or interviews, and I always replied that I had only experienced my father's sudden death. Now that I have experienced both, I can reflect on each.

With a sudden death, you feel the person was suddenly ripped out of your life, and your existence changes abruptly. I remember that when my father died, I was left with the feeling of not having been able to say goodbye, of not having been able to tell him once again how much I loved him, to hug him again. I could not process his passing little by little.

Having experienced with my mother the other kind of loss—a long and extended death—was also very painful. This type of grief is experienced very slowly. I felt as if someone was pinching me harder and harder. It was seeing how my mother was declining, the changes taking place... This, in itself, is already a loss, and we begin the grieving process. We can experience this type of grief when we have a family member diagnosed with a terminal illness. It hurts to see the change that is taking place. What if it is our own diagnosis? Do we process grief or ignore it?

PROCESSING YOUR GRIEF

Have you experienced persistent grief?
_____
_____

How did your loved one die?
_____
_____

What type of loss was it? What happened?
_____
_____

What was your role, how did you process it?
_____
_____

Did you have the opportunity to share it with others?
_____
_____

Do you feel that this type of grief is the same or different from what you are experiencing now?
_____
_____

Grief: Our New Companion Whom We Do Not Welcome

> Grief is not something you go through,
> it is something that becomes a part of you.
> It is forever
>
> ELEANOR HALEY

What is grief? It is the natural and unique response to a loss. It is unique because we are unique individuals. We are responding to the loss that we experience that has broken our hearts into a thousand pieces. We have it totally splintered inside and must rebuild it. Facing a loss is like riding a roller coaster and embarking on a journey of ups and downs, sometimes abrupt, sometimes slower. Sometimes, the ride is longer than anticipated, and it is necessary to be aware of the feelings we may experience; let us not close ourselves off from them.

Most people avoid grief as much as possible; they ignore it, repress it, or do not pay attention to it. However, if we do not open our hearts and welcome it, it will not be possible to process it or let go of that part of it that keeps us stuck because, when we lose our loved one, an aspect of our grief remains latent in our heart, in a space known only to us, and we learn to live with that "form" of grief that does not interfere in our daily life.

The more we keep grief unprocessed in our lives, the heavier the burden becomes, and sometimes it becomes impossible to go on. And what happens if we are not even able to take a step? Because grief can take us to that dark place inside us, it can strip our souls bare and make us not know who we are, where we are going, or where we came from.

When you are grieving, you are in an automatic mode; you do not know if you want to move forward or stay static because grieving is like that; it can strip you of any intention to move forward. Grief stops you abruptly, head-on; you come walking, and suddenly, you come up against a wall. And how can you avoid the wall? You want to pass on the right side, but you cannot; you want to pass on the left side, but you cannot because grief will not let you pass; it is right in front of you. And you cannot escape it either; it is there, and you have to touch it, feel it, and assume it because it is yours. Do your best to stay present, as Beatriz, who lost her husband, tells us: "What has helped me the most is prayer and being in my pain"[1]. Indeed, the important thing is to learn to live in the moment and be present in your grief. The first thing we can do when we experience it is to accept it without trying to pretend otherwise; we suffer such great pain because we feel a very deep love for our loved one. The pain we feel comes from the desire to be with the person who is no longer by our side, to smell them, to feel their arms around us and tell us that everything will be all right. Maybe nothing was going to be all right, but just by that person telling us, we felt it would be so.

---

1 See her full story in the appendix of this book.

And what happens now when there is this void when we go to places we visited with our loved one that becomes a trigger for a great, sometimes unexpected pain?

That emptiness actually exists, so much so that we suddenly wonder how we can feel that hole in our stomach if we have it in our hearts. How can we be whole at such times? Since our grief is real, the lack of desire to move forward is also real.

Intense grieving takes everything we have inside and breaks it into a thousand pieces. Since this is my field, I know it is natural for these questions to arise; I know all this intellectually. This knowledge has helped me understand what I think and feel.

Being so close to my mother, I sometimes wondered: "How am I going to live without her? That is the kind of question one asks oneself; that I asked myself, especially in the beginning. And it was not that I would not be able to live, because I knew I would be able to; what I did not know was what my life would be like without my mother being the pivot of it because—as renowned grief counselor and educator Alan D. Wolfelt, PhD (2016) tells us—when we experience a loss of great significance, we grieve every day. However, Wolfelt also emphasizes that, although challenging, what will help us heal one day at a time is to be present in our grief by connecting with our thoughts and emotions. This is something I did from the very beginning of my process, and I tell you with my soul that it is what determines how we will navigate this journey.

There are times in our grieving process when we will fall to the floor. That is understandable; it is human. It is up to us to stay there or get up again. It depends on your choice, how you want to define yourself in this process. Throughout the book, I will be sharing with you different tools and strategies in order to give you a hand in those moments in which it is difficult to get up once more because we may discover along the way that the grieving process never ends; it is eternal. What happens is that with time, it diminishes; however, it is there. It is part of our being. On the other hand, other things always remain in our lives, such as the great love we feel for our loved one, the memories that live in our minds, and the legacy he/she leaves in our hearts. What I want most is for you to feel that I am with you because I understand your pain. Sometimes, it is not easy to take a step forward. However, if we set our minds to it, it is possible.

PROCESSING YOUR GRIEF

Have you sometimes felt like you have a hole inside your heart or stomach?

_____

_____

How do you see your grief represented? In this space describe it or draw it.

_____

_____

Are you living your grief consciously or are you trying to ignore it?

_____

_____

> **Are there times or situations when you feel the absence more?**
>
> _____
> _____
>
> **What do you do when that happens?**
>
> _____
> _____

CHALLENGES WITH MY GRIEF

> Part of what makes grief so hard is that it is invisible. Inside we are torn apart, but outside we look basically the same.
>
> ALLAN D. WOLFELT

When facing the death of my mother, I realized that the challenge was great since many people, in the early days, expected me to overcome grief quickly—when we lose our loved one, we do not get over it; we learn to live with the loss since love is eternal. Listening to the clichés repeated to me by certain people with the best of intentions, I would say to myself, "What makes you think that if I am a grief specialist, I will not grieve the loss of my mother? What about my emotions?" That is one of the biggest challenges that we grievers have: that we are not given the space to grieve the loss of our loved one since people expect us to move on and people expect us to be okay. Who are these people to measure us with their yardsticks? They are people with good intentions who wish to free us from the burden,

I know. What these people want most of all is to be able to fix what has gone wrong when, in fact, there is nothing to fix but to recognize. People expect us not to be sad for long, to go back to being who we were before the loss, but we will not be the same. I talked about this in the section "Change and Attachment." How do we let them know that what we want is to be given the space to live our grief? Grief is not a puzzle to be solved. It is an experience to be shared and understood; therefore, we do not want to hear, "How fortunate that she had a long life; now she is resting." We do not want to hear those things, as most of my clients state: "I do not want people say that to me!"

Freud and the importance of grief work

The psychoanalyst Sigmund Freud was actually the first person to refer to what is involved in the grieving process. In his essay "Mourning and Melancholia" (1917), Freud emphasizes the importance of grief work in order to lead a more meaningful life, since when we lose a loved one, we constantly long for their presence.

This task is not easy for some because it implies decision and responsibility. We try not to face the pain by not giving it importance, ignoring it, or simply minimizing it. In doing grief work, we connect directly with our emotions. It may be that, at first, we avoid feeling the pain; however, by doing so, we release trapped emotions and open the heart to welcome other emotions, such as peace, hope, and love.

Elisabeth Kübler-Ross's five stages of grief

Among the different theoretical models that have emerged

for the elaboration of grief, I consider Elisabeth Kübler-Ross's five stages of grief to be the most influential in our society since they have been applied in different contexts. Kübler-Ross, a pioneer in thanatology, introduced her model in the seminal book *On Death and Dying*, published in 1969. These stages are denial, anger, bargaining, depression, and acceptance. Despite not being conceived as a linear model, that is, not expecting the stages to follow one after the other—something that Kübler-Ross clarified at the time—the griever expects them to occur this way, which has created a lot of confusion. I have had clients express to me how worried they were because they had not experienced either anger or bargaining.

This five-stage model has been misinterpreted, as discussed by David Kessler, who wrote with Kübler-Ross *On Grief and Grieving* (2005). Kessler emphasizes that in grief, there is no typical response; therefore, not all of us experience the stages or go through them in a particular order. What this model has helped us to do is to recognize the different emotions we may feel, which serve as a frame of reference.

Based on my experience, I would tell you that the stage that seems to be the immediate response to loss is *denial*, for it hurts us to accept, in the first instance, that something as painful as losing our loved one has happened, and many times we just say, "I cannot believe it!" However, grief is not passive. It is active; it is not like what many think and expect: experiencing Elisabeth Kübler-Ross' five stages of grief as the rest of the world. Each grief journey is unique. She later wrote at length that she never expected these stages to be linear or to always happen. In pointing out to you that this trajectory is unique, I share with you this reflection by Esther[2]: "We are authentic, unique, and genuine beings, and we need to go through the dark night of our own soul in order to, later on, already transformed, return to a new life, with new feelings, from a unique experience to be able to follow the path of our own existence."

The fact that our process is unique is also shared by María de los Ángeles[3]: "What I would suggest to someone who is grieving is to deal with their grief in whatever ways are comfortable and meaningful for them. Everyone is different, so each individual grieves differently... There are no timelines when it comes to grief."

Mio[4] tells us how necessary it is to experience grief: "To someone who has suffered a loss I would suggest to acknowledge the loss and allow themselves to go through the grieving process. You cannot stop or avoid the process, you have to live it; you have to feel the emotions and the pain that comes with it. Express your grief and find support in family and friends." To keep in mind that everyone is different and deals with loss differently.

Likewise, JWM[5] points out the following: "I suggest that people should be allowed to cry, to think, and to remember and that no one should contain their mourning. Grief is unique to each person, and everyone experiences it in their own way."

---

2   See her complete story in the appendix of this book.
3   See her complete story in the appendix of this book.
4   See her complete story in the appendix of this book.
5   See her complete story in the appendix of this book.

Is grief as we imagine it?

> Grief as we imagine it and grief as it is.
>
> JOAN DIDION

How do we imagine our grief? Coming to the end of this powerful book, *The Year of Magical Thinking*, and reading that grief is not how we imagine it took me back to an entry I had made in my journal on October 3, 2017, on a plane during a trip from Miami to Nicaragua. In that entry, I commented on how I realized my mom was becoming more frail—she was ninety-eight years old at the time—and wondered what my life would be like without her. I wrote about how I imagined my grief and what my process would be like not having her by my side. I did not know what to think because you do not know what it will be like until it finally happens. What I did believe was that I would no longer work in the field of thanatology. I never expected that, after my mother passed away, I would be able to help people in grief again.

I even thought I might change careers... but no, it just happened to be the opposite. By helping others, I am entering an even deeper, more soulful place. I never expected to find so much meaning in my own grief by helping those who are also grieving. I never expected that I could do it so soon, as I never thought I could help others living through grief this raw.

So, yes, *grief is not as we imagine it but as it is.* Because we do not know what is going to happen. We do not know until it knocks on our door, and, above all, we do not know what the other person is feeling. It is a mistake to say, "I know how you feel," -even if we do it with our soul- because we do not know. J. Shep Jeffreys, in his book, *When Tears Are Not Enough*, defines the reality of grief: "It is what we humans do" (2011, p. XIV).

The unexpected of grief

> In our own woundedness, we can become sources of life for others
>
> Henri J. M. Nouwen

By anticipating the death of a loved one, we can also anticipate how we will react to it. However, the reality is that we do not know in advance how we will handle our grief, and sometimes it is difficult for us to understand what happened, as Alfredo[6] tells us: "The most difficult part of my grief has been trying to understand why."

Grief is unpredictable

I remember, as I mentioned, that before my mother died because I was so attached to her, I thought I would probably stop helping the bereaved and devote myself exclusively to life *coaching*. However, I realized that we cannot predict how we will react to the loss of a loved one. To my surprise, what I felt in my soul was the desire to help the bereaved even more intensely than before. That desire was heightened since the pain I felt in my soul was so great-even having the tools to manage my grief- I wanted to be there to help my clients in those moments of great pain. This reminds

---

[6] See his complete story in the appendix of this book.

me of a very profound conversation I had with my great friend and colleague Howard Winokeur, the internationally renowned bereavement expert, who, upon learning that my mother had passed away, called me to offer his help from a distance. As I shared with him my strong desire to help the bereaved, inspired by my own story, he said to me, "You are the wounded healer," the title of the famous book by the Catholic theologian and priest Henri J. M. Nouwen. Intrigued by his comment, I looked up the book on Amazon, and upon reading it, that sentence struck me deeply, for I identified with it completely: : "Thus, nothing can be written about ministry without a deeper understanding of the ways in which ministers can make their own wounds available as a source of healing" (1979, p. XVI). My dear friend was right, and I repeat the purpose of this book: that by sharing my wounded heart with you, I hope to help you heal your own wounds.

In 1951, Carl Jung, a German psychoanalyst, used the term "wounded healer." He believed that the illness of the soul could be the best possible tool for a healer. In fact, the term "wounded healer" was created by him, who believed that the therapist could help his patients by means of the knowledge he acquired through his own wounds. I believe that this is what has happened to me: through my very deep grief, I feel that I can empathize even more with the acute pain that others feel when they lose a loved one. It is almost like touching someone else's pain and feeling a deep desire to caress it with the hand and soothe it.

> **PROCESSING YOUR GRIEF**
>
> **Are you handling your grief the way you thought you would?**
>
> _____
> _____
>
> **Write in your journal how you imagined it and how you are doing it.**
>
> _____
> _____

THE TRAJECTORY OF GRIEF

> Grief expresses itself in countless number of confusing and surprising ways.
>
> TOM ZUBA

YOUR GRIEF IS PROPORTIONAL TO YOUR CAPACITY TO LOVE

The pain you feel in your heart is due to your great capacity to love. The more you love your loved one, the greater the sense of loss. At the same time, I remind you that, inspired by that great love within us, we possess the capacity to transform that great pain, that suffering, into the possibility of honoring their life and their memory.

WORKING THROUGH GRIEF: WHAT DOES IT CONSIST OF?

> Grief is not a problem to be solved; it is an experience to be carried.
>
> MEGAN DEVINE

When we suffer a loss, we have two choices: ignore it or confront it. By ignoring it, many people think the grief is going to go away on its own. What happens with that is that we *sweep* it under *the rug* and move on. Do you think that really helps? What happens is that by repressing grief, it can manifest itself in different ways, including somatically—in our body, with physical ailments. On the other hand, confronting it is what we mean by doing grief work. It is simply seeing the pain face to face, giving it the attention it deserves, and doing everything in our control to process it. We call it "work" because it requires effort and commitment. If you pay attention to how your grief feels, you may feel drained physically, emotionally, and spiritually. This is because it requires a lot of energy on our part, and it is up to us how we use it.

As Harold Ivan Smith (2004)—a thanatologist and specialist in the subject—points out, by doing griefwork, we begin by seeking an answer to the questions we ask ourselves about how we will continue without our loved one or what we will do with the life we have ahead of us. It is important to understand that there are different ways to do this work: we can join a support group, either in person or online; seek professional help, or share with someone we trust who can listen to how we feel. We can also write in our diary, do meditations centering ourselves and reflecting, or we can pray, connecting with our higher being.

One Moment at a Time

> When we feel sad, it may seem as if our sadness will last forever; in actuality, by definition, all emotions are ephemeral- that is, they are short-term reactions... usually lasting only a few seconds and at the most a few hours
>
> George A. Bonanno

When going through grief or any type of challenge, people often say, "One day at a time." In the case of the death of a loved one, I emphasize the phrase "one moment at a time" because grief is like that. We experience an accumulation of emotions that manifest themselves according to what we are thinking, to the triggers, to the conversations, to the rituals, to the moments in which we are accompanied, to the moments in which we are alone, to the memories, to the experiences, to the expectations, to the unanswered questions. Sometimes, I have heard clients worry about how they will feel for a long time or that they will never be able to experience joy again. If we dwell on those kinds of thoughts, we will feel hopeless, and, in the end, we will feel even worse. Therefore, remember that we experience grief moment by moment. So when you feel better, you can say, "*Right now, I can handle it. In this moment, I am fine. In this moment, I am at peace. In this moment, I am fully functioning.*"

With my grief, the first few days, I felt like I was functioning at half speed. I was very distressed and I knew the journey would be long; I knew it and embraced it as a life experience.

How are you doing?

One of the most difficult questions to answer and one that people often ask us, is: "How are you doing?

This is how Alex shares his experience[1]:

I was asked how I was feeling so many times following my son's passing that it became an annoyance to me, but I knew that people were only asking out of concern. That is when I came up with the response that made all the sense in the world. When people asked me how I was doing, I would say, "I am having good days and bad moments." I realized that saying that I am having good days and bad days would be unfair to myself because every day brings something good with it. So, saying, "I am having good days and bad moments," brings the truth of every day to light.

Actually, that question does not sit well with any bereaved person. I remember once a very dear client who had lost his daughter came into the office, and I noticed he was very upset. I asked him what had happened, and he told me that a friend had just asked him, "How are you?" to which he would have liked to respond, "How do you think I feel if my daughter just passed away?"

If you have lost a loved one, you do not feel good, and it is okay not to feel good! It is your right!

---

1 See his complete story in the appendix of this book.

The journey of grief has its valleys and hills; it has its darkness and light. What I can share with you is my journey and how I have lived this process. In the first few weeks, people would ask me, "How are you?" I would say "I am" because maybe at the time I was experiencing a terrible pain, knowing that grief is lived moment by moment. One step at a time. The way I like to ask my clients is, "How are you right now?" That is what I experienced in my process. The first few weeks were very difficult. Even when I would wake up, my family would ask me, "How are you this morning?" I may have responded: "I woke up," not knowing how I felt. It was like being in an unreal situation, like when you feel numb and unable to feel. Other times, the pain was so present and so intense that I could not stop crying. And I did not want to stop; I wanted my pain to be expressed in the best way possible. With every tear I shed, I expressed some of my grief. When I started my process, I lived each stage intensely. I went down to the depths of the valleys, touched the ground, and then climbed the small hills full of memories and love. That was my path; no one could walk it but me. The same thing happens to you; no one can walk it in your place, even if they wish, no one can do it. Do not be afraid of it. Let yourself go. You, too, are capable of falling and getting up. Remember my words in your ears: "You can do it. I could do it, and you can do it too."

We go through our own unimaginable pain and begin to take the first steps, climbing the mountain, little by little, slipping sometimes, and pulling ourselves up again, which is what happened to me during the first year after my mother's death: it was the period of falling down and getting up. That is my nature. That is who I am, that is who my mother was, that is who my father was. My parents are my role models on how to restore myself after such enormous pain. My mother taught me resilience. She was stoic when she lost her husband—my father—and her mother—my grandmother—in the space of a month and a day, as she used to say. That was my example, and I am sure it had a great impact on me. We learn and grow by example. As the pain of grief is something unimaginable, the life that can emerge from that grief is also something we cannot imagine, but rather something we can build. One step at a time.

PROCESSING YOUR GRIEF

How have you responded when asked how you are doing?

_____

_____

How would you have liked to respond?

_____

_____

Which valleys have you descended into?

_____

_____

What hills have you climbed?

_____

_____

Name an occasion when you were able to stand up.

_____

_____

Types of Grief. Disenfranchised Grief

> Psychological flexibility empowers us to accept our pain and live life as we desire, with our pain when there is pain.
>
> Steven C. Hayes

According to the renowned thanatologist and educator Kenneth Doka (2002), disenfranchised grief is a type of pain that is not validated by society, as the grieving person is not allowed the right to grieve. The griever experiences a deeper sense of loss because their grief is not validated. This can occur when the loss is not recognized socially, such as in the case of loss of homeland, retirement, or the pain of children leaving for college... In the context of this book, related to grief due to the death of a loved one, this applies, for example, when grief for an elderly parent is not validated because "they had a long life." This was what I experienced with the death of my mother, as being a centenarian, many people would say to me: "Instead of being sad, you should feel happy for having had her with you for so long." Indeed, I feel very happy for having had her with me for a long time; however, what about the absence? What about not having that presence that was a constant for sixty years?

Doka emphasizes the disenfranchised grief in the elderly since "...they are seen as less valuable by society... Society presumes that people have lived full lives and that therefore their deaths are less significant" (2002, p. 151). Additionally, Alan D. Wolfelt (PhD) sees this as a prevailing myth in society and describes the message we receive from others: "Everyone dies, and people who have lived a long, full life are expected to die. You are a grown-up; you know these things. You should not be so upset when your parent dies."

So present is this lack of validation that the author Edward Myers wrote a book called *When Parents Die. A Guide for Adults* after losing his mother. Because of the great pain he experienced as an adult, he realized the need to address the issue of when we lose our parents at that stage of our lives. Myers perceived that society does not validate this type of grief, so he called the first chapter: "Neglected Grief." He notes how other types of extremely painful losses, such as that of a child, a spouse, a parent as a child, or tragic deaths such as suicide are very prominent, and acute grief is to be expected. However, this does not happen with elderly parents, as he tells us:

> But an older parent's natural death-surely this is another matter. An elderly mother or father has lived a long life. After illness and suffering, death may be not only acceptable but welcome...In addition adult sons and daughters have the advantages of experience and maturity to help them deal with their parents' deaths (1986, p. 1).

However, it is painful since—as the author mentions—there is another type of vulnerability, as shown by the words spoken by a woman after losing her parents:

> My parents died within ten months of each other and the loss was truly devastating for me. Despite a supportive husband

and two great children, I felt orphaned-truly isolated. I had lost the only unconditional love in my life (1986, p. 2).

In speaking of the disenfranchised grief of a loved one, I do not wish to limit myself to the death of an elderly parent. I also wish to include losses due to miscarriage, natural loss, or death of friends, colleagues, or partners. Among the types of death that touch our hearts because they have a social stigma and can also be unrecognized grief or, as we call it, *disenfranchised grief*—including death by drug overdose and suicide[2].

Luly[3], one of my clients, shares with us how she felt after losing her son to an overdose:

> The greatest challenge I find is that I feel most people do not associate an overdose death as a death from a disease. There is so much social stigma about the person he was, "...after all, he was a drug addict." Friends" and even close "family" do not call, text or write, they just ask how you are. I find it hard to talk to most people because I find that losing a child leaves you speechless.

One thing we sometimes feel we have to do is let people know that our loved one had qualities and that the way they died did not define them. This is what Chip[4], one of my clients, felt when he lost his daughter, Katie:

> When sharing with others about my grief is strange and I will tell you why. Every time I told someone about Katie

---

2 See https://www.ncbi.nlm.nih.gov/pmc/articles/PMC9526383/
3 See her complete story in the appendix of this book.
4 See his complete story in the appendix of this book.

overdosing, especially those that did not know her, I HAD to clarify the fact that she went to a private school, went to the University of Miami Law school, and taught Crossfit. I could not leave it that she overdosed without pointing out the good things. She was such an enigma.

PROCESSING YOUR GRIEF

Have you experienced a loss that has gone unrecognized?

_____
_____

What emotion did you feel?

_____
_____

How did you express it?

_____
_____

How did the people close to you react?

_____
_____

What do you miss the most?

_____
_____

Present and anticipatory grief

We always talk about anticipatory grief when we are going to suffer the loss, and we imagine what our lives will be like without our loved ones. However, what happens when we have our loved one with a terminal illness, with a degenerative disease, when they become old, when we see the changes of age, when we see that they are fading away... This is a present grief. So, we can suffer from two types of grief:

Present grief is experienced when we witness the changes in that person and also the changes in our relationship with them. Maybe we used to go out together to eat, to the movies, or to the beach, but we can no longer do that. In my case, this happened with my mother. When she decided to become bedridden after achieving her goal of turning 100, she became increasingly frail and eventually needed hospice care. My mom, my companion, was no longer my partner. My mother was changing: she was no longer the mom I recognized, the active mother. I had to learn to enjoy the moments I could have with her, the moments when she was awake, the moments when we prayed together, and her endearing actions when she did them...I had to start living off those moments instead of having the complete, full relationship I had before. That can definitely create a sense of grieving because I also thought, "What will happen when she is no longer here?" My love for her was so great that I was able to imagine how much it would hurt to no longer have her by my side. However, what was it that helped me? What did I do in those moments to change the perspective? I thanked God for having her and for being able to enjoy her in whatever way I could. Instead of focusing on how sad it was that she could no longer go out, on the changes that had taken place, or how painful it would be when I no longer had her with me, I focused a lot on being thankful and enjoying the moments I still had with her.

If you are with your loved one and they are going through some physical condition, instead of allowing suffering to consume you by thinking about the pain you will feel when are no longer with you, take advantage of it and focus on the present moment, for that is what you have with them. Sometimes, our minds play tricks on us and create many future scenarios. However, the future is uncertain. You will know when it is your time to live it. The only thing you have is the now; therefore, make the most of your loved one, always relying on love. Those memories are what will remain with you afterward, because what depends on us is how we live the moments we have with our loved ones. Additionally, it is important to process the grief you are feeling, to realize that the sadness overwhelming you is grief, and to work through it by writing about it. If you need to go to a support group, do so, as help is often needed to navigate this transition. It is essential to express how one feels when facing this type of loss, which is both present and anticipated.

PROCESSING YOUR GRIEF

Are you experiencing an anticipated loss?

_____

_____

What kinds of thoughts come to mind?

_____

_____

> **Are you focusing on an uncertain future?**
>
> _____
> _____
>
> **What can you do to focus on the present tense?**
>
> _____
> _____

WHAT DOES FROZEN GRIEF MEAN?

When experiencing a loss, it is natural to grieve. When this happens not in the moment but sometime later—months or even years—it has become into frozen grief. When we set it aside, we sweep it under the rug and do not enter that space, this can happen. It might occur because, as the pain is so intense, we freeze it as a defense mechanism. We leave it for later and use all our energy in other activities. It can also happen when we have to take care of important matters, such as attending court in the case of a tragic death. All the energy is concentrated on the legal process, and the grieving is postponed for later. The person may also declare that the loss does not hurt or that they are strong. The reality is that they are ignoring it.

I have had clients who have lost loved ones months ago, even years before they came to see me. What we do in that instance is to relive the loss and have the person reconnect with the thoughts and emotions attached to that death.

Recurrent grief

> Many Americans still seem to think that grief can be finished.
>
> Paul C. Rosenblatt

You may be surprised to hear this term, but what do we mean by recurrent grief? How does it present itself? Psychologist Paul C. Rosenblatt, based on his extensive studies on bereavement, concluded that we do not reach a definitive ending. In other words, we do not have specific a moment to say: "I have finished grieving." In effect, what we do is that we learn to live with it since it is something that is part of us. In addition, Rosenblatt states that according to evidence-based on his research studies: "Strong feelings of grief for major losses will recur over a lifetime" (1996, p. 45). Moreover, he tells us how necessary it is to know that this is going to happen to us because if we are not aware that it may happen, it may cause us even greater pain. This is why I have included this perspective so that we are prepared and know that it is a natural part of the grieving process. This is why I want to share with you an experience I had after my father died.

It had been five years since my father's death, and on his fifth anniversary, I felt that I especially missed him. I wanted to see him. I wanted to hug him. I took his picture, which I had in a wooden frame, and holding it against my chest, I walked all around the house in a fit of despair. Five years had passed! And who could tell me that "enough" time had passed? There is no such thing as time for grief.

I had managed to live through the intense pain, and little by little, I had been learning to live without my father by my side. However, for some reason that anniversary triggered a tsunami of grief. I share this with you because it is likely you have experienced something similar despite the passage of time. At a special moment, whether it is an anniversary, birthday, or family celebrations like Christmas, the pain resurfaces deeply, and you feel as if the wound had been reopened. Do not close yourself off to the feelings and the pain. Remember that the grieving process is like a rollercoaster: one goes up and down, but as time goes by, the downs are less frequent and less intense, until a time comes when they only happen occasionally. Though they rarely disappear completely; they can remain dormant within us and, at times, be almost imperceptible.

Sometimes we may feel that we are not making progress in our healing process

> Healing is not forcing the sun to shine, but letting go of that which blocks the light.
>
> Stephen and Ondrea Levine

Due to these moments of recurring pain, you may feel that you are not processing your grief or moving forward in your healing journey. I wish to remind you that this is a path that cannot be rushed. In those moments, I suggest that you reflect on the past months or even years, and you might recall an anecdote you had forgotten. It will show you how far you have come on your path.

I remember Alina, who lost her infant daughter. When she experienced recurrent grief, she thought she was not processing it, as she was surprised by how intensely she felt her absence.

After reminding her how the grief process works, that is no linear, I mentioned something that had happened months earlier. She used to avoid entering the baby's room, as it was very difficult for her, and she asked me if she should do it. I told her at that moment to look inside herself and follow what her heart was telling her. In the next session, the first thing she said to me was: "I sat in the rocking chair in my baby's room... I cried a lot; however, it was good for me to have done it." By reminding her of this anecdote, she realized how, little by little, she was walking her path of grief, that experiencing recurring moments of pain did not imply either regression or stagnation in her process. Little by little, she was removing what was blocking the healing light.

Is this complicated grief? When the grief is prolonged

> The central issue in prolonged grief is its considerable impact on daily functioning.
>
> KRISTENSEN ET AL

All these emotions that we experience, the thoughts that haunt us, and the triggers that set us off are part of natural grief, and most of the population can process it without even needing to seek professional help. On the other hand, what we call complicated or pathological grief is when a person cannot function fully, is unable to overcome acute grief, and may develop psychological and physical problems (Paya, 2010). According to Kristensen *et al.* (2021), prolonged grief is the most common form of complicated grief, one of whose symptoms is the difficulty in accepting the death, continuing without the loved one, constantly ruminating on the details surrounding the death, and even blaming others and ourselves. While it is natural to suffer intensely the loss of our loved one, what makes prolonged grief complicated, according to these authors, is the inability to function on a daily basis.

Men and women, do they express grief in the same way?

This is a question I have heard so much that I wanted to include it in discussing grief, as it will help us explore it. According to Kenneth J. Doka and Terry L. Martin (2010), we can find the following styles of grief processing: instrumental, intuitive, and a mixture of both, which is a continuum. I will describe how each of these styles has been understood, warning you they do not apply exclusively to each gender, man or woman; in other words, we do not want to establish stereotypes. Sometimes, it happens in reverse, and other times, it is a combination of both.

Instrumental grief has been attributed to men, who express it through actions. In this sense, they demonstrate their grief by taking action. Intuitive grief has been associated more to women and focuses on expressing feelings, either by crying or talking. A mixture of both can occur as a continuation from one style to the other.

How do you feel you are? I can tell you that, as someone grieving, I have a combination of instrumental and intuitive, because I have not only expressed my grief through tears and talking about my mom but also by creating things—such as writing books, making videos—that have helped me express it. In my experience working with couples who have lost a child, I have noticed that sometimes the mother is the one who takes care of the funeral arrangements, while the father is overcome with tears or is unable to take any action.

On the other hand, we can also see examples of the instrumental style in men. I remember that during the training I conducted with Dr. Dale Young, he shared an anecdote told by another pastor who also worked with grief. This pastor once organized a weekend camp for bereaved fathers. For the first two days, Friday and Saturday, no one spoke of their grief. When Sunday arrived, just as they were about to leave, the pastor came up with something creative to help these parents process the loss of their children. He suggested they build a pergola. They began constructing it, and suddenly, one of the parents wrote a name on a wooden post. Another father approached him and asked whose name it was. The father replied, "That is my son who died." After that, the father who had asked the question went to the post and wrote his son's name. And so, in succession, each father wrote his son's name, and at the same time, they shared and processed their grief. I tell you this story because it may help you understand what it means to be instrumental. Again, it can also happen to women; therefore, we never know how we will act because we will not know until we experience it ourselves.

Weathering an Emotional Storm
The Tsunami of Grief

> Grief is like the ocean; it comes on waves ebbing and flowing. Sometimes the water is calm. Sometimes it is overwhelming. All we can do is learn to swim.
>
> Vicki Harrison

The grief tsunami strikes when experiencing acute pain and it often occurs unexpectedly. We also refer to it as waves or stabs of grief, wisely described by the German psychiatrist Erich Lindemann, a pioneer in the study of this subject: "Somatic distress occurring in waves lasting from twenty minutes to an hour at a time; a feeling of tightness in the throat, choking with shortness of breath, need to sighing, an empty feeling in the abdomen, lack of muscular power, and an intensive subjective distress described as tension or pain."[5]

When experiencing all these sensations, we may wonder how it is possible to feel so much pain and see life continue without our loved ones, as Kastenbaum indicates. Sometimes, you literally feel them coming like a tsunami that knocks you over and drags you to shore; it makes you feel like your heart has shattered into a thousand pieces.

What to do at that moment? Ride the wave. Cry it out and remember that the wave will pass. As Rodriguez tells us in relation to a moment of extreme pain a day after her son's anniversary, when she thought she would not be able to keep on living: "The wave submerged me for an instant. Then I

---

[5] Cited in Kastenbaum (2011, p. 343).

pulled my head out of the water and took a deep breath" (p. 141). Allow it to pass, take a deep breath, and think of something beautiful about your loved one. One thing I have done when these waves suddenly come is watch videos of my mom saying funny things or reciting. Those videos bring a smile to my face. In this way, I have managed to shift the emotion. You can do it, too, if you give yourself the opportunity.

Let us pay attention to the fact that there is no time limit for the appearance of grief waves and that they arise when triggered: a song, a greeting, a person, a card, a video, a date... there will always be a trigger. Over time, the intensity of the grief will begin to lessen; however, do not be alarmed if another strong wave suddenly reappears. It is natural.

Something that has helped me tremendously when the tsunami begins to form is doing something physical. It is said that as we change our physical state, we change our emotional state. I like to exercise. A few weeks after my mother's death, I decided to buy an elliptical machine to use at home. It helped me release all that heavy energy. Lifting weights is something I especially enjoy because I believe that as I strengthen my body, I also strengthen my mind. Another thing that helped me a lot, especially during the first few months, was writing in my journal and transferring my emotions to paper. Also, when the sting of grief returns, I grab a prayer card and sit with my mother's photo, light a candle, and dedicate a moment to our daily ritual.

Or I simply say to myself, "*Let me close my eyes and let the tears flow... Let me go to church and remain still, feel the grief, acknowledge it...*"

That feeling, that pain will come again, probably less frequently, less strong, less raw, but it will always come, it will always be there, even if it is slight... It will always be there because, with grief, we learn to live without our loved one; however, that latent, internal grief will be with us until we close our eyes. I remember how, even at 100 years old, my mom still longed for her mother because when we love so much, the love and longing do not go away. What we learn to do is take all that feeling of loss and turn it into something that gives meaning to our lives. Brené Brown describes something similar when she shares how a friend compared grief to surfing, "...sometimes you feel steady and you are able to ride the waves, and other times the surf comes crashing down on you, pushing you so far underwater that you are sure you'll drown" (2015, p. 147).

I feel, in the face of that immensity, as if I am facing a huge ocean. I see that great wave coming, sometimes pulling me along, and other times, I just sit by the shore, watching the sea.

I navigate these waters with the heart in my hand. I am immersed in grief to process it fully and let it go because I want to be happy again. That is me. That was my mom. I carry her favorite phrase as a banner: "Hearts up! So much so that I had it placed on her plaque in the cemetery. That is her eternal message.

The triggers

The grieving process does not happen in a straight line; we have laughs and ups and downs, and many times, the downs are due to triggers, which provoke sensations that were thought to be overcome. A trigger that has been present in my process occurs when my iPhone generates surprise videos with photos of my mom.

If it has happened to you, it is natural that it touches your heart. For me, it gives me mixed emotions. On the one hand, it fills me with tenderness and joy to see her and remember those happy moments, and on the other hand, it evokes strong emotions in me because of how much I miss her.

Be proactive in the face of expected triggers

There are situations in which we can imagine that a trigger will go off. One such situation is a special date, such as an anniversary, a birthday, Mother's Day, or Christmas—something we will discuss later. Because I know how those triggers can make us feel, I wanted to prepare for my mom's first birthday, which was August 8, 2020, two months after she passed away. The way I prepared myself was to create a compilation video with photos of her life, from when she was a young woman to her 100th birthday. It became a project, and I started working on it in July. It was something beautiful because I did it to honor her on August 8, to give her that gift. I posted it on YouTube and shared it with my family and friends and on social media. That gave me a lot of meaning and helped me deal with that trigger. Additionally, I wanted to prepare something special for her birthday. My sister Alicia and her daughter Alicita came home, and we did a very special ritual to honor her, which I will share with you later. I can assure you that the fact I prepared myself by making the video and celebrating the ritual made a huge difference in how I felt on her first birthday after her death.

Therefore, I suggest you prepare yourself for those unexpected and intense moments when you may feel your heart breaking. You may have had two or three days of feeling good, and then suddenly, all those thoughts, all those "I wish," all those "why," all those "I miss her" invade your mind. As they multiply, they trigger the emotions of longing again—then you begin to yearn for your loved one.

PROCESSING YOUR GRIEF

Have you experienced detonators?

_____
_____

When did this happen?

_____
_____

How have you handled them?

_____
_____

Have you prepared in advance for a special date?

_____
_____

How did you do it?

_____
_____

Do you feel like you are on a pendulum?

Have you ever felt in your process, like you are going from one extreme to the other? That suddenly you may feel engrossed in your grief and everything that has to do with your loved one? In another moment, you see yourself going about your life in the new world you face without that person, and you perceive that you can carry out those activities and fully function? It may seem to you that you are on a pendulum. Well, this is something that often happens to us when we are grieving. In fact, there is a theory called "The Dual Process Model of Grief" (Stroebe and Schut), which indicates that when we lose our loved one, we experience life as an oscillation between two processes: the loss orientation and the restoration orientation.

When we are loss-oriented, say the authors, we are focused on experiencing our loved one's disappearance, "including the process of confronting, trying to accept the fact of loss, reminiscing about the deceased person, and visiting the burial place to remain close to them" (2016, p. 99). In shifting toward restoration orientation, we focus on what we need to do in our lives as a result of the loss: this includes reorienting ourselves in a world that has changed in many ways because of the death.

Many aspects of our daily lives may need to be taken up and planned again (p. 99).

It is interesting that Bonanno (2019) calls the pendulum "oscillation" and emphasizes that instead of staying sad for long periods, our experience of the emotion comes and goes. It oscillates. Over time, the cycle widens, and we gradually return to a state of equilibrium (pp. 287-288). Bonanno refers to how, when grieving, it is possible to go from sadness to smiling or laughing in an intermittent manner, which can confuse the griever. That is a question I have been asked by many of my clients, who worry and get surprised by being able to smile despite experiencing deep grief. What happens is that the way we tolerate grief is oscillating and precisely shifting from focusing on the pain to focusing on the present world.

Overload

Have you ever felt overburdened by your grief? Have you felt drained and like you cannot handle all that is expected of you?

When this happens, there can be what we call "overload," a feeling that can cause one to feel overwhelmed and unable to cope with so much grief at once. It is so present in bereavement that psychologists Stroebe and Schut (2016) added it to their model of the dual process—loss orientation and restoration orientation—as they realized that it was the *missing link* in this model. Therefore, besides the need to oscillate between the two processes to manage grief, recognizing overload that can be placed on us as grievers is fundamental because what we want to look at is what helps most to manage it. First of all, what we want to do is to talk about what we feel, to have—as they call it—openness, to say how we are, and to ask for help when necessary. Life itself generates causes of stress, and when we are grieving, those stressors can be magnified, as we have a limited capacity to deal with events or situations. Something that can also help us is to develop tools that make us feel empowered, to apply *mindfulness,* and to learn to say no. This reminds me of a phrase that tells us that sometimes when we say yes to others, we are saying no to ourselves, which can cause anxiety and a feeling of overload.

Be aware of what you can bear and take measures on how you are managing your process, as researchers have recognized how necessary it is to take a pause, to take a *break* in both processes to avoid feeling 'overload': "But one cannot cope the whole time, it is exhausting to do so a lot of the time; time off is needed, where non-bereavement-related activities are followed or when the person simply relaxes and recuperates" (Stroebe and Schut, 2016, p. 99). These notions, such as taking a *break* and even welcoming brief moments of joy and happiness, help us manage grief and see the possibility of moving forward (Bonanno, 2019, p. 63).

PROCESSING YOUR GRIEF

Do I feel overwhelmed in my grieving process?

_____
_____

Do I feel that it is impossible for me to deal with so many things at once?

_____
_____

How do I behave when I feel overloaded?

_____
_____

> **Do I sometimes feel like taking a break? When?**
>
> _____
>
> _____
>
> **What do I think could help me at such times?**
>
> _____
>
> _____

Note:

Action plan

Write down three things you could do on those occasions when you feel overwhelmed:

1. _____
2. _____
3. _____

Witness Our Own Grief

> What everyone has in common is that no matter how they grieve, they share a need for their grief to be witnessed.
>
> David Kessler

If you have experienced a major loss in your life, you may feel misunderstood and disoriented. These feelings can cause you to feel stuck. Still, you can help yourself take the necessary steps to be active with your grief. Give yourself permission to experience, share, and live your grief. The documentary *Speaking Grief* explores grief with great sensitivity, raising awareness of our struggle to avoid it, even though we know we will experience it at some point. Their recommendation is that *we need to get better at grief.*

The grief we avoid sharing, we keep it inside and carry like a heavy backpack; we avoid it, ignore it, suppress it, drown it until a trigger occurs, and then all that pain that has been suppressed comes to the surface. It was about time we allowed pain to be expressed, witnessed, and understood. Kessler (2019) emphasizes that all of us grievers, regardless of how we express grief, have a need for it to be witnessed (p. 29). Not just that others witness our grief, as Megan Devine points out in her book *It is Ok That You Are Not OK* (2017), but to witness it ourselves, especially when that grief is very deep. A similar concept is the one that Sameet M. Kumar recommends in his book *Grieving Mindfully* (2005), which is precisely about being fully aware of our grief.

Applying mindfulness to grief (*mindfulness*)

> Grieving mindfully can be understood as making the decision to allow yourself to mourn, and to fully experience the lessons of grief with the goal of living life better.
>
> Sameet M. Kumar

One of the most helpful techniques to witness our grief is to apply mindfulness. We can connect by entering that space of grief and remaining still. Feel it and pay attention to it. Remember that what we ignore does not cease to exist; it is only repressed. Therefore, instead of ignoring it and minimizing it, we must face it in order to live it to the fullest because it is the same as fear: when confronted, it loses power. As long as we avoid facing grief head-on, it will continue to feel like a heavy shadow over us, pulling us down and making us lose our strength. We may become numb at first. Some people do not express it and carry it inside for many years, internalizing it without realizing it. Often, if we do not pay enough attention to it, it can manifest itself physically in our personal relationships or in our productivity.

Representation and expression of grief through art

When we experience the death of a loved one, the emptiness we feel in our soul when that person is not there is so great that it is impossible to describe it. Sometimes, we can only, like children, draw or paint it. Many other times, we use art to express our feelings, which are impossible to name. I remember that, shortly after my mother passed away, someone shared with me the image of the sculpture *Melancolie* by the Romanian sculptor Albert György. In it, we can see a man sitting on a bench with a dejected posture and a large hole in his torso. György had lost his wife and wanted to represent his grief in this way. It is very powerful because it inspires a lot of emotion as that hole can be felt very deeply, and you also feel that nothing can fill it. When I saw that image, I completely identified with the projection of pain in that artistic manifestation. I was not the only one since thousands of people have contacted him to make replicas of the sculpture.[6]

This gives us an indication of the number of people who wish, in some way, to see their grief represented and

---

6 https://totallybuffalo.com/a-sculpture-that-creates-intense-emotion/

contemplated. When my mother died, the pain I felt was so deep that it was as if someone had ripped out the center of my body and left it empty, just like György's sculpture. In recent days, I had an experience with a client who, in describing how she felt physically, reminded me of that image, and I asked her if she knew it. Smiling sadly, she told me that she did, that a friend who had lost a child had sent it to her. That made me think that we, the bereaved, have a unique way of communicating. Despite being different and unique, the grief we feel is like an adhesive that binds us together as we suffer the absence of our loved one.

Poetry as a form of expression in grief

Do you know what reawakened in me with my mother's grief? Writing poetry, as it is something I used to do when I was younger. When my mother died, all that pain, all those words that flowed through my soul, needed to be on paper. That is how I returned to poetry as a form of expression for my grief.

On this occasion, I will share one with you, which is the one that, I would say, represents in the most palpable way how I felt in those days at the beginning of my day.

Thank you, Mom

Is the world moving faster, or am I the one moving slower? Suddenly, the spaces are bigger. Suddenly, the steps I take have lost their haste; they are only tiptoeing on the floor. It is as if, by tiptoeing, I do not feel the floor underneath.

I will not feel the coldness of this reality, which is like a cloak, like a blanket, like a layer of coldness over me.

That coldness is the coldness of death. The feeling that everything has stopped.

How do people keep walking if everything stopped? What do I care about eating?

What do I care about drinking?

The greatest source of my joy, the greatest source of my purpose, my little doll, as I called her, is not here to hug me, to reach out her small arms and hug me against her chest, to make her forehead move toward mine, to touch our noses in that unique and intimate movement of love and total surrender to what love means.

The absence of warm from that body I cuddled so many nights.

The face I caressed with adoration. True love. The eyes I kissed day after day. Her body so small and yet so strong. Strong will, warm heart. Unlimited love, without limit.

A capacity to love beyond words. A life filled with joy, appreciation for everything, thanks for everything, "how beautiful!" for everything, "what a joy!" for everything.

This was the beauty of this woman who lived for 100 years and made a difference in each one of us.

This woman I used to call "Mom"; this woman I used to call "my beloved mother."

This woman I used to call "my little doll." The emptiness... the emptiness is beyond words...

Nothing can fill the emptiness, nothing and no one. That was her place. It belonged to her alone. Our love was deeper than deep, stronger than strong, closer than close, an understanding just by looking at each other, an understanding just by seeing each other... and that was it.

Thank you, Mom, for showing me what love means. Thank you, Mom, for showing me what strength means. Thank you for showing me what faith is.

In the book I wrote about my mother celebrating her life, I included all of them; however, on this occasion, I am sharing only this one with you. I want you to know that I wrote it with the heart in my hand.

In my process, there have been very dark moments in which I have felt that the pain could not fit within my soul because it was immense. Once, I stood there looking at it deeply and thought: "If I stay there, I am taking in the sense of defeat, and that is not me because I carry my mother's love within me, and her famous phrase 'Hearts up!' has been my mantra, my inspiration."

Deepak chopra and grief

I would like to share with you three tips from Deepak Chopra, the renowned spiritual leader and expert in alternative medicine, who brings us a short video on how to deal with the death of a loved one[7].

The first piece of advice he gives us is: *Bring them into your awareness and talk to them.* Chopra tells us how he talks to his parents every day, and it is something that, in fact, I do with my mom, not only when I go to the cemetery. I often do it to tell her about something beautiful that happened to me or even to remember something funny. It is something that most of my clients do, and—as Chopra himself points out—we suggest it as part of the grieving process because,

---

7   https://www.youtube.com/watch?v=LBFufOhggvM

although our loved one is not next to us on the physical plane, they still exist in our thoughts, in our hearts, and because the relationship does not end, it transforms. You can do this by speaking out loud, writing a letter, or writing little notes and putting them in a box, as mentioned in the rituals section.

The second piece of advice is: *embrace grief*. This is precisely what I have wanted us to do together with this book, to live grief, because, as Chopra himself reminds us, if we repress it, it becomes stronger.

The third tip is: *express love*. Love is the most powerful emotion, and we can express it in many ways: by giving love to ourselves (self-love), by expressing it to others through our gestures and actions, and, in a unique way, by transforming our grief into eternal love.

The effect of denying or repressing grief

> It is gathering the courage to turn toward the pain of your grief that ultimately leads to the healing of your wounded heart.
>
> ALAN D. WOLFELT

A natural and common reaction when experiencing a loss is denying it. Denial is one of Elisabeth Kübler-Ross' stages and, as I mentioned before, is the most common in grief since, in many cases, it helps to come to terms gradually with reality and to cope with the anxiety that can be experienced in the face of a painful transition. John Wilson, PhD, puts it this way:

How may the denial phase have been useful in human evolution? The intense pain of grief can be debilitating to the point that we are unable find food or keep safe from predators. Individuals who could get themselves into a stable position and safe place before they grieved would have been more likely to survive and pass on their genes, particularly if kinship individuals chose to care for them. Even today, in wars and natural disasters, individual grieving is sometimes delayed until it is safe to do so.[8]

In the case of the death of a loved one, we may continue waiting for the person, calling them or denying the possibility of their death. Repeatedly, I have noticed that the person avoids saying the word "died" or "deceased" and uses euphemisms such as "is resting," "he left," and "the day he departed."

PROCESSING YOUR GRIEF

Have you avoided using the word "death" when referring to your loved one?

_____

_____

What makes you avoid using it?

_____

_____

What other word have you used?

_____

_____

---

[8] https://johnwilsononline.org/2014/01/06/happy-grief-a-stage-to-work-towards/

> **What does it mean to you?**
> _____
> _____

Inside of us it seems impossible that we are facing such great pain. It seems unreal to us that we have lost our loved one and that we will never see them again. I understand you with my soul if you feel this in your heart.

We know that at first, we may experience *shock* or feel numb in the face of so much pain. Many times, we end up, in fact, in denial about what happened and suppress our grief. Our hope is to erase reality, to imagine that it has not happened, and continue as usual. However, this is not the case, and that immense pain can manifest itself in different ways, whether physically, affecting your health, or affecting your relationship with others. If you find yourself denying what has happened, you can talk to someone who can help you. There is a great void inside of us, and we do not know how to fill it. If, on the other hand, you pretend to be "fine" and avoid showing, in your opinion, weakness, remember that feeling sad or desperate at times is not weakness; it is the natural response to the great loss you have suffered.

Topics for reflection in the face of our grief
What does it mean to be strong?

> Be strong is a euphemism that means to deny or hide your grief because it makes others uncomfortable.
>
> Harold Ivan Smith

If I tell you a joke and you find it funny, you are likely to laugh. Laughter is an expression. The same goes for grief: if you feel sad and your way of expressing it is to cry, then do it. We all have the right to cry, including you.

Zuleika,[9] who lost her husband, expresses the following: "What helps you most in grief is to share with others, to talk and cry and talk and keep on crying. Just to be heard, even if the story is repetitive."

Remember that crying expresses the great love you feel for your loved one and helps you unburden yourself because it cleanses the soul (as the saying goes: "Tears cleanse the soul").

In this regard, Dr. Daniel G. Amen points out: "When we bottle our feelings and refuse to cry, our emotional brain becomes inflamed. After someone has died, it is healthy to let the tears flow freely." https://www.amenclinics.com/blog/7-common-myths-about-grief-that-prolong-the-pain/ However, we continually hear the message: "You have to be strong! And I ask you: what is it to be strong? People generally consider not crying to be a sign of strength. I consider it the ability to connect with our emotions and to

---

9 See her complete story in the appendix of this book (this is a foot note).

be able to express them in a way that helps us process what we are experiencing. Castelblanco emphasizes: "We must know that expressing is important. Expressing with our body, with our words, with our tears. If there is an important moment to express the emotions we are feeling, it is this first moment of our grief. Now is the time to cry" (2015, p. 12).

Your ability to grow through grief is in recognizing it, validating it, sharing it, and entering your inner self to find that hope that will help you continue to carry your loved one always in your heart.

PROCESSING YOUR GRIEF

What does it mean to you to be strong?

_____
_____

Have you been told to be strong? In what context?

_____
_____

Is it easy for you to cry?

_____
_____

How do you feel crying?

_____
_____

If you do not cry, in what ways do you express your pain?

_____
_____

Is this normal?

What is "normal"? I hear this question a lot from my clients because sometimes you think and behave in ways you do not understand. Of course, remember that grief is a taboo topic that is often misunderstood. In my case, it helped me a lot to have knowledge about what happens when we grieve, and I told myself: "Ligia, this is natural" (in my case, I avoid saying the word "normal"). It helped me to feel self-compassion because what was happening was that I had become my observer. It was a dual relationship: the observer and the observed person. As I entered into this dynamic, I would say to myself, "This is to be expected. You are grieving." Being aware that this was natural or "normal" helped me to understand and process my grief in a healthy way. It is precisely because of this experience that I wanted to share with my clients with greater fervor what has helped me in my process. It hurts me deeply to think how they might feel as they continue tormenting themselves with their thoughts; for not being aware how to get out of that space of deep suffering.

Has it happened to you?

After the death of our loved one, we sometimes act automatically, accustomed to what we did before. For example, has something important happened to you, and you instinctively reached for the phone to call your loved one? As my mother's caregiver, I always kept my cell phone by my side in case of an emergency. I remember that a month after her death, my cousin invited me over for dinner, and while preparing, I rushed to the living room grab my phone from my purse as I realized I did not have it with me. It was automatic. The realization that it was not necessary since my mother was no longer alive was like a bucket of cold water. The pain of the loss, the absence, hit me once again. Other times, I would call home from the supermarket to see if she needed anything or call to say I was on my way home from the office. These situations are very common when we lose our loved ones since their presence and what we shared were integral parts of our lives.

Something that also happened to me was listening repeatedly to the song *Después de ti* by Cristian Castro and Raúl Di Blassio. I used to listen to it so much because I identified myself with the phrase "despues de ti no hay nada" (after you, there is nothing), and that is how I felt.

Have you ever listened to a song over and over and over again because it reflects how you feel about your loved one? If so, I share this with you to let you know that you are not alone, and you are not doing anything "strange." It is natural. Like you, I have also felt that absence. I also felt that my heart broke into a thousand pieces and that, at times, I was in a dark place I could not get up from. However, the message I want to convey to you and invite you to do is not to stay there forever. There are times in our grieving process when we will fall to the floor. That is understandable; it is human. But it is up to us to stay there or to get up again. It depends on your choice, and it depends on how you want to define yourself in that process.

Do you feel you have lost your mind?

Another comment I have heard repeatedly from my clients is, "I feel like I am going crazy!" At times, you may feel like you are losing your mind when you are having the magical thoughts we talked about earlier or when your grief deeply consumes you. In those moments, put your hand on your heart and say these words, "This is happening to me because I am grieving." As Albor Rodriguez tells us she said to herself, "It is not that I am going crazy. It is just that the brain takes time to assimilate losses" (p. 21).

PROCESSING YOUR GRIEF

Have you found yourself doing things that did not seem to make sense?

_____
_____

Have you ever called your loved one for no apparent reason?

_____
_____

How have you reacted to these situations?

_____
_____

Have you ever wondered if what you feel is normal? When?

_____
_____

> Have you thought that you may be losing your mind?
>
> What happened to you?
>
> How can you now give yourself self-pity?

CAN WE LAUGH WHEN GRIEVING?

> There is time to cry, time to be spent in serious reflection, and time to laugh – all are healing.
>
> ELEANOR HALEY

This is another of the most common questions my clients ask me because they are afraid that if they laugh, they are either forgetting their loved one, or they feel guilty because, when grieving, they should not be able to laugh. Laughing is something natural and inherent to being human, even when grieving, because it can happen in different ways. We can use humor when dealing with a loss so that it does not feel so heavy or because we feel nervous. I remember what happened to me when my father died: At the wake, I had a fit of laughter and could not stop. Now I realize that I must have been very nervous among so many adults accompanying us in our grief. We can also laugh to handle the situation better and make it lighter.

In short, we can also smile when someone tells us something that relieves us, when we remember our loved one, or when we feel in our heart the love that lives in us.

Why am I not dreaming about my loved one?

That is one of the most frequent questions I hear from my clients. That longing to maintain the connection manifests itself in the desire to dream about the loved one. While I would like to tell them that they will at some point, I cannot say for sure. Based on my experience, some people dream frequently, while others never do. What matters most, however, is to understand that there are other ways in which we can maintain the connection.

What happens if you dream?

If you dream of your loved one and vividly remember the dream, I suggest that you keep a journal by your bedside and write it down as soon as you wake up. This will help you to elucidate what it meant to you. Dreams are very symbolic and have meanings, as Freud (1989) tells us:

> I will provide the demonstration of the existence of a psychological technique that allows the interpretation of dreams and through which each dream is revealed as a psychic product full of meaning, to which a perfectly determined place can be assigned in the psychic activity of waking life. In addition, I shall attempt to elucidate the processes upon which the singular and impenetrable

appearance of dreams depends, and to deduce from these processes a conclusion about the nature of those psychic forces whose combined or opposing action give rise to the phenomenon of dream. Having achieved this, I shall consider my exposition finished, for I shall have reached the point where the problem of dreams leads to other, broader problems, the solution of which must be sought by the examination of different material (p. 2).

Places You Frequented with Your Loved One

> Her absence is like the sky, spread over everything.
>
> C. S. Lewis

Several of my clients have told me that they avoid going to places that remind them of their loved one because they think it will make them feel worse. Now, if in your case, it is a challenge and you want to confront it, you can do it with a close friend whom you trust. Remember that this may be fear of feeling because we are so vulnerable that we do not want to experience pain. However, the only way to overcome fear is to confront it. If you wish to do so—at your own pace—you can go with someone and gradually get closer. There is also a type of therapy that helps a lot when there are traumas, for example, places that we do not want to go to when there is something that we avoid and that has trapped us in a place with no way out. It depends on what you want to do and what might help you in your process.

Have you ever been afraid to go to places where you used to go with your loved one? That is what happened to C.S. Lewis after losing Joy, his beloved wife, until he decided to face the situation and realize that the absence was not worse as it was not limited to one place but was present everywhere.

Despite feeling my mom's absence everywhere, I was impacted by the first time I visited Macy's department store, one of her favorite stores. I have a vivid memory of how I felt walking into Macy's two and a half months after losing my mother. I felt a cold chill inside when I saw the blouses she loved so much and knew that buying one for her was impossible, as I often did. Unexpectedly, I felt like I was lost, and I realized that place had been a trigger. By coincidence, at that moment, my best friend from Nicaragua called me and asked me, "Where are you?" I started to cry. I allowed myself to express my grief to her because if I put on my mask and told her that everything was fine, I would have done nothing but swallow my pain. We talked for a while, and I went from crying to smiling. I remembered, with my friend, a special outing when my mom tried on a hat that made her feel Parisian. It was a very cute memory and full of joy. It moved me from a place of sadness to a place of soulfulness.

Remember to express how you feel to those close to you who can accompany you in your pain. Part of the process involves showing our vulnerability because, yes, we are vulnerable. You know what? It is what makes us human, and by accepting it, we show strength. If we want others to accept us, let us start by accepting ourselves.

> **PROCESSING YOUR GRIEF**
>
> **Have you visited places where you remember your loved one in a special way?**
>
> _____
> _____
>
> **Has it been a trigger for you?**
>
> _____
> _____
>
> **How did you react?**
>
> _____
> _____
>
> **How did you handle the situation?**
>
> _____
> _____

FEAR OF FORGETTING YOUR LOVED ONE

You do not leave your loved one behind and close the chapter. You carry them with you in your heart and soul and move forward inspired by their memory and, above all... by their love. Sometimes, we feel that the only way to be united with them is through suffering.

This passage from the book by Albor Rodriguez (2015, p. 148) shows us:

-I do not want to forget my son, doctor. I understand it is my brain chemistry, as you say, but I do not want to feel good if I really am not.

-You will not forget him, Albor.

-Sometimes I feel that the pain is the only thing I have left of him, maybe that is why I do not want to stop feeling it... Do you assure me that I will not forget him?

-How can you forget him? He was your son, he is part of you.

But I fear the illusion of well-being.

This is precisely one of the greatest fears I have heard from most of my clients: to begin to feel good and enjoy themselves because they consider that they are not respecting the memory of their loved one and may forget them. However, we never forget them, as I discussed on Instalive on November 8, three days before my father's fiftieth anniversary, November 11, 2021. In that talk, I shared how the memory of my father has been kept alive over the years; therefore, they should not fear the idea of forgetting them, for love is never forgotten.

When we talk about forgetting, we can remember the phrase "moving on." What do we mean by this? Below, we will explore these concepts we often hear when we lose a loved one.

Move forward or move on

> I would advise someone who has just lost a child to find a purpose so they may be able to move forward. You never move on!
>
> Maggie, Bereaved Mother

In comparing these two phrases, I want to clarify the difference because sometimes we confuse them, especially in English. *Move on* is a phrase that we grievers hear a lot, and it has the connotation of "getting over the loss." When faced with the loss of a loved one, people say, "It is time to move on." What do they mean by this, that we put them behind us and move on? In the field of grief, we prefer the phrase *move forward*, which means to advance. What is the difference with this phrase? It means that moving forward does not imply "getting over" or "closing the chapter" and forgetting our loved ones. It means that, instead of staying stuck, we continue to live with our loved ones in our hearts.

Social media and grief

Social media have added a social component to our grief. Many people resort to them to share, have pages on Facebook, or write memories of their loved ones on different walls. In addition to that, family and friends continue to accompany us in this way. For me, in particular, interacting on Facebook has helped me a lot in my grief. I have shared many experiences of the past with my mother on this social media, as it constantly generates memories of yesteryear. This is a beautiful thing for me since sharing fills my soul, and reading people's comments brings me great comfort as I feel accompanied from a distance. I have also shared writings and poems that I have written to her inspired by my grief. I have wanted to openly share my pain to let people know my humanity, which is behind my professional image as a grief expert. People sometimes get confused, believing that knowing how to deal with grief means not expressing it or, even worse, not feeling it.

> **PROCESSING YOUR GRIEF**
>
> Have social media played a role in your grief?
>
> _____
>
> If so, what do you like to share?
>
> _____
>
> How does it help you to do so?
>
> _____

Making important decisions in the first year

> The loss of a close and loved person through death is regarded as one of life's most stressful events
>
> KRISTENSEN *ET AL.*

This is one of the reasons why it has been repeatedly said that during the first year, it is best to refrain from making important decisions. If you find yourself needing to make a decision immediately after losing your loved one, it is best to write down the options on paper and look at them again once your mind is clearer. It has been said that when you are grieving, especially in the beginning, you should avoid making decisions of great significance because you may make the wrong ones.

Mourning as an expression of grief

When we talk about grief, it is about what we really feel inside. Mourning is what we express to others. We have different ways of showing that we are mourning, and these have to do with our culture, our religious beliefs, and our personality. We manifest our mourning either by doing rituals—a mass, for example—or by writing in a journal, not attending parties, expressing how we feel, not listening to music, or wearing black clothes.

Black clothing

"And you are still wearing black? She would not like to see you in black." That phrase was said to me by several people with the best of intentions a few months after my mother passed away. On one occasion, I replied, "Well, she would like to see me in black because she instilled it in me." My mom believed in mourning. When my father died, she kept three years of rigid mourning for him. As a twelve-year-old, I wore black and white for a year.

The concept of mourning is something very personal. Some people believe in wearing black clothes, others do not. In my case, it was something that was in accordance with my beliefs, and I did it from my heart. It is something innate in me. I remember many years ago when I found out that my best friend's husband had died in a plane crash, the first thing I did was go home and dress in black. Even though I lived in Miami and she lived in Nicaragua, I did it because I felt it in my soul.

> **PROCESSING YOUR GRIEF**
>
> **Does wearing mourning clothes mean anything to you?**
>
> _____
> _____
>
> **If there was one color that represented what your heart feels, what would it be?**
>
> _____
> _____
>
> **What would it mean?**
>
> _____
> _____
>
> **How is your compass in your grief?**
>
> _____
>
> **Are you living by it?**

Therefore, wearing black clothes is, for me, a way of expressing what I feel, and at the same time, I felt I was honoring my mother. For a year and two months, I mourned her, oscillating between black and black and white. When I wanted to bring peace to my soul in a tangible way, I wore white. Then, I began to transition little by little, wearing soft colors. I did not feel in my soul to wear bright colors. Red is my favorite color, and my heart would not allow me to wear it. To this day, about a year and a half after her death, my heart has not asked me to wear red, and I have not. When the time is right for me, I will. It is in my own time, not because it is been a year, as people may expect, but because it is time for me to do it. It is my grief, and I have lived it according to my compass.

Does it help to visit the cemetery?

When I told you about my mother's desire to stay in Miami because she wanted me to visit her in the cemetery, it was precisely because she knew me. She knew that I love going to cemeteries; that is one of the first things I do when I go to my country, Nicaragua. I like to visit my father in the cemetery. It is special to me. She knew that. So, she wanted me to do the same with her, and here in Miami, it was easier. I have kept my promise. Every Sunday, after going to mass, I stop to buy her flowers and go to the cemetery to visit her, as this symbolizes a ritual to honor her memory. Albor Rodriguez says that when our loved one is not present, there is a "forced spiritual bond, that of talking to someone in the cemetery without knowing if they are listening to you" (p. 24). I agree with her; I like to talk to her and pray to her; it fills my soul with peace and joy. My mother died on a Sunday. The meaning of Sundays for me is not sad; it is not tragic. The meaning of Sunday is sacred; it is a day on which I feel even closer to her on a spiritual level.

A question I get asked a lot by my clients is whether they should go to the cemetery or not, to which I answer that it all depends on what it means to them. The value of doing something is the meaning it has for us. If you are one of those people who do not like going to the cemetery, you do not have to; many of my clients choose not to go. Juan Morales, a young man with muscular dystrophy who is an example of overcoming and transformation, shared with us, in a conversation we had on Instalive, that after losing his father, he did not visit the cemetery because where he felt close to him was on a beach in Hollywood. If that is your case, do what your heart asks you to do.

TAKING OUT THE BELONGINGS. WHEN TO DO IT?
When they lose a loved one, many of my clients ask me when to get rid of their belongings, when to clean out the closet, what to do with the clothes, and whether it is good to leave the photos. The bereaved have many questions because people have a lot of opinions. Family and friends give unsolicited advice. Have you ever felt that people have wanted to impose what they think is right for you to do? That happens a lot, and sometimes, they make comments that make you feel worse. I remind you that no one can make you feel any way or tell you how you should live your grief. Do not compare yourself with anyone because everyone has their own story.

Keep in mind that others want to help in the best way they know how. However, sometimes, it is not the most appropriate, and what you should avoid is making a decision under social pressure. Do what makes you feel best and when you are in the mood. There is no precise time to remove things and get rid of your loved one's belongings. Some people give away the clothes and redecorate the room in a relatively short time, weeks or months. There are others who keep the clothes in the closet and leave the room untouched until a year or two has passed. Everyone has their own style of processing. There are people who feel close to their loved ones by touching their belongings or wearing their clothes. In my case, I took out my mother's things little by little. It was a very emotional process and, at the same time, sacred. I kept things that reminded me of her and distributed the rest among my close family. One thing I have done that I love is to wear certain of my mom's blouses. I feel so close to her when I do it!

PROCESSING YOUR GRIEF

What have you done with your loved one's belongings?

_____

_____

Have you worn the clothes, any jewelry?

_____

_____

What about the photos?

_____

_____

Did you leave them or did you remove them?

_____

_____

What made you do it?

_____

_____

The first christmas, anniversaries, birthdays

When special dates are approaching, it is important to prepare yourself because they are going to be different. Your feels more sensitive, and your mind is filled with memories. For this reason, it is good to have strategies in place about how you will live those days.

You can write down in advance how you would like to experience those moments, what you think would help you, and with whom you would like to share it. You can perform a ritual or simply let that date go unnoticed and go to the movie theater with a friend. You are the one who has the right to live it as you wish. You are the one who will decide what will help you the most. What I recommend is that it does not take you by surprise.

Christmas

What if you do not feel the Christmas spirit in your soul as December begins? Living in the United States, the holiday season begins with Thanksgiving, celebrated on the fourth Thursday in November. One of the strategies to follow is to change the tradition if it brings you too much pain. That reminds me of something a lady said in a talk I gave at a church just before Christmas. She told us that because her husband was the one who used to cook the Thanksgiving turkey and no one could match it, they decided to create a new tradition. On the other hand, you may continue with the same custom, as Jennifer did, a client who had lost her husband and wanted to keep the tradition of celebrating the same way they had celebrated as a family for so many years.

It filled her soul with a lot of peace. Something you can also do, which is a beautiful way to honor your loved one, is to cook a dish that they liked and, when serving it, mention it in a special way since your loved one will still be in your heart.

On the other hand, many of my clients have told me that they wish they could go to sleep just before Thanksgiving and wake up on January 1st because they would like to be able to skip the holidays. Has this happened to you? It is natural because we are anticipating the pain we will experience when we do not have our loved one with us. And that pain is real. Therefore, it is important to have strategies. It is important to prepare ourselves. Many times, we say, "It is the first Christmas. It will be different later." It does not have to be that way. I remember Lucia, a widow who came to see me and let me know that she was immensely troubled because the second Christmas after her husband's death had been worse than the first one, and she could not understand it because people were telling her: "After a year, you will see that everything changes, you will feel different." She had all those messages inside, and what happened? All those messages had been wrong, and when the year came, she said to herself: "What is wrong with me? I feel worse!" What happened was that she had not done the grieving process. She had put it aside and had continued functioning. This issue is something we must understand and validate: It is not a question of getting over the pain when a certain predetermined time has passed, in the style of "three months have passed, six months have passed, a year has passed." Father Alberto Cutie said this when I was on his program *Hablando claro con el Padre Alberto* when he pointed out that this is what people say and expect to happen[10]. People expect that after a certain period of time, let us say three months, it will not hurt anymore, and that is not what necessarily happens.

The first Christmas I spent without my mother was very painful. Talking to my friend Lucrecia, I told her how I felt about my anticipation of the second one, because the day before Thanksgiving, I had missed her so much due to triggers such as a video my phone had generated with pictures of my mom. My friend told me that, likely, the grief having been so profound the year before, as I use to say, that I might have been in *shock* or numb and had not made room for her absence from the festivities. The following year, now in better spirits, I missed being able to share with my mom that time of the year that we enjoyed so much together. What also happens is that when the second Christmas arrives, the reality of the absence becomes more present since it is perceived that it will be permanent.

PROCESSING YOUR GRIEF

Have you created new holiday traditions or continued with the same ones?

_____

_____

---

10 https://www.youtube.com/watch?v=WcKVt8f6rq0

> If you have created new ones, describe them in your journal.
>
> _____
>
> If you have kept the traditions, in what way have you honored your loved one?

Wearing the Mask
Pretending when being with others

> An abnormal reaction to an
> abnormal situation is normal behavior.
>
> VIKTOR FRANKL

As grievers, we often pretend to be fine, so we do not upset our family or friends. They may be unaware of how we feel or try hard to make us feel differently. This usually happens by avoiding talking about the person who died. It is as if they suddenly cease to exist in our world or our memories, as Albor Rodriguez says when referring to her infant son Juan Sebastian—whom he had just lost—during a family dinner: "Why does no one mention him? Is it because the future no longer includes him? For not hurting me?" (p. 53). On the contrary, remembering beautiful moments with our loved ones helps us a tremendously in our healing process. In my family we have kept the memory of my mother alive. It even brings us joy to remember the nice or funny things she did, as well as remembering with love her sweetness. When we think of our loved ones, let us remember something that brings a smile to our faces.

If we have faced the death of a loved one, it is natural, as Viktor Frankl points out, that our behavior is altered; it is not the same. What happens is that most of the time, we are expected to get back to "normal" or as we were before in an almost instantaneous way. This means that on many occasions, we have to put on a mask so we're not put in an uncomfortable situation. What happens is that, in that case, we are behaving in this way to please others instead of making them witnesses to our own pain and inviting them to be witnesses to our grief as well.

You may feel like crying and cannot because you do not want to disturb your family or others. They may tell you: "You are always sad. You are always crying." They do not take into consideration that you have just lost your loved one and that you have probably realized that you will never see, hug, or kiss them again. You sense that it has only been a couple of months, and you do not feel free to say that you miss your loved one. People do not want to hear that, and you regret that they deny you the right to express that you miss them.

They may not realize that you are experiencing great pain. That loss, that longing to be by your loved one's side, is huge, and people sometimes have difficulty understanding the fact that your heart is aching, that the emptiness you have is enormous, while they just want you to remain happy, enthusiastic, motivated, and joyful.

In life, we are supposed to experience different emotions, as the Bible says in Ecclesiastes (3:4): "a time to weep and a time to laugh, a time to mourn and a time to dance." So, do your best to express your grief. If you wish to cry, cry. If you want to scream, scream. If you wish to hit something—without hurting yourself or others—hit a pillow. If you want to write, write. If you want to run, run, but do not repress it. Always try to express what you feel inside in a way that you do not hurt yourself or others. That is the only thing I caution you against in your expression of grief: even though you have the right to grieve and feel pain, you do not have the right to hurt others.

PROCESSING YOUR GRIEF

To whom can you freely express how you feel?

_____

_____

Do you find yourself faking it all the time or can you let someone special know how you feel?

_____

_____

How do you respond when someone asks you how you are?

_____

_____

Is it easy for you to share how you feel or do you hide your real emotions and pretend everything is fine?

_____

_____

I understand that we will not tell everyone how we feel. However, I emphasize that it is very important to validate how we feel, and if we do not start by validating ourselves, who will validate us? As Gandhi said: "Be the change you wish to see in the world." Above all, validate your feelings to yourself. Look at yourself in front of the mirror and take off that mask you sometimes have to wear when you are in front of others who do not want to know about your pain. When you are alone, take it off, look in the mirror and ask yourself:

PROCESSING YOUR GRIEF

How do I feel?

_____

_____

What makes me feel this way?

_____

_____

It is time to choose an emotion you want to feel and ask yourself: What emotion would you like to feel at this moment?

What can I do to feel that way?

_____

_____

What action can I take to feel that way?

_____

_____

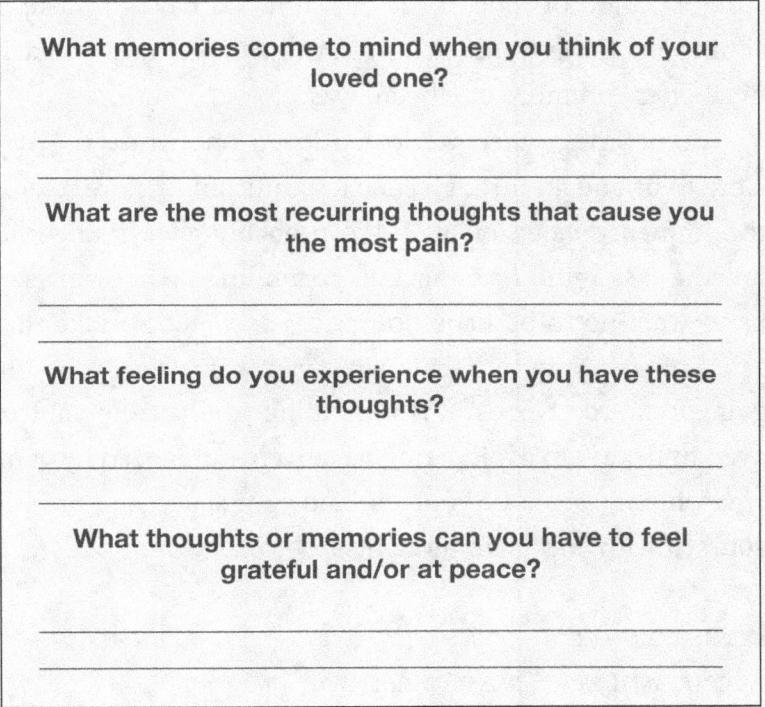

EXTERNAL FACTORS THAT MAY INFLUENCE YOUR GRIEF

I would like to ask you if, due to external factors, you feel that you have not wanted or have not been able to live your grief. This can happen due to different situations in your life: work overload, a relationship that is negatively influencing your grieving process, a health situation, or caring for another person... All these factors can influence and affect the development of a conscious grieving process. In this regard, I suggest the following: avoid making impulsive decisions. Take your time, knowing that during the first months after the loss, it is not advisable to make important decisions.

After a period of time, if the decision you have to make is about something you can control, you will be able to make it in a better and more intelligent way.

Sometimes, when we lose a loved one who was very close to us and go through such a significant loss, we realize the immense value of life. We probably always knew it, but the loss reinforces that understanding. That can lead us to wanting to be happy ourselves as well. So take that as an opportunity to decide what you want from your life going forward. Now, if it is something you have no control over, find ways to avoid being negatively influenced by your environment: separate yourself, find your space, and protect yourself with your own thoughts.

I feel lonely!
Alone, isolated, misunderstood

Situations may also arise that produce a feeling isolation and loneliness, especially if others choose to talk about other topics and do not even mention grief. This is likely to happen as many people do not want to listen to you and want to distract you; in fact, they will talk about other things. This can make you feel lonely and misunderstood because, in reality, during the grieving process, what we want is for our loved one to be named; we want to remember happy moments; we want to express how much we miss them; we want to talk about the change we feel, because, usually death does not only affect us but also the rest of the family. This is what Rodriguez expresses when she says that the loss of her infant son was a blow to her whole family (2015, p.

53). I feel the same way about the death of my mother. Her absence is still present even after a year has passed since she died, because she was the matriarch, the source of constant love, the head of our family.

It is also interesting that sometimes we withdraw, and although we wish to be accompanied internally, it is impossible for us. In our grief, we are alone. They can accompany us physically, but we are alone internally because sometimes there are no words that can express what we feel inside. I remember once I was driving home, and I thought: "I am alone in my grief, nobody knows how I feel." In reality, no one needs to fully know it, because it is my experience. I also thought similarly: "I like to be alone with my grief; I do not want to share it or have it meddled with." It was a feeling of wanting to protect my pain, as it was something sacred, sublime, my unique and personal way of expressing my great love for my mother. Has this happened to you?

Avoid getting stuck in grief

I want to make a distinction here between having the right to grieve and remaining trapped in your pain. These are two different things. Crying is your right if it is the way you express your grief. I express a lot through tears: joy, emotion, or sadness. Each person is different. Some cry, some do not. However, if it is your way of expressing it, go for it. Now, it is one thing to express your grief and another to stay in a dead-end space, to remain immersed in the pain, and to increase it even more with negative thoughts.

It is incredible how what we think influences the way we feel because if we stay in the memories, ruminating about how we miss our loved one, and we stay in that dark space for a long time, it will prevent us from evolving in our grief. Let us open our hearts to realize that expressing how much we miss our loved one is one thing and another is to elaborate on it allowing one thought to be mounted on top of another. For example, if I were to start with the thought: "Mom, I miss you so much," and then continue to elaborate on all the things I miss doing with her, I would probably end up saying to myself: "I really do not know how I will be able to continue living without my mother." And getting in that space means spiraling down. That is getting stuck. Please pay attention to what you are doing. Diving into negative thoughts is sometimes natural, as we are human and we miss the physical presence of the one we have lost; however, if you find yourself doing it in a continuous way, I suggest that you make an effort to change your perspective and remember something beautiful, such as being grateful for having them in your life, for the beautiful love they gave you, for a special moment that has been engraved in your heart... Let that be what fills your spirit with peace. Let that be what fills your memories. That way, you can fill your heart with love. It is your choice to stay stuck in the pain or to find a new purpose. If you find it impossible to do this on your own, look for professional help or you may be experiencing complicated grief, as mentioned earlier. Below is the definition of "complicated grief." If you identify with it, I encourage you to seek professional help so that you can feel better.

Complicated grief (CG) is a syndrome that affects 10% to 20% of the bereaved, regardless of age, although proportionally more will face the death of loved ones in late life. CG is characterized by preoccupying and disabling symptoms that can persist for decades, such as inability to accept the death, intense yearning or avoidance, frequent reveries, deep sadness, crying, somatic distress, social withdrawal, and suicidal ideation (Miller, 2012).

PROCESSING YOUR GRIEF

What kinds of thoughts come to mind when you think of your loss?

_____

_____

Do you process your grief or avoid facing it?

_____

_____

Is it impossible for you to stop crying or to accept what happened?

_____

_____

Getting stuck

Grief can express itself in all aspects of our existence and keep us in a dark place if we allow it, for we can make it the center of our lives. We may find no purpose in anything else, and our days are consumed by that sense of hopelessness. When people feel trapped, the way they deal with their loss can cause them to develop some of these habits that, instead of helping, can increase grief:

- Abuse of alcohol or drugs
- Overeating or not eating at all
- Avoid talking about the loss
- Oversleeping as a means of escape
- Having outbursts of rage
- Ignoring grief
- Pretending that everything is fine

PROCESSING YOUR GRIEF

Have you experienced any of these behaviors during your grieving process?

_____
_____

Did it help you?

_____
_____

How has it impacted your process?

_____
_____

Do you think you would like to try a different way to process your grief?

_____
_____

ADAPTING TO THE NEW LIFE

At the beginning of the bereavement, during the first few weeks, people will visit you, call you, text you, and leave social media messages and voice mails. Your friends will be aware of how you are feeling, ask how they can help you, and let you know that you can count on their company. After the first few weeks, they will distance themselves, and you will have to deal with the new reality: that friends, and often even family members, will not even ask you how you feel without your loved one; they will avoid doing so. It will be as if the person, by ceasing to exist physically, had ceased to exist in your heart. And they will not do it to hurt you: it is because it will no longer be a part of their conversation.

When this happens, the bereaved may feel a great sense of loneliness, as they may feel like others do not care anymore. Moreover, they may wonder how it is possible that the world keeps on turning and people keep on living as if nothing has happened. Have you ever felt this way? It is natural, and it is common. Most of my clients have commented on this feeling. What happens is that, many times, we have too many expectations. We think people will slow down to match our pace, but that is not the case.

And what would happen if we let them know we still need them? This is suggested to us by Raymond R. Mitsch and Lynn Brookside in their book *Grieving the Loss of Someone You Love: Daily Meditations to Help You Through the Grieving Process* (1993):

Too often, however our friends come near only during the first few days following the death of our loved one. Then they gradually drift back to their own lives, most of them convinced that we are functioning quite well without their help... It is important for us to give ourselves permission to ask people to meet our need for comfort so they know that need is legitimate... We have to fight the tendency to think that if people loved us, they would just know what we need without telling them...Our reminder do not have to be confrontational. We can simply tell our friends that we are having a particularly difficult day and that we are missing our loved a great deal, just now. As crazy as it sounds, we can even ask them to help us through our grief. Most people to whom we are close will respond to such a reminder. They need only to be invited to deal with our hurt. Naturally, we all have some friends or family members who have difficulty dealing with our people on an emotional level. Those are *not* the ones to turn to for comfort. But most of us have at least one person in our lives who will respond with love when we make our needs clear to them (pp. 16-17).

I found this passage very helpful because that is what we may feel when we go through those days when we feel alone. Avoid thinking that no one understands you. Trust that special person who can listen to you without trying to pull you out of your pain and open your heart to them.

PROCESSING YOUR GRIEF

How have you expressed your grief?

_____
_____

What has been the biggest challenge in your evolution?

_____
_____

How did you feel about sharing it with others?

_____
_____

Have you experienced loneliness despite being with people around you?

_____
_____

Did you feel understood?

_____
_____

What did you miss the most?

_____
_____

Physical sensations that can be perceived as an expression of grief

> [Grief is] a multidimensional experience that affects not only our physical body and our emotions, but also our relationships with others and with ourselves, our cognitions, beliefs and presuppositions, and our internal existential or spiritual world.
>
> Alba Payàs Puigarnau

Besides experiencing it physically, we can indeed express grief in all dimensions, the physical dimension being a tangible manifestation of how we feel inside.

Throughout this journey of grieving, especially during the first few months, I experienced an inner cold, a feeling of being frozen inside. It felt like it was chilling my bones. We experience many physical sensations: internal cold, the stomach sticking to the spine, and how you are going to be able to eat if the last thing your body asks for is food?

People said to me: "You have to eat. You are too skinny." In those early days, I forced myself to eat because I was aware that, when experiencing grief, one can either overdo it or stop eating altogether.

On the other hand, you may experience an insatiable desire to eat—due to the emptiness you feel inside—you may feel dizziness, migraines, and nausea, your heart rate may speed up, or your blood pressure may rise. You can express many things physically. Remember the mind-body-spirit connection. Your body may ache, and you may feel extreme fatigue.

All of these and more can happen to you on a physical level. I suggest that you document—either in a notebook or in your journal—any physical symptoms you experience and if they happen repeatedly.

Below, I share with you a series of physical manifestations that are common when experiencing the loss of our loved one:

- Headache
- Fatigue
- Weakness
- Body pain
- Chest tightness
- Hyperventilation
- Stomach pain
- Pain in the heart
- Nausea
- Dizziness
- Loss of appetite
- Insatiable appetite
- Insomnia
- Excessive sleep

PROCESSING YOUR GRIEF

How has your grief been represented to you physically?

_____
_____

> **Have you eaten or stopped eating?**
>
> _____
>
> **Do you sleep a lot or suffer from insomnia?**
>
> _____
>
> **Any physical ailment: headache, stomachache, backache?**
>
> _____

IMPORTANT
If you have a physical ailment, always consult with your doctor before assuming it is due to grief.

OUR EMOTIONAL STATE

> We need to know how we feel. Mindfully acknowledging our feelings serves as an "emotional thermostat" that recalibrates our decision making. It is not that we cannot be anxious, it is that we need to acknowledge to ourselves that we are.
>
> NOREENA HERTZ

When grieving, we experience a range of emotions other than sadness. We may feel guilt, anger, fear, or anxiety. These are just a few of the many emotions we may feel and can sometimes be difficult to accept; however, they are very common when grieving. Chip, Katie's father, says, "The way

I have expressed my grief has been feeling anger, Depression, Tears, and Isolation, self-blame, all passed through me for a long time at any given time like a roller coaster titled FEAR."

It is essential to acknowledge all the emotions linked to our grief because, as Steve Case tells us: "Even if you start pretending you do not feel nothing, even if you disconnect from the world around you and turn those feelings off, at some point, you will have to address your buried emotions again" (2020, p. 3).

In the next section, we will explore how to deal with each of these emotions. I suggest that you recognize the ones you experience and process them; this is what I do and what I suggest my clients do through different techniques or activities.

Exploring the Feeling of Guilt

> [Guilt is] a remorseful emotional reaction in grieving, with the recognition of having failed to live up to one's own inner standards and expectations in relationship to the deceased and/or the death.
>
> JIE LI, MARGARET STROEBE,
> CECILIA L. W. CHAN AND AMY Y. M. CHOW

In all the years I have been working in this field of helping the bereaved, this is the feeling I have heard most often: the feeling of guilt.

Because it is such a predominant emotion in grief, I decided to start with it.

What happens with this feeling? What makes us feel guilty?

I found this definition on the DK *Salud* blog, which shows how our beliefs can generate this feeling of guilt: "It is the action or omission that provokes a feeling of responsibility for a harm caused. You have to believe that you have done or omitted to do something and that you have caused harm and that belief generates the feeling."

Notice the word "believe" since we may feel guilty if we did not do something we thought our loved one would have wanted or needed, if we did something that might have hurt them, or if we did something that was not the best decision at the time, as Armando points out[1]:

> My pain does not stem from her death, but from not having done enough for her or from making the wrong decisions during her last days. At that moment I believed she would get better as she used to do in other medical situations... The biggest challenge in my grief has been accepting that there is no way I can correct what I did wrong or failed to do.

Pay attention to whether you are making the situation even more painful by relying on beliefs of this type. Also, I want to remind you that when we make a decision at any given time, we think it is the best of all options. However, that feeling of not having certain things can hurt our souls.

What matters most to us in reference to what we say or what we do is the intention. If you have guilt, remember that before an action, there is an intention. Was it your intention to hurt your loved one? Sometimes, we hurt intentionally when we are hurt. If that was the case, remember that we are human and, as such, we make mistakes. Make a list of everything you did for your loved one, and if there are things you feel you did not do or say, make a list of them too and include them in a letter, either addressed to yourself, forgiving yourself, or addressed to your loved one, asking for forgiveness. You can also forgive them for something that hurt you, and maybe you keep it in your soul. Remember that we are not perfect; we are human and make mistakes.

---

[1] See his complete story in the appendix of this book.

This is your opportunity to forgive or to forgive yourself. It is beautiful to understand ourselves. It is very deep and valuable to be able to let go of that burden and forgive ourselves for anything we might have said or done, remembering that forgiveness is both a choice and a process.

Why? Because compassion starts with yourself. That is being self-compassionate.

Remember, again, that you are human, and if you think that your actions were not the best, forgive yourself, and as you do it, focus on everything that you actually did that brought happiness to your loved one.

PROCESSING YOUR GRIEF

Do you feel guilty about something?

_____

Write: I feel guilty about:

_____

What makes you feel guilty?

_____
_____

WHEN WE TALK ABOUT GUILT,
WE WANT TO KNOW WHAT GUILT IS

Guilt is the emotion we feel when we think we did something wrong or that we said something that does not align with certain standards. Guilt is a common human emotion, and it is important to validate it. As we grow up, we, as humans, receive messages that become standards by which we measure what can make us feel guilty and what cannot. These are parameters by which we regulate ourselves. If we acted or said something that was not aligned with those standards, we may feel guilty. What is important is to see what it is causing you to feel guilty. In that sense, avoid asking yourself, "Why?" Instead, ask, "What makes me feel guilty?"

You may have said no to something your loved one asked of you; that makes many people feel guilty. Let us remember that sometimes we do or say things that are not done or said in the best way: you may have spoken harshly, and then feel guilty. Maybe it is an unfounded guilt, and you are reprimanding, judging, and criticizing yourself: "I tried to help her, but not having an accurate diagnosis made it harder to understand her pain. This is my biggest regret. I ask myself, "Did I do enough?" The word ENOUGH haunts me every day..."[2]

It is very important to realize what it is that makes you feel guilty, if it is something that is in your head or if it is something real. That strong and heavy emotion can keep us stuck in one place. Sometimes we say: "If I had done this, if I had not done that; if I had taken her, if I had not taken her..." All the "what ifs" grow inside us, and then, instead of focusing on the beautiful things we did, we focus on the things we did not do.

We feel this very deeply when experiencing grief, as María[3], a mother who lost her son to suicide, points out to us:

---

2   Maggie, grieving mother. See her complete story in the appendix of this book.
3   See her complete story in the appendix of this book.

There are many challenges that I have faced and continue to face after my son's suicide. The biggest of all has been the feeling that, in multiple ways I paved the way for my beloved son to make that decision. That I did not spend enough time with him, that I did not dedicate enough time to him, that I did not understand him enough, that I did not support him enough, that I should have foreseen that he was going to die by suicide, that he was having a hard time... that I should have known... even though we did not live in the same country... and a long list of "that I did not..." "if I had..." and "I should have..."

Do not ignore guilt, for you are carrying it. Sometimes, in our minds, we create unfounded guilt. Sometimes, it surfaces due to triggers that set it off.

Make a list of all those "what ifs," step out of the movie, and look at them in an objective way. How about changing them to what you did do?

If you were responsible, accept it, let go, and see what you can learn from it to make amends or avoid doing it again.

Look at what happened to me on November 11, 2020, approximately six months after my mother had passed away. That would be the first anniversary of my father's death in which she would not be present. It hurt me deeply that my mom was not with me to go to Mass. So I decided, first of all, to validate my emotion, to acknowledge how sad I felt; I processed it, wrote it down, and released it.

Since I wanted to change my emotions, I remembered that a cousin had told me about a beautiful place, the

Christmas Palace, which exists in Miami, Florida. I thought about it because I love Christmas, just like my mom. I wanted to get into the magic of the holiday to change the feeling. In fact, I greatly enjoyed looking at all the decorations and got caught up in the atmosphere. After a while, I left, as I had gone just to distract myself. When I left, guess what? I thought, "My mom would have loved to come here," and I started to say to myself, "Why did not I bringer her to this place?" It is amazing what our mind is like! Because noticing our thoughts is part of my professional training, I observed myself and realized what I was doing.

I thought that I had not brought her, and I started to feel guilty. I stopped suddenly and said to myself, "Ligia, you did not even know this place existed; how could you have taken her? Then, I immediately sat down in the car to make a list of all the places I had taken her to enjoy the Christmas season. I share this with you because it can happen to you, and what I suggest is that you observe yourself, notice the triggers, process them, and focus on what you did.

Another thing that can make us feel guilty has to do with decisions that were made or not made. One may say, "If only I had gone to another doctor," "If only I had traveled as I had promised and did not," or "I was not there."

Let us remember that we do not have the magic ball to see what is going to happen. At certain moments, we make the decision we think is the best and use the tools we have at hand to make it. If it is not the right one, let us remember that we are human and let us have self-compassion.

That is where I invite you to take a moment and reflect.

> **PROCESSING YOUR GRIEF**
>
> What was my intention in acting this way?
> What did I do or not do?
>
> _____
> _____
>
> What did I say or not say, which I now regret and feel guilty about?
>
> _____
> _____
>
> What made me act this way?
>
> _____
> _____

NOTE:

VERBALIZE THE FOLLOWING STATEMENT:

"Today I let go of the guilt that grips my heart and replace it with the love I feel for... (your loved one)."

ANGER AS A REACTION TO GRIEF

> Remember that you can often do very little to alter life's losses, but you can adjust to things beyond your control, move through your anger, and find a place in your heart where grief and peace can coexist
>
> LES PARROTT

Anger is a natural emotion and often manifests itself in the grieving process. Although sometimes it may seem impossible to accept, we may experience anger toward the doctors who could not save our loved one, toward family members who were not present at the time of death, toward our loved one for having left us, or even toward God, who took them away from us. Do not even be surprised if you ask yourself questions such as: "Why did this happen to me?"

Although it is not an accepted emotion in our society—as Devine (2017) reminds us—we should not repress anger; on the contrary, we should find a healthy way to express it. It will depend a lot on how you handle it, whether you can prevent it from harming you, either by repressing it or by expressing it in a destructive way.

NOTE:
Something that has proven to help a lot is the following: In addition to talking with a friend or a professional who will listen to you without judgment about what makes you feel angry, write down on a piece of paper everything that emotion makes you feel and then tear it up. Moreover, if possible, burn it.

Additionally, it has been proven that something that helps a lot is to channel the energy of anger, as we are told by the expert in organizational behavior R. David Lebel, who has won awards for his research studies on fear and anger. According to Lebel (2016), the idea is not to suppress the energy, as it leaves us exhausted, but to redirect it, and an effective way to do this is through exercise. Psychologist Brett Ford, who has specialized in emotions, tells us that rage or anger can be mobilized by activating it in a physiological way (Robson, 2020). In other words, you can release all that energy you feel inside by doing some kind of exercise or sport.

Taking a brisk walk, jogging if you can, or even putting on some boxing gloves and unloading all your anger by punching the bag can help you drain all that emotion.

When I offer the 11 Principles of Transformation® workshop, one activity I like to do with my group to let go of disturbing emotions, is to write everything down on a piece of paper, and then put it in a paper shredder. The feeling of liberation that this activity causes in many people is impressive.

On the other hand, you may punch a pillow or scream in your car or in the shower. I recommend paying attention to your anger and noticing if it is not covering up another emotion, such as fear, which is very common. As Les Parrott tells us, anger can give us certain signals: "Constant anger, in fact, could mean that we are not giving ourselves permission to absorb our loss and fully grieve."[4]

WHAT ABOUT FEAR?

In his well-known memoir, *A Grief Observed*, which C. S. Lewis wrote after the death of his wife, Joy Davidman, Lewis describes grief as follows: "No one ever told me that grief felt so like fear. I am not afraid, but the sensation is like being afraid. The same fluttering in the stomach, the same restlessness" (p. 3).

This book is a classic on the subject of grief, and I discovered it when I took my first class on *Death and Dying* at the University of Miami. It is a small yet highly profound book that reflects on the topic of the suffering we experience

---

[4] Taken from the booklet "Dealing with the anger that comes with grief": "Dealing with the Anger that comes with Grief."

when we miss our loved one and the relationship with God when facing loss.

When experiencing anxiety

> It is understandable that death makes us anxious. We experience anxiety after a loss because losing someone we love thrusts us into a vulnerable place.
>
> Claire Bidwell Smith

Anxiety is a very common emotion in our society. According to the Anxiety and Depression Association of America[5], anxiety disorders affect forty million adults over the age of eighteen in the United States. This represents 18.1% of the population per year. Anxiety originates when we feel fear of something that may happen, whether real or imagined. Again, I want you to pay attention to the possibility that this something that could happen is imaginary because everything depends on our perception. Our thoughts greatly influence our anxiety because they are based on fear. This, in turn, produces in us a feeling of agitation or that something is going to happen (Bidwell Smith, 2018).

You may ask yourself, "How can this be linked to grief?" What happens is that by repressing fears or other emotions created by the loss of our loved one, they manifest themselves in the body, causing multiple symptoms of an anxiety or panic attack. Many times, the person carries these repressed

---

[5] Anxiety & Depression Association of America, ADAA for its acronym in English.

emotions for years until they are able to process all the grief they have been carrying inside. As frozen grief is processed, the issue of anxiety may start to lessen.

Some of these symptoms are as follows:
- Lack of air
- Dizziness
- Nausea
- Hot or cold
- Rapid breathing or pulse

What to do about it? Smith (2018) recommends that, first of all, we normalize emotions and notice how our thoughts have caused the way we feel and act. If we feel sad, we cry; if we feel afraid when realizing we lost our loved one, that emotion manifests in the body. The realization that we have lost our loved one may occur later since, at first, there may be a state of *shock,* and the person may process, only with time, the reality of what has happened. All this can eventually provoke feelings of fear, anguish, and anxiety.

We can sink into deep grief, into immense sadness... It all has to do with how we handle the emotion presented to us because it originated in the thought, and if we continue to elaborate on the thoughts that have to do with that emotion, it will grow. Fortunately, that is something that we can realize, and the only way we can manage this is by observing ourselves.

Our emotions are just a signal of what we are thinking. If you pay attention to your thoughts, you will realize the direct relationship they have with how you feel. Do not like the way you feel? Change your thoughts... Remember: you have the ability to choose. Choose to be happy. Choose to be grateful. Choose to forgive. Choose to love.

Right now, you can make a conscious decision, as Carlos, a client who lost a loved one, told me. He realized that what had helped him in his grief was to consciously decide what to think and, consequently, how to act. If you decide how you want to feel, you can move from pain to love, from darkness to light, from suffering to peace.

Recognize and validate each of your emotions

> Authenticity is the daily practice of letting go of what we think we're supposed to be and Embracing who we are.
>
> Brené Brown

Brené Brown, the well-known researcher on vulnerability and shame, makes us see how we get used to numbing the pain just by sensing it coming. What happens, Brown tells us:

> For many of us, the first response is not to lean in to the discomfort and feel our way through, but to make it go away. We do that by numbing the pain with whatever provides the fastest relief. We can take the edge of emotional pain with a whole bunch of stuff, including alcohol, drugs, food, sex, relationships, money, work, caretaking, gambling, affairs, religion, chaos, shopping, planning, perfectionism, constant change, and the Internet (p. 63).

Four steps to process a disturbing emotion

Whenever you experience a disturbing emotion, such as anger, fear, or guilt, I suggest these four steps that will help you to connect with it and process it:

Recognize: Recognizing your emotion is the first step in processing it. Sometimes, it is difficult to name it. Be patient. The more you do it, the easier it will get.

Validate Your Emotion: Immediately validate what makes you feel this way with the question, "What makes me feel this way? Avoid asking yourself, "Why do I feel this way?" you will be delving into your feelings by asking, "What makes me...?" This reminds me of a social worker who attended one of the seminars I conducted for PESI[6] on grief transformation. When I asked the group of mental health professionals what they thought was the difference between "Why do I feel this way?" and "What makes me feel this way?" she responded that the second question was like digging for the answer.

Process: Once you have realized what it is that makes you feel anxious, then find a way to process it, whether by applying breathing, writing in a journal, talking to someone, or simply recording yourself on your smartphone, as they all have voice recording capabilities.

Release: By processing the emotion that disturbs you, you will avoid repressing or ignoring it. You will then be able to let go of the emotion and focus on the emotion you want to feel instead.

For this, you will think of a beautiful memory or something you will do to honor your loved one. That will make you experience a positive emotion, either love or peace, and then you will act accordingly. Make it a point

---

[6] Professional Education Systems Institute.

to practice this technique. It has helped many people with their grief—including me—. Give yourself the opportunity.

PROCESSING YOUR GRIEF

Acknowledge your emotion: "Right now I feel…"

_____
_____

Validate it: "What makes me feel this way?"

_____
_____

Process it: Write in your diary, write a letter, talk to someone who listens to you.

_____
_____

Let it go: Let it go and focus on another emotion that makes you feel differently.

_____
_____

CHANGES ON A SOCIAL LEVEL. DO YOU FEEL OUT OF PLACE AND THAT NO ONE UNDERSTANDS YOU? CHALLENGES PEOPLE FACE IN NAVIGATING YOUR GRIEF WITH YOU.

This includes family members, friends, colleagues, people at the supermarket, waiters, church groups, and even anyone who realizes that you lost a loved one, even more so if they knew them and asked you about them. It is a very sensitive situation for them and for you. I remember once, at the supermarket, someone asked me about my mom, as I loved to take her in her wheelchair. When I told her that she had died, she was left speechless. They just do not know what to do or what to say, as no one educates us on this subject.

I remember when I was giving the seminar for mental health professionals, which I mentioned earlier, I would always ask them to raise their hands if they had received any formal education on grief or death. We would start from elementary school and move up to graduate school. Very few people had received education in school. It was only talked about if a classmate or teacher died. At home, of course, it was a taboo subject. In higher education, not everyone has taken advanced courses on these important subjects.

Now, imagine ordinary people who have no idea how to handle this situation. So, let us open our hearts and understand that they, too, have their own story. Sometimes, our stories can remind them of something from the past that they never processed, and that causes them grief; they feel incompetent to help or simply do not want to relive their pain. On the other hand, our grief can be felt among our family and friends. It is important to pay attention, as Oralí[7] suggests: "We must be patient with ourselves and those around us;

They also have to be patient with us, and we must understand that, when the family is affected. Everyone processes it differently; therefore, respect and understanding are fundamental during the process."

Friends disappear or remain present

The first thing I want to ask you to do is to put your expectations aside. Do not assume all your friends will be

---

[7] See her full story in the appendix of this book.

there for you when you need them and will know what to say or even understand you. There are three types of friends: those who are unconditional, who, no matter how much it pains them to see you like this, will be there for you and will make you feel their support. There are other friends who are also present; however, they have comments that are not very helpful, or they expect you to behave as they suggest—with good intentions—because they want to help you and move you out of the space of pain. Finally, there is the third type of friends, who simply disappear. It is too much for them because they want the "other person," the one you were before the loss.

Sometimes, what hurts us is that the friend we thought we could count on is one of the friends who disappeared, and we feel disappointed. Let us keep in mind that many times, they act this way because of the pain it causes them to see you grieve or because they cannot face death.

Let us understand that this is not necessarily personal; it may be more based on their story than on yours. What happens, as Bonanno (2019) points out, is that when we see someone sad, we tend to feel sad, too. So, maybe that friend who has not visited you wants to avoid feeling that way. It is almost a defense mechanism. Sometimes, over time, it is possible to reconnect and talk about how difficult the experience of your loss was for both of you.

As we mentioned before, sometimes—and it happens more often than we would like—when we are grieving, we lose friendships because they distance themselves, as they often do not know how to respond and do not know what to say to you. What is more, it may be too much for them because it reminds them of something from their own story, and they remain in it. It may also be that they simply do not have the sensitivity to accompany someone when they are going through such an important challenge and are not feeling well. Even though this can happen, remember that there are also friendships that are always there. There are friends we can always count on, who will offer their help, and create the space to listen to us and provide their support.

Do you isolate yourself or seek companionship?
We are not an island

Remember that grief takes time to process. Just as you cannot rush the growth of a plant in a clay pot, you cannot rush the grieving process. Make it a point to share with others, as I suggest in my fifth principle: *Share with others, for you are not an island.*

For Mayra Elena[8], sharing was of great value in processing the grieving for her son, Yasser Hernán: "I have had the opportunity to discover that one of the ways, because there is no perfect way to process grief, is to share with others what we are feeling and thinking as we walk blindly, trying to find light in the dark well that is grief." Do not keep your feelings to yourself, talk about how you feel, share stories about your loved one, plan activities such as going for a walk with someone, watching TV series with a family member or friend, playing cards or just chatting on the couch. You can even share, with a friend, the things that happen to you, because one of the situations in which we miss our loved one a lot is when we want to share something

---

8   See her complete story in the appendix of this book.

with them. We want to get home or call them on the phone to tell them anything and we realize, once again, that they are not there. This process of becoming aware of small details is sometimes more painful than a big event or a special date; therefore, what you must avoid is falling into isolation, as Stanley Kissel (PhD) recommends: "What is important is that you just do not sit around at home brooding, staring at the TV alone. Investing your energy in work, hobbies or a new career are alternative ways of coping, moving on and getting back into the swing of life."[9]

Meaning and importance of support groups

Support groups are of great value to many people because they can help us feel understood and supported. If you do not have someone you can confide in, you can join a bereavement support group.

These groups are very helpful because the people who attend are sharing a common grief: the loss of a loved one. And while you may find it difficult at first to share your feelings or experiences with strangers, you will find that they have great value. Now, there have been times when clients have told me that they do not feel comfortable attending support groups.

It all depends on you because each person is different. The only thing I suggest is that you give yourself a chance and give it a try. Sometimes, the facilitator may not touch your soul, or you may find the meeting place too cold. If you participate virtually, you may not feel a connection with others. Any of these situations can present themselves

---

9 https://nationalwidowers.org/moving-on-after-losing-her/

to you. However, if it is something you feel will help you, keep looking until you find a support group where you feel comfortable and understood.

Among the main reasons many people like to belong to support groups is the fact that they can share their feelings, hear how others are feeling, and realize that many other people may be thinking and feeling similarly. Keep in mind that belonging to a support group is meant to help you process, share, and live your grief without getting stuck. The support group should not be a place of weekly complaining because, as Smith (2004) says: "There are groups, unfortunately, that encourage a "'poor us" mentality focusing on the past rather than the future" (p. 191). What you should be looking for is the opposite: the support and feeling of others help you get out of the dark place in which you find yourself. Find out what types of groups exist, either virtual or in person. I hope that, as you read this paragraph, face-to-face groups will be available again on a regular basis.

PROCESSING YOUR GRIEF

Do you have the support of people close to you?

_____

_____

What kind of support do you receive?

_____

_____

Do you belong to a support group?

_____

_____

Our spiritual being and how it expresses grief

> Many people suffering loss will turn to their belief system for help with death-related rituals, prayer support, comfort, and for advice on placing the loss within a larger spiritual context.
>
> J. Shep Jeffreys

Noreena Hertz, in the section on emotions, talks about the emotional thermostat, that is, being aware of what we are feeling, and this reminds me of the spiritual thermometer mentioned by my great friend, Reverend Dr. Dale Alan Young, in his book *How to Take Your Spiritual Temperature* (2021), which is a self-assessment of our spirituality in different dimensions of life.

Connecting with Your Spirituality

> The spiritual quest we are embarking upon is a rare and precious undertaking, so be gentle yet persevering through any beginning difficulties.
>
> JOSEPH GOLDSTEIN

When we connect with our spiritual dimension as we process grief, we are entering into a profound realm for we are connecting with our essence. Keep in mind that we can strengthen ourselves emotionally and deal with our loss in an inspiring way on a spiritual level. Our spirituality is essential, and we can relate to what we feel fulfills us internally, whether it is connecting with God, the universe, nature, or the legacy we wish to leave behind.

During grief, this dimension becomes very present, as it pushes us to penetrate the depths of our being by asking existential questions such as:

What is life?
What does death mean?
Why do tragedies happen?
Where is God?

When we lose a loved one, our spirituality can come to the surface and can make us more perceptive, more intuitive, and more open to other realities. As we deepen our spirituality, I like to delve into two important topics: forgiveness and gratitude. I call them "spiritual tools," and they are part of my third principle: *Develop your Spiritual Dimension*.

Opening the heart to forgiveness

> The quality of mercy is not strained.
> It droppeth as the gentle rain from heaven
> Upon the place beneath. It is twice blessed:
> It blesseth him that gives and him that takes.
>
> William Shakespeare

Forgiveness is an essential element of our spirituality and is one of the most sublime acts we can perform for others and for ourselves. By forgiving, we can find peace and, at the same time, free ourselves from that burden that we carry in our soul without realizing it: "Forgiveness is only a conscious act that frees us all, and just with the firm intention of forgiving—even without feeling it in our hearts—little by little that intention becomes a beautiful truth that fills our heart with love and light."[1]

When we forgive, we are making the decision to forgive and let go of feelings that hurt us but do not benefit us. Sometimes, it is difficult for us to forgive immediately, and we hold some resentment; it may take some time.

What will give rest to your soul is to have decided letting go of things from the past. The more we engage in

---

[1] María, bereaved mother

griefwork, the more we will be able to recognize different emotions—such as guilt and anger—to accept and process them.

The most important thing is that you are clear about your intention. If it was that you were angry and somehow produced an intentional harm, to cleanse your soul, I heartily suggest that you write two letters: first, write a letter to your loved one asking for forgiveness and remembering your human qualities. If you have the opportunity to go to the cemetery, you can also talk to him/her there, express how you feel, and ask for forgiveness. You can do this as a ritual. When writing the letter, after writing everything you feel, tear it up and burn it, saying, "By releasing all this, I cleanse my soul and open my heart to peace."

The other letter is written to the person—including yourself—or institution against whom you may feel anger. It can help you cleanse your soul. That reminds me of when I taught meditation classes at my center before the pandemic. They were weekly classes in which we meditated on different topics: gratitude, spirituality, union with a loved one, and forgiveness, among others. The class on forgiveness always provoked a lot of emotion among the participants. One thing I always noticed, when sharing at the end of the class as a group, was that what they found most difficult was to forgive themselves.

I give you ideas on how to do the work of forgiveness in the hope that it will help you, for, as Dr. Robert Enright (2019)—a pioneer in scientific research and study on forgiveness—says in sharing his method with the people, he cannot promise that everybody will be able to forgive.

Likewise, I recognize that, with the suggestions I give you here, I cannot say for sure. However, the intention to help you do it comes from my heart.

When we forgive, we feel that our soul feels lighter. Furthermore, there is something very interesting that Dr. Enright mentions in his book *Forgiveness is a Choice: A Step-by-Step Process for Resolving Anger and Restoring Hope* (2019), and that is that, based on his vast experience, he has realized that when a person begins their healing process, they are able to focus on giving the gift of forgiveness. In other words, instead of focusing on themselves, they focus on the person they are forgiving.

What does gratitude have to do with grief?

> Expressing gratitude is healing for us...
> Focusing on gratitude opens the
> heart and enables connections with
> ourselves and with others.
>
> Candice C. Courtney

When you experience the loss of your loved one, the last thing you may want to do is be grateful. This is because the pain is so immense that there is no room for this emotion. However, as Candice C. Courtney—who lost her husband to a brain tumor and wrote the book *Healing Through Illness, Living Through Dying* (2012)—tells us, being grateful helps us in our healing process. In this space, give thanks for everything you can to your loved one, for the experiences you had with him, and for the memories. Give thanks for what they offered you, for the love you shared. Maybe you told them this while they were alive, and it is a blessing that you did. I had the joy of doing so. However, there are times when we are not given the opportunity. Be thankful for everything they represented in your life.

> **PROCESSING YOUR GRIEF**
>
> What did your loved one give you for which you feel grateful?
>
> _____
>
> What special moment do you keep in your soul?
>
> _____
>
> Write a sentence in which you thank her for teaching you to love in this way.
>
> _____

LOVE AND SELF-COMPASSION

> To be "bereaved" means to have special needs, with perhaps the most important need being compassion with yourself.
>
> ALAN D. WOLFELT

The third tool that I consider to be part of our spirituality—forgiveness, gratitude, and love are the components of my third principle: *Develop your Spiritual Dimension*—is love. In this opportunity, I have added compassion, as it has taken center stage in our society with the advent of the *mindfulness* movement. There are retreats, guided meditations, and support groups based on love and compassion. These are precisely the emotions we wish to bring to ourselves when we find ourselves in the valley of pain. There, when you find yourself dejected, powerless, and immersed in grief, is when you should give yourself all the love you can and the compassion your heart needs. You can give yourself what you need in those moments when all you want to do is lie in the fetal position and cry. Or you may just stare blankly into space, or you may find yourself pacing the entire house—as I did during acute grief. Establish an inner conversation and talk to yourself with all the love you can; give yourself the affection you need. That is what I have done all this time: I talk to myself the way my mother used to talk to me, with that loving tone, and I help myself, either by understanding that juncture of grief or by inspiring me to transform it. You can also give yourself one of those "me moments" and do something that makes you feel good. Taking care of yourself does not mean you are selfish; it means you are paying attention to your needs.

NOTE:
Have you been compassionate with yourself today?

Practice meditation

Meditation is a practice that can help you feel at peace, and it is highly spiritual. If you do not practice it, start with ten minutes at a time. When taking time for yourself, it is essential that you prepare the environment, as this is your sacred moment. Choose a quiet place, if possible, without external noises. You can start by turning off the phone and the TV and concentrate on yourself. After getting into a comfortable position, just close your eyes and focus on your breathing. Breathe gently through your nose and let the air out through your mouth, saying the word "peace" inside yourself. Do this three times, and then continue to breathe gently. If thoughts distract you, focus back on your breathing. Meditating will help you relax and connect with your inner self. Give yourself love and compassion, and connect with your deepest self. Take time for yourself. That is what you need most right now.

BREATHING-FOCUSED MEDITATION

Place one of your hands on your belly, keeping your eyes closed. Then, place the other hand on your chest. As you inhale, count from 1 to 7 and, at the same time, expand your belly. Feel when the hand on your belly rises and the hand on your chest remains flat. Now, hold your breath and count from 1 to 4. Then, exhale, counting from 1 to 8. As your belly becomes flat, make the "AHHHH" sound. It is important that you make the sound as you release your breath. Now let us do it together:

Inhale: 1, 2, 3, 4, 5, 6, 7.

Hold your breath: 1, 2, 3, 4.

Exhale: 1, 2, 3, 4, 4, 5, 6, 7, 8.

Make the "AHHHH" sound while flattening your belly completely...

Again:

Inhale: 1, 2, 3, 4, 5, 6, 7.

Hold your breath: 1, 2, 3, 4.

Exhale: 1, 2, 3, 4, 4, 5, 6, 7, 8.

Make the "AHHHH" sound while flattening your belly completely...

Once again:

Inhale: 1, 2, 3, 4, 5, 6, 7.

Hold your breath: 1, 2, 3, 4.

Exhale: 1, 2, 3, 4, 4, 5, 6, 7, 8.

Make the "AHHHH" sound while flattening your belly completely...

Repeat the sequence three times and then relax[2].

THE POWER OF PRAYER

> Prayer is not asking. It is a longing of the soul.
> It is daily admission of one's weakness.
> It is better in prayer to have a heart without
> words than words without a heart.
>
> MAHATMA GANDHI

In times of grief, many people may find it difficult to pray, as they may be upset about the loss of their loved one or may not feel the strength to pray. However, when a person is able to open their heart to faith, prayer is considered a resource of great spiritual value, as Chip points out:

Prayer was another huge staple toward stability and hope. At first I was so angry, because I would pray for God

---

[2] Taken from my book *Transforming Grief and Loss. Workbook* (2016).

to help Katie with her addiction, never in a million years thinking He would take her. I have come to the realization that God did not do this, in fact Katie made this choice to use. Prayer was and is so essential toward living a healthy and productive life. I need God in my life everyday so He can take my pain, so he can give me purpose but mostly so that He can help me to be of service. I do not have any of the answers.[3]

María de los Ángeles also finds relief in prayer because it helps her feel close to her mother: "There is another way in which I am honoring my mother, and that is by praying the rosary…I feel closer to her every time I pray it." The fundamental element in prayer is faith. As the saying goes: "Without faith, nothing is possible," and this is testified to us by Oralí when she points out:

> *Faith as support in the face of pain*: I recognized that the experience of that moment was too much for me and that I would not be able to get through such a tragic situation on my own. A situation that affected my husband, my daughter, my family, and me. I realized I needed someone to help me understand what was happening and to be able to live through it. Drawing on the faith I have embraced since childhood, cultivated in my family, I decided to seek support from a spiritual guide, particularly a priest, who guided me for a year on my spiritual path to healing my wound[4].

---

[3] Chip Corlett, Katie's father.
[4] Oralí, Albalicia's mother.

WHERE IS GOD WHEN WE ARE GRIEVING?

> Meanwhile, where is God?
>
> C. S. LEWIS

In touching on the theme of spirituality, I could not fail to include the theme of God because our relationship with Him is something of great value to many and is manifested in our response to experiencing grief. We either hold on to Him more strongly or distance ourselves. It depends on how we feel in our hearts.

The question: where is God? is something I hear a lot, either from my clients, from people attending my seminars, or when facilitating support groups. What I wholeheartedly offer them is a space where they can share and express how they feel. I can tell you that I understand, as I remember how angry I was with God when my father died. The news was given to me by the Mother Superior as I was at school. I was confused, as I had just been praying in the chapel for my father's well-being. Even more, when I returned from the cemetery, I went to my bedroom, and crying disconsolately, I asked myself: "Why did God take my father away?" Within me, a profound grief and lack of understanding took hold. If God was a benevolent being, why had He left me without a father at such a young age? I asked myself over and over again, "How is it that, having so much faith, being a Catholic child, being a believer, praying every night, going to Mass... suddenly my father has died?" In my heart as a child, I felt that God had not heard my prayers. That was a process that I had to go through to reestablish my relationship with Him because I needed that source of comfort, strength, and hope in my heart. Religion and faith were my rocks during those early years, and they have also been present as I faced the loss of my mother.

However, because of our unique way of processing grief, many people experience anger toward God and hold Him responsible for what happened. Harold Ivan Smith recognizes how common this reaction is and even applauds the person who questions God and shows their anger because not all grievers admit it. One thing he recommends doing is the following: "Sometimes, you must pray, "God, help me to forgive you." Sometimes, you must live your way into forgiving God" (p. 63).

For this book, I developed a questionnaire that I used with certain clients to illustrate how they have processed their grief in different ways. In the question, "What has been the greatest challenge during your grief?" María de los Ángeles shows us what a grieving person can experience when they feel anger before God:

> The greatest challenge with my grief has been my relationship with God. At the beginning, right after my husband passed, I was very angry with Him. I was close to becoming an atheist; my faith became a struggle…WHY, if He was truly a loving God, He had not healed Daniel, despite all my prayers…The next minute, I would be asking God to help me get through this HORRIBLE pain. At this time, I think I would like to feel closer to Him, but there is still some resentment toward Him…I also feel betrayed by Him[5].

---

5   María de los Ángeles, bereaved wife.

This feeling of Maria de los Ángeles can be exacerbated even more by comments from people who, with the intention of helping us, say things like: "God does not give you more than you can handle." It is, therefore, a good habit to refrain from saying something like that if we do not know how the person feels internally because it can intensify their anger.

As a pastor, Richard Gilbert recognizes these kinds of questions when we are grieving and have so many questions. He advises us not to ignore it or put the questions aside:

> If you feel overwhelmed, walk away from some routines and people, but do not walk away from your pain. Stay with the doubts and questions: "Why did dad have to die now?" "Why did Mom get cancer?" "Why did the treatments fail?" and the many other questions that arise from your heart. Ultimately, these are doubts about God. You may never have "the answers" that are going to solve everything, but the questions are paths on which you meet God, and ultimately, yourself (2014, p. 59).

He shares this paragraph, which is taken from his book *Heart-Peace*: "Lord, this is a very bumpy road. Detours, depressions, new doubts…With each recognition of the loss, the pain rises to its highest point. Will I ever heal, Lord? Stay with me, God, please?! Amen."[6]

On the other hand, there are grievers who, upon losing a loved one, seek to draw even closer to God:

---

6 Gilbert, Richard. *HeartPeace: Healing Help for Grieving Folks*, p. 32.

I have also been greatly helped by the love of my loved ones and the acceptance of God's love...the meaning I found in my loss is that I found God, I found him sincerely. And that saddens me sometimes very much, because it is another "if I had" that I add to my long list: "If I had truly had God with me, within me, and I had taught it to my son... maybe none of this would have happened..."[7]

Alex, a father who lost two sons, shares with us his relationship with God as follows:

The grace beyond the grief is seeing for the first time things we thought were invisible. Things beyond this world that are opened to us when our suffering is deep and our tears are sincere. God's grace is released, and we are privileged to see things that are not meant for this world. God cries with us because he is a God of compassion, but our suffering gives us the opportunity to have a deep and unique relationship with God. Your darkest moments can become the deepest moments of enlightenment you will ever experience. In our brokenness, He gets to put us back together in life-changing ways.

Sometimes, as we begin our grief journey, we feel a lot of pain and also a lot of anger toward God, and we do not want to talk about Him. This reminds me of Luz María, a dear client who lost her son. When talking about this issue she told me: "I am at a truce with God." We navigated like this for months. I would ask her from time to time: "Are you

---

[7] María, on losing her son to suicide

still at a truce?" Until one day came when, at last, she decided to take out her little white flag and made peace with God. That happened in her time, not mine. I like to accompany my clients where they are at without telling them how they should feel or not feel.

If such thoughts have assailed you when you have lost a loved one, do not feel guilty or think that you are not a good believer. It is just that your pain is so great that you seek answers from a supreme being in whom you have always placed all your trust. But God never told us that pain would not be present in our lives, nor did He promise us eternal life on this earth. However, asking the question, "Why, God?" is something human since we have many questions and doubts when we suffer great pain. We want answers that often do not exist.

This passage I share with you is taken from the book *When Bad Things Happen to Good People*, which Rabbi Harold S. Kushner wrote when faced with the death of his fourteen-year-old son, who was suffering from an illness. Kushner lets us know how he feels before God and whether he holds Him responsible for his suffering:

> God does not cause our misfortunes. Some are caused by bad luck, some are caused by bad people, and some are simply an inevitable consequence of our being human and being mortal, living in a world of inflexible natural laws. The painful things that happen to us are not punishments for our misbehavior, nor are they in any way part of some grand design on God's part. Because the tragedy is not God's will, we need not feel hurt or betrayed by God when

tragedy strikes. We can turn to Him for help in overcoming it, precisely because we can tell ourselves that God is as outraged by it as we are (2004, pp. 147-148).

It also speaks about the capacity we possess to find meaning and purpose in our lives despite tragedy. Kushner does not expect God to intervene in the things that happen to people; we need to see how we manage what happens to us. It is a profound book that, in a human and natural way, depicts the tribulations we may face in losing a loved one and how we can transform them.

In this passage, he invites us to explore the concept of meaning:

> "Let me suggest that the bad things that happen to us in our lives do not have a meaning when they happen to us. They do not happen for any good reason which would cause us to accept them willingly. But we can give them a meaning. We can redeem these tragedies from senselessness by imposing meaning on them"(pg. 149).

We will delve into this question when we cover the section on finding meaning.

In a tangible and raw way, in the memory of C. S. Lewis, we can witness the struggle this man, experiencing such intense grief, has with God over the loss of his wife. In his innermost self, he longed to find an answer about the nature of God and the power of prayer, for he felt that He had not heard him. In this book, which is really a kind of journal, Lewis opens his heart in a raw way and asks himself, as he reflexes on his writings and his inner struggle "Are not all these notes the senseless writhings of a man who will not accept the fact that there is nothing we can do with suffering except to suffer it?" (p. 33), and he comes to realize that what he has wished to do in insulting God is to strike back because of the great pain he has experienced in his grief. Moreover, he comes to the conclusion, "I begin to see. My love for H. was of much the same quality as my faith in God" (p. 41).

Many people get upset with God because they think he did not answer their prayers. Do you feel identified? If so, you can write Him a letter expressing your feelings.

There are people who express guilt for feeling that way; however, it is important to validate emotions. Precisely, validating emotions is what the Reverend Doctor Dale Young—who was the director of pastoral care—and I recommended in the training we offered at Baptist Hospital to train support group facilitators in churches. We conducted this training for nine years.

In that training, it was common for the topic of anger toward God to come up. We would tell the attendees that they were being trained to be group facilitators, that they should show empathy rather than judgment, and that it is not necessary to say a single word of disapproval. Sometimes, with just a glance, we imply that we are judging. Let us pay attention to how we feel and how others feel. Many times, that feeling is fleeting. We have the case of Maria Gough, who came to our first training group. She had lost her fourteen-year-old son Jaime, who was killed by a classmate, and she was devastated. Well-meaning people came to her with bibles, saints, crosses, and religious objects to help her in her grief. María did not want any of that, for she was very angry at God. She remained this way for several months, and it was then that she attended the group and shared her story. A complete change took place in her, and she went on to create a successful bereavement support group in a Christian church. This shows us that anger does not have to be permanent. The important thing is to give ourselves the space to express it and process it to let it go.

If you feel hopeless, seek help

I have had clients tell me: "Ligia, I do not want to live without my loved one. It is not that I want to end my life, it is just that I do not know what to do, how to live without him."

This is a natural reaction, and it helps a lot to talk about it because, by sharing it with another person, the two of you can exchange ideas about what can be done. Yes, it is true: your life has taken a 180-degree turn; however, if you give yourself the opportunity to see alternatives on how to use your time to create activities and see options, you will discover that little by little, the interest could start growing inside of you. If, on the other hand, you feel that you do not really want to live and want to end your life, I urge you to seek help.

There are many crisis call centers, support groups, and professional help. Give yourself the opportunity. Always think of your loved one as a loving light in your life, one who lights your path and always accompanies you. Also, think of those you may harm if you cause harm to yourself. Think of yourself as someone who is capable of loving so intensely. Love is the most powerful emotion; share it and give it to those who do not have it. It can change your life and theirs.

PROCESSING YOUR GRIEF

It is important to take an inventory of your behavior throughout the grieving process. No one knows you better than you know yourself. Introspect on how you are acting, what you are feeling and thinking and ask yourself the following questions: Is this helping or hurting me?

_____
_____

Is it helping me in my growth and honoring my loved one or is it sinking me deeper into anger or resistance?

_____
_____

Are you offering me the opportunity to develop spiritually or are you filling my heart with bitterness?

_____
_____

Accompaniment

> We mean well, but we do not know the right words to give comfort.
>
> *Speaking Grief* Film

In this section of the book, I wish to speak directly to the friend, the colleague, the family member, the companion of that person who is facing the loss of a loved one, and to the person who has lost a loved one. The purpose is to help the bereaved and the people who accompany them to give them the space to cry and express how they really feel because what people want is to be heard and understood. Pay attention to what you have to say and be present.

How do you behave with someone who is grieving?
First of all, I want to thank you for your desire to help the bereaved. You are in a situation that is not easy; it is a challenge, and sometimes you do not know what to do or what to say. Because there is a lack of social education regarding situations of losing a loved one and because we avoid talking about grief, I understand that sometimes you feel lost and do not know how to help that special person who is going through the grieving process.

In reality, it is something that takes us out of our comfort zone. Sometimes, we even avoid seeing the griever, or if we get to see them, we do not mention what happened. This makes the person feel alone and emotionally abandoned. I remember a client who suffered the death of a loved one due to suicide. Every time she arrived at her place of work, people pretended not to see her to avoid saying a word. As she continued walking to her office, she could hear the whispers and comments. The social silence in the face of such a loss is something that greatly affects the bereaved. Pay attention and avoid falling into that situation.

Accompanying instead of encouraging

> A single person is missing for you, and the whole world is empty. But one no longer has the right to say so out loud.
>
> Philippe Ariès

What Philippe Ariès said in his book *Western Attitudes toward Death* (1975, p. 92) is what, we, who have lost a loved one, feel. The thing we desire the most is to be allowed to express our feelings. When we lose our loved one, it is absolutely necessary to express that we miss them. Why do we have to pretend that we do not miss them? Let us speak and express what it is like to lose a loved one: what it is like to lose a mother, a father; what it is like to lose a spouse, a son, a daughter, a grandmother, a soulmate. Brianne Benness provides this message on her blog Grief Keeps on Coming[1], representing all the grieving: "I want us who to be

---

1 The Grief Keeps Coming: https://medium.com/swlh/the-grief-keeps-coming-3ef76174d62a

surrounded by people who see our grief as valid, human and worthy of compassion. I want them to understand that our grief is not over because our loss is not over."

Therefore, when you are next to a grieving person, be patient and validate their feelings. Grief is a process; it is a journey. Walk it alongside the griever, for that person is going through something terrible in their life. Their world, as they knew it, has changed. There are many emotions that come together, and it is a process of adaptation, stability, and learning. Please make sure that your story does not overshadow theirs. Avoid saying, "Let me tell you what happened to me." Please avoid being the center of attention. Do not wish for everything to be like it was before because it will never be the same as before. However, what helps most in the grieving process is support, which consists precisely of being present and validating the feelings of the griever. If you cannot be close due to the pandemic, as mentioned earlier, accompany them by WhatsApp, Zoom, or Facetime; what matters is that you are present.

Something that also often happens is that the family or close friends want the bereaved person to participate in celebrations, whether birthdays or other festivities. Often, they insist with phrases such as: "The whole family will be there. We will miss you," "It is not good for you to be alone," "It has been a long time since we have seen you, and we miss you, think of us too," or "It is a special time of the year to share and we want to be with you."

All these phrases are expressed with a beautiful intention. However, it is not about what you feel but about what the grieving person experiences. I have heard many comments from clients who reject the insistence, as they take as the person being self-centered, only thinking about themselves instead of considering the other person's pain. Similarly, it may happen that the grieving person does not want to be socially active or does not feel part of the conversation because they find it trivial. When experiencing such profound pain, they may sometimes feel that they do not fit in, that their friends do not understand the space they are in, or that they do not feel part of that form of interaction. Topics that once seemed joyful and fun before the loss may now seem superficial. It is important to be patient and understand that what they are going through is natural. Remember that grief is a process and that it is different for everyone.

Understanding the grieving process

One of the barriers to knowing how to behave is the lack of knowledge about how grief manifests. Therefore, if you wish to accompany your loved one, do your best to inform yourself and to know that grief can manifest itself not only from an emotional point of view but in all other dimensions, as we explored in the section dedicated to grief. When we want to be experts in something, we study it. In that sense, if you want to have broad understanding of how to act, you need to learn about grief thoroughly. By doing so, you will not only support your loved one, but you will also help yourself.

Phrases that illustrate the lack of social understanding about grief. If you want to help me...

> ... do not tell me that is enough: "That is all you talk about."
> ... do not tell me to hold back my tears: "You are always crying, and your loved one would not like that."
> ... do not tell me how I should feel, either: "You should be grateful she had a long life."
> ... do not tell me: "She would not like to see you sad; you have to be strong."
> ... do not tell me: "God does not give you more than you can handle."

I share with you some phrases that we may hear when we are grieving. I am aware that people are doing the best they can and that they want to help and encourage. However, on behalf of so many other grievers, I ask you to simply accompany them, understand them, and give them the space to explain how they feel. It is natural that they do not feel well. You do not need to help them, just be there. Above all, validate them. This is one of my purposes with this book: for the grieving person to feel that their pain is being validated.

You are not encouraging them to remain stuck; you are just holding the space for them to express what they are feeling. Letting it out helps the grieving person much more than suppressing what they feel and staying stuck in their thoughts. So, please listen and realize that what helps the griever is not your story, but theirs.

In reality, it is not your fault if you have repeatedly make these comments without realizing it, because living in a death-denying society, is what we are accustomed to.

That is why I wanted to share this section with you so that you can just open your heart, give space to the griever, and validate their feelings, not yours.

I Know How You Feel

After accompanying so many people in grief, I know that the phrase they least want to hear is precisely: "I know how you feel," because in reality... you do not know. No one knows how the other person feels even though they have experienced the same type of loss. Let us remember how many variables are present in our grieving process. Also, being unique people, I remind you that our grief is unique.

A phrase often said is, "It is time for you to move on," and it is the last thing we want to hear and the least helpful to us. That comment comes from people's desire to encourage the bereaved. They may not know what it is like to have lost a significant loved one, or perhaps their way of coping with loss is different. As the Rev. Dale Young, chaplain and former director of pastoral care at Baptist Health System in Florida, said, "Each of us has our own clock."

For nine years, the Reverend and I trained people to be facilitators of bereavement support groups in churches, a beautiful faith-based program. In that training, we emphasized how necessary it was to allow the person to express how they felt without judging them or telling them what to do.

Other common and generic phrases

"Everything happens for a reason." "He is in a better place." "God has a plan."

"If you cry you will make your loved one sad." "You have to be strong for your family."

Everything Passes

"Everything passes" is another example of those consoling phrases that are said a lot, and that does not help the griever at all as they generate a reaction contrary to what the phrase implies, given that the death of a loved one does not "pass." People mean well when they tell us that we must move on. That we should not let ourselves fall; that everything passes…

However, this message is not well received when the person has lost a loved one. How are you going to tell a mother who lost her son that "everything passes"? What "passes" in this case? What people really want to say is that the stab and rawness of those early days will gradually lessen because the message from society is: "You will feel better, everything passes." You may have heard the phrase "everything passes" and rebelled against it. As time goes by, it is natural that the intense emotions experienced at the beginning will diminish. However, how can you "get over" the death of a loved one? How can you "get over" the death of a child from a drug overdose? How can you "get over" the death of a child from a drug overdose? How can you "get over" the death of a loved one? "Pass" the death of a spouse in a plane crash?

How can the death of a daughter who had an aneurysm in the bathroom just before she got married "happen"? How can the death of a child "pass" minutes after birth? How can a mother's death "pass"? They probably mean that the intensity of the pain is lessening, and by saying that phrase, they want to give us hope that we will feel better.

If you tend to say that phrase, think again because, based on my experience helping so many bereaved people and my own, this is one of the least helpful phrases.

You have to think positive!

"Think positive!" is another phrase to be avoided. The message being sent is that of repressing the pain and the expression of grief when what the griever needs is the validation of their feelings in order to cross the abyss and gradually emerge from that depth. Following this line of thought, Megan Devine comments on the expression "Being brave -being a hero- is not about overcoming what hurts and turn it into a gift (2017, p. 36)… it standing at the edge of the abyss that has just opened in someone's life and not turning away from it, not covering your discomfort with a pithy "think positive" emoticon" (2017, p. 37).

Many well-meaning people invite us to think positively and to know that this pain will pass and that, in time, we will be fine. It is one thing to have a positive outlook on life and another to "be positive" when one is in the ocean of grief. If we tell someone to "be positive," we are denying them the possibility of living their grief and expressing it. In the section on the power of the mind, I elaborate on what I consider to be positive thinking when grieving. You can go there and review it. In those moments, we need to be allowed to swim in that ocean, often even needing a lifesaver to keep us from sinking. However, we need to swim it. We do not want to sit by the shore, watch it pass us by, and stay under a palm tree. Grief is active, not passive. We can take actions that will help us to swim little by little until we reach the other shore. Yes, if we want, we can emerge from the depths of that ocean and learn to swim on the surface for the rest of our lives, for that is what grieving for a loved one is like, for love is eternal.

Let us avoid assuming how the griever feels

People are also surprised by our behavior. Sometimes, they expect to see us in pain indefinitely and make comments such as, "But you sound great!" This can happen when we call the bereaved to offer condolences and hear them calm and able to carry on a flowing conversation. The bereaved then asks, "How am I supposed to be?" and may feel guilty for not being upset or appearing to be upset or even frustrated by the expectation.

"You are better now." This phrase is also said by people, of course, to make you feel better and because they consider that you are "doing well" in your process. We do not welcome it in a positive way for two reasons: First, we do not like to be judged or measured by other people's standards. Second, maybe at that moment, that person felt that the grieving person "was doing better," without knowing that maybe ten minutes later, he would fall into deep sorrow because grief is lived moment by moment. It is as if there was a need to show people how we are doing. It is not like that. Our grief is unique, and it is personal. It is ours. What we want from others is simply companionship and understanding of our story.

At the end of this section, I warmly suggest that, when you meet with that special person who is grieving, do not avoid talking to her about her loved one. Ask her how she feels and if there is anything you can do to help her at this time—even if it has been months or a year, the pain is still fresh. Do not be afraid if, when you ask her, she gets emotional. It is natural. It is likely that, deep down, she is thanking you for remembering her loved one and for being present in her grief.

Facebook Live

Inspired by the lack of tact or information that exists about how to help or treat the bereaved, I decided to do a Facebook Live with the desire to help those who were going through grief just like I was. That was two weeks after my mother passed away. I brought a message to others based on my own story. I talked about what we need the least and what helps us the most. My soul was set on helping all those grieving people who want the support they are looking for. I spoke of what I needed. I spoke of what so many of my clients need. I talked about what the nature of this book is. I realized that giving that message of help to others was my purpose. It was to continue with my mission, renewed by that great pain. I began this path of accompanying the griever by honoring the death of my father, and now, in the most painful moment of my life, I renewed my mission with more inner strength to honor the memory of my mother.

Here is the message I shared on June 21, 2020:

The Art of Bereavement Support

I wanted to bring this message today that is dedicated to those mourners, to those people who are going through the death of a loved one. It is also directed to those who wish to accompany their loved ones. I wanted to call this talk "The Art of Accompanying the Bereaved." What makes me call it an art? It is an art, and, as I have always told my clients, people may say things to you with the best of intentions, but they do not help you. However, sometimes we do not know what to do. In our Western society, we do not like to talk about death, and who does? But we all go through grief, and because I have heard it so much and I live it, I wanted to talk about it.

What is the art of accompanying someone in bereavement? Understanding that grief is to be there; it is to be present. Many times, people call me to ask me what to be to say when going to a funeral or a wake. The greatest thing we can do is to be there, show affection and understanding, and give them love. Sometimes, we say words that do not help. I want to raise awareness because I have always done so. That strength to help others is even more renewed since the death of my mother. I feel it in my heart, and I ask: "How can I help you?

It is important to communicate to others our desire to help them in those moments and for those accompanying to listen. Sometimes, what we need the most is to be allowed to talk. To listen, to let us cry if we want to cry, to let us scream if we want to scream. Not to be told, "You should not feel this way," "You have to be strong," or "She would not like to see you like that." I have always said this, and now I emphasize it even more.

What does it mean to be strong: to put on a mask and pretending everything is fine or having the capacity to connect with our real feelings and having the spiritual strength to express them, to talk about them, to write, to let out everything that weighs us down? For me, the latter is what being strong means. What does being strong mean to you?

Additionally, knowing when to offer help, when to listen, when to give a hug...that is the art of accompaniment.

Instead of them trying to comfort us, we want to feel accompanied. One thing I have noticed that our family and friends have a hard time with when accompanying us in grief, is knowing what to say to us. What they want is to soothe us, to take us away from the place of pain. But what we really want is to be listened to, to be loved and understood. Is not that so?

What kind of comments touch our souls

> Some of us might be grieving for the rest of our lives, and that is okay. It does not need to be fixed.
>
> Brianne Benness

One of the most beautiful comments came from my optometrist, when he told me, "Oh, your mom was 100 years old? Actually, it does not matter how old she was; it always hurts." And that is what touches our soul because the fact that she was a centenarian is not a reason to minimize the grief because there are more experiences lived with her, more memories, and more nostalgia for not having her. So I am grateful for those comments, those that validate how the bereaved feel for the physical absence without analyzing the loss itself. That is what we need when we are grieving! Not that they want to fix us up, not that they tell us: "You will feel better," not to hear: "This will pass with time," because, although all those intentions are wonderful, there are moments when we do not want to be told any of that. There are circumstances in which we just want them to listen to us and let us talk, so that we can then recognize and know that, yes, with time, that intense pain will pass, and it will lessen. We need someone to simply give us a hand, open their arms, and say: "Here I am."

WHAT TO SAY IN TIMES OF GRIEF?
- "I am with you in your pain."
- "I am here if you need to talk."
- "I understand that it is painful to lose a loved one so close."
- "I do not know what to say to you. Let me listen to you with my heart."
- "I support you in whatever you need."

PROCESSING YOUR GRIEF

What comments have you heard people say that have not helped you?

_____

_____

What would you have liked to answer?

_____

_____

What comment or word has touched your heart?

_____

_____

Where Are We Focusing on Our Grief?

> Where attention goes, energy flows.
>
> JAMES REDFIELD

There are times when emotions flood us in such a way that we feel we cannot control them; they feel like a torrent, and we cannot control them. If we allow them, they possess us. It is as if the floodgates of a dam were opened, and the water flowed freely. It can happen when we are alone or in public places, so it becomes difficult for us to express them freely. In those moments, you can do several things to divert your attention: you can call someone in your support network—something I highly recommend you have- or you can focus on something external, which is in your environment and on which you can focus all your attention. What you can also do is to mentally count from 100 to 1. By focusing on the number, you will change the focus of your thinking.

To demonstrate to my clients, or to the people who attend my seminars, how we can choose where to focus and how this influences our perception, I do this exercise with them: I ask them to pay attention to the objects in a room that are a certain color and focus only on that. For example, to perceive everything that is white. Then I ask them to close their eyes and tell me everything that is black. Most of them fail to mention black objects even when they have had them in front of their eyes because their attention is focused on the white, and they are surprised that this happens to them.

The same goes for our lives and emotions. If we focus only on sadness, anger, or guilt, that will be our reality. Therefore, if you do this exercise, you can "choose another color" and focus on external objects that divert your attention at that moment, from the intensity of emotions, if the occasion is not conducive to expressing them freely.

Do you see it as a movie?

When grieving, we may feel different emotions, thoughts that may confuse us or emotions that we have never felt before. Sometimes, we can get caught up in replaying the final moments, running them over and over in our minds. It feels as though there is a movie playing constantly in our minds, looping endlessly. In my experience, that is something that happens to most people.

What happens in that respect is natural because you have experienced something deeply painful, and it is as if your mind cannot take it all in at once. One thing you can do with your brain when you are presented with that movie—I do it with many of my clients—is to imagine that you push it back as far as you can.

You can also put the image in black and white or make it blurry. These are NLP techniques—neuro-linguistic programming—that can help you. I always try to emphasize that if you want to feel better, you can apply different tools to help you in your process.

You can also redirect the "movie" to a time in your life when you felt at peace or recall a memory with your loved one that brings a smile to your face. As I shared with you earlier, it has helped me tremendously when my iPhone generates videos of photos with my mother. Those videos can be bittersweet, especially as we begin to walk the path of grief. However, little by little, you can focus on how beautiful it was to have shared those moments with your loved one. One thing I suggest to my clients, and now to you, is that when you see photos of your loved one, instead of falling into sadness at the thought that they are no longer by your side—if that is where your mind tends to go, I accompany you in that, because I understand how pain leads us there—do your best to evoke the experience you had when taking that photograph and embrace that memory within your soul. Again, it depends on where we focus. This can help you heal your soul little by little because we know that healing will not happen from one moment to the next, as it is a process. Above all, I wish to emphasize that *we do not forget* this is not the intention of healing. Healing implies learning to carry that loss as part of our lives while always focusing on love-that, to me, is healing. It is about not staying in a place of suffering; that is the difference. When we heal, we learn to process difficult emotions and decide how to act because we have learned to assimilate what hurts us and what has happened. The first step is wanting to do it, and that is where I have seen the difference when I am with my clients; the person who learns and allows themselves to assimilate is the one who wants to move forward.

Using thoughts to our advantage

> Nothing can harm you as much as your own thoughts unguarded.
>
> BUDDHA

> What you focus on, what you think about, becomes your experience.
>
> MARK D. LEE

If you are a client of mine, you probably know the importance I place on our thoughts, as they greatly impact how we process our grief. We have come to understand how necessary it is to "sit with our grief," experience it, and embrace it. It is part of us. However, there is a difference between living our grief and increasing it based on the type of thinking we have in our minds. That is why I called my ninth principle "Modify your Thoughts" because we have the ability to watch them, as the Buddha tells us, to notice which ones hurt us and which ones help us in our process. It is worthwhile to observe them and recognize that we can control them since we are the ones who created them. As we experience the loss of our loved one, over which we have no control, I want to make you realize that we still have control over something: how we think.

The idea is to be able to redirect those thoughts after having processed our emotions instead of ignoring them. When I say, "Think about something else," I am not referring to ignoring the pain that the thought may have caused you, but acknowledging it and processing it, if necessary, so you can let it go. Then, look for something that makes you feel better. This will come naturally once you embrace it. I do it, and it helps me a lot. Although I specifically mean that we apply it in the context of the loss of our loved one, we can apply it to any situation. When intrusive thoughts flood our minds, let us acknowledge and validate the emotions they make us feel, but let us avoid dwelling on them. Let us redirect them to images that bring peace and love to our hearts.

Sometimes, not only do disturbing thoughts come to mind, but images also seem to repeat over and over again. Instead of ignoring them, acknowledge them and validate how they make you feel. Then, think of a beautiful memory and focus on that image. Remember life with your loved one was made up of many other moments the one that may be troubling your soul.

The pain we may feel for our loved ones can be so intense that it seems to persist over time. Yet, within us, we also possess much love, which is born of our relationship with them. Let us put our effort into letting it be love not pain, that moves us to find purpose, become better, and leave a mark in the world, inspired by them.

THE POWER OF OUR MIND
TO CREATE WHAT WE WANT TO FEEL

In his popular podcast *Breaking Patterns and Finding Inner Peace*, Tony Robbins interviewed the spiritual leader Michael A. Singer, author of the bestseller *The Untethered Soul: The Journey Beyond Yourself*, who elaborated on the power of our mind. When Robbins asked how he discovered that the mind can be as dangerous as it is beautiful, Singer explained that by looking inward, he realized that it is all in the mind-that the mind can be both a beautiful and dangerous place. Singer described he observed himself as a scientist, to understand why feelings changed, and he focused on understanding why beautiful emotions were leaving and, at the same time changing, and realized that it was all in the mind.

When I heard that, I identified myself to a great extent because that was exactly what I did with my grief. There I was, the person who specialized in the subject after having helped so many people, acting as a scientist and observing myself from the outside. Do you remember that at the beginning, I told you I was in two states: the bereaved daughter and the professional? Well, I concentrated on noticing what I was feeling when I was grieving, what were those experiences, what were those thoughts that were occurring, what were those emotions that were manifesting in my body. I observed all of that carefully, just as Singer proposes. I did it with two purposes: one, to help me in my own grief, to notice what helped me, how I felt when I was experiencing certain types of thoughts, and how my grief was expressed. The other purpose was to help the griever even more since I was adding to the theoretical principles a recent personal experience. Aside from my training and my experience in my grief as a child, I now had something current and felt it in a very raw way. What I have been learning from my experience I have shared with many clients, and now I am sharing it with you. Reflecting on it is very important, and I invite you to do so, to reflect, observe, and know yourself. For example, if you are sad and down, take a pause, connect with your inner self, and ask yourself: "What is making me feel this way right now?" Ask yourself the question, document it, and write it down in your journal; Actually, use a journal specifically for this. Write down what you did, what you were thinking, and what made you feel so sad, angry, or guilty. We have mentioned all those emotions.

Now, let us do the opposite, as Singer proposes. When you are feeling good, stronger, encouraged, hopeful for the future, and motivated, stop for a minute and ask yourself: "What am I doing right now? What am I thinking right now? What has helped me? This can be very helpful, as you will focus on what helps you feel better. I suggest it to you, as it has been very helpful to me and many of my clients. From the bottom of my heart, I wish and hope that you open your mind to this possibility and say to yourself: "I can do it. I want to do it." You will begin to notice an internal change that will express itself in your external world. Our mind, by means of thoughts, is the one that helps us deal with our inner dragons, a topic we will explore below.

Positive thinking

Because the issue of positive thinking when grieving can cause us to resist, I want to share below how I see positive thinking and how it applies when we have suffered a loss.

- Positive thinking does not mean ignoring how we feel.
- Thinking positively does not mean looking the other way when faced with a loss.

- To think positively is not to live in denial.
- To think positively is to be able to evaluate our situation.
- To think positively is to validate our emotions and know that we can have an impact on how we feel.
- To think positively is to be able to rethink our thoughts.
- Positive thinking is recognizing that we are facing a loss and processing our grief, knowing that there is hope in our lives.
- Positive thinking is accepting what is happening to us and choosing our response.

If we embrace these ideas, our positive attitude will come from within. It will be real. It will not be a mask we wear so that others will think we are "very positive." It will be the equivalent of developing a sense of gratitude and empowerment and seeing the possibilities that exist in your life. It will be equivalent to knowing that our thoughts greatly influence our emotions and that it is on the basis of those emotions that we act.

Daniel G. Amen and the dragons of the past

As I was writing this book, Dr. Daniel G. Amen's latest book was published (2021), which speaks precisely about our inner dragons. Dr. Amen is a renowned brain health expert neuroscientist, recognized by *The Washington Post* as "the most popular psychiatrist in America." He is the author of multiple *bestsellers* and is the medical director of Amen Clinics, nationally recognized as a pioneer in brain health.

Dr. Amen calls "dragons" that part of us that comes out and represents internal plots that can affect us and influence the way we handle certain situations. He talks about the dragons of grief and loss, among others. Those dragons are riddled with automatic negative thoughts (ANT). All of those messages are found within the dragons. I see them as something metaphorical, like monsters that come out, catch you, and, unfortunately, accompany you and are with you, when in reality, you would like to have an angel by your side.

However, these dragons are present with messages that do not help you in the least. Dr. Amen calls some of them: "Abandoned Dragons…Grief or Loss Dragons…Anxious Dragons…" We must learn to deal with them as we pay attention to the thoughts and messages we give ourselves. In grief, as we have seen, this attentive vision will have a great influence on the way we will process them.

To help us by example, Dr. Amen shares with us how he handled the loss of his father.

It happened in 2020 after he had managed to survive COVID-19. He was deeply hurt by this loss. However, he began his healing process immediately because, in his opinion, if we break an arm, instead of waiting a while to do something to heal it, we do it immediately:

> My dad joined the angels that day. And suddenly, Grief and Loss Dragons that I had been helping so many of my patients and social media followers cope with during the pandemic unleashed a fireball in my brain. Fortunately, as a psychiatrist who has spent decades helping people deal with death and

loss, I knew I needed to start the healing process as soon as possible. Some people think you need to wallow in suffering following the death of a loved one, but I always ask, "If you broke your arm, would you wait six weeks to have the bone set?" One of the most important steps in healthy grieving...is to express your feelings rather than bottling them up (2021, p.3).

NOTE:
EXERCISE TO OBSERVE YOUR THOUGHTS

First of all, I suggest that you take a moment to dedicate yourself completely to this experience. Pay attention to your breathing. After breathing in three times through your nose and releasing it through your mouth, pay attention to what is going on in your mind. Observe your thoughts. Avoid judging it; that is not the idea. The purpose of this exercise is for you to develop the ability to be aware of what you are thinking, as that will shed light on how you are feeling. Once you know what your thinking is, ask yourself if it is helping or hurting you in your process. If it is hurting you, you can take another breath and, as you exhale, let go of that thought. Then, choose another one that makes you feel better.

If you are saying all the time, "I cannot live without my loved one."

Try saying, "I live with my loved one in my heart."

I have used this technique with most of my clients, who feel it helps them in those moments when thoughts can literally knock them down. It is what is known as "Cognitive

Behavioral Therapy," and it helps us to feel differently by learning to change our thoughts.

What I usually do is draw the words on a magnetic board like this:

- Thought
- Emotion
- Action

When I show them to my clients, I tell them the following: "According to how you think, you feel, and according to how you feel, you act." This technique has been very helpful in helping people to feel and behave differently, whether they are a fifteen-year-old teenager or a ninety-three-year-old woman. Our mind is powerful. Thoughts are our cognitive aspect, and by changing your thinking, you can immediately change your emotions and act differently. For example, if you are feeling fear and you want to feel peace, think of something that gives you peace of mind. It is amazing how well this type of therapy works to manage anxiety, fear, and sadness. I have been teaching it for a long time, and last year, I had the opportunity to apply it in the hardest and most painful moment of my life, when I lost my mother. I assure you it works. I have applied it in circumstances in which thoughts have led me to the greatest sadness. After processing it, I change the thought to a beautiful memory, which completely changes my emotions and, therefore, I act differently.

> **PROCESSING YOUR GRIEF**
>
> Recognize how you feel right now.
>
> _____
> _____
>
> Note what you are thinking and write it down.
>
> _____
> _____
>
> Then, choose which emotion you would like to experience.
>
> _____
> _____
>
> Write down the thought that would help you feel that way.
>
> _____
> _____

Trust yourself, you can do it. Many of my clients pronounce the thought out loud, and that is what I suggest to them: to express it, to verbalize it, to write it down in their notebook—most of them bring one to the session to take notes of what they want to take away and apply later.

WHAT ELSE CAN HELP YOU AT THIS TIME?
Something that helped me significantly during the first few months after my mother's death, and that can also help you, was to have structure because that creates a sense of grounding—something that we can very easily lose during the early days because it is natural to feel up in the air and

aimless. Move forward step by step, one at a time. I suggest you use lists and see what is really important. As for your responsibilities, avoid ignoring them because then they will pile up on you. On the other hand, do not demand too much of yourself. Do not think that you have to move forward at the same pace as before. It is understandable and even necessary to slow down a little. Therefore, planning your days and finding something to do every day will help you find a place in your new world. However, you do not have to do it all at once, as that can overwhelm you. If it feels like too much, ask for support. At such times, people like to be supportive. The grieving person sometimes avoids asking for help, as they do not like to bother others, Usually, people do not know how to offer it and do not want to bother you. Ask for help, accept it, and learn to delegate.

NOTE:
Plan something this week that makes you feel good, such as taking a walk on the beach, getting a massage, shopping for something, or cooking a new recipe.

FROM PASSIVE TO PROACTIVE

What I am going to develop below will be useful to you depending on where you are in your process, remembering that each grief is unique. Therefore, something that I suggest because it can help you, and that many of my clients do, is to be proactive. How does being proactive help us, and what do I mean? Well, instead of waiting for some of our friends or family members to call us to make plans, how about making them ourselves? We can organize a get-together at home, go out to have lunch, or even go on a trip. We will then be able to share and be proactive instead of reactive, something that is easy to fall into when friends do not respond as we would like; therefore, we get stuck in the space of sadness or anger. Let us be proactive and plan with the people who are there for us.

This reminds me of Terry, who lost his husband and took on a highly proactive attitude: he planned a trip with friends to go on a yoga retreat, which he enjoyed very much because, apart from connecting, the type of trip they took was highly spiritual. Likewise, he regularly connects with friends to go out to eat and plans different activities. Terry feels he has made great progress in his process.

I also share with you the case of María de los Ángeles, who has discovered friendships through a support group and has found herself planning activities such as watching movies, eating, and even traveling. They call each other on the phone and take the initiative, and that is what I suggest to you, as it is something that will help you to stop being isolated, inactive, and passive.

You may not want to be so involved right now. That is okay, one step at a time. Each little step you take will help you in your recovery—from the acute stage—or, even better, of transformation because, in reality, as we heal our soul, we are transforming our loss and, therefore, transforming our lives in the same way as María has done: "I understood that there is no one outside of me who can heal my pain. Only myself, hand in hand with God, can heal my wounds and my pain and transform everything into love, light, understanding, gratitude and forgiveness."

Actions you can take to feel better
- If you want to cry, do it. Tears cleanse the soul. Remember that faking a smile can hurt more than shedding a tear.
- Share how you feel with someone who knows how to listen.
- Make a commitment to yourself to take one positive action every day.
- Create a daily structure with a specific goal in mind. It can be something small, like feeding your dog or making your bed.
- Connect with your inner self through meditation and/or prayer.
- Find something you enjoy doing and do it on a regular basis.
- Take time for yourself.
- Breathe deeply and let the air out gently for three consecutive times.
- Write how you feel in a note and put it in a little box. You can also write thoughts to your loved one and put them in a box.
- You can use the concept of mind mapping: on a large sheet of paper, place a goal in the center and, around it, write concepts that have to do with that goal or project. When creating something like this to honor your loved one, you can write their name in the center and around it, list their defining qualities and characteristics, as well as what they enjoyed doing.

- Choose an object that will serve as an anchor to remind you of your loved one. I like to give my clients a ceramic heart to remind them that love is eternal.
- Make a list of the things that make you feel good and at peace, over which you have control.
- Practice some type of physical exercise (always consult with your doctor).
- Write in a journal.

One of the activities that has helped me the most in my grief process is writing in a journal. You can do it in different ways, as a ritual every day at a certain time or as a way of documenting as you go through the experiences. You can do it when you are alone or after you have shared with someone. The most important thing that helps is to connect with how we feel, to recognize the triggers, what helps us feel better, and to put those thoughts on paper.

Exercise to remember your loved one

I found this exercise, suggested by Dick (2014), very valuable to remember our loved ones. He refers to our parents; I expand it here for anyone who is no longer physically in our lives.

Find a large sheet of paper, and write the name of your deceased parent—or any other loved one—at the top. Take as much time as you need, and list the things that come to mind that you want to remember about that person and your relationship with them (p. 16).

RECREATING THE STORY

> Telling and retelling of the story of a grieving person's loss is an important part of his or her healing.
>
> J. SHEP JEFFREYS

In accompanying grievers and living my own grief, I have realized that we need to recreate the story. We want to go back. We want to have details. We want to recreate what happened and rewind the movie little by little, over and over again.

In doing so, we may find a missing link. We can find hidden messages, which is exactly what happened to me as I was recreating my mother's story during the first months after her death. As I read the texts exchanged with the nurse, with the lady who helped me take care of her, and with my best friend, Lucrecia, I put a lot of effort into finding the details, connecting the missing dots to recreate the story, finding significant moments with my mother. We keep the memories in our souls, not as consolation, but as shared experiences that we have with our loved one, and to which we return time and time again.

We also want to tell our story with them, what we mean to each other. We can choose the narrative we tell ourselves and what we will focus on. Death is only the end of the story of a life. Therefore, in the story, when you reconstruct it, include everything your loved one liked: what they ate, if they played an instrument, what kind of activities they enjoyed... All this can be part of the new story.

There is a lot of talk about narrative therapy, and I found myself doing it intuitively. My mother's story is full of love, laughter, resilience, and cleverness, and recreating it helped me make sense of it. It helped me process the painful details and remember the beautiful ones. Among them is this message I shared with Lucrecia in a WhatsApp text. It said: "Three days before she passed away, when I entered my mom's room, she looked at me and said: "I love you so much, so much, so much..."

NOTE:
Call that person who listens to you without judgment and tell them your story.

PROCESSING YOUR GRIEF

In this section, I invite you to write the story of your loss. Write it as clearly as you can.

_____

_____

Have you recreated the story of your loved one?

_____

_____

What moments from that story do you replay in your mind?

_____

_____

Do you share your story with anyone?

_____

_____

> **What kind of narrative do you want to recreate?**
>
> _____
>
> _____
>
> **What are the qualities you liked most in your loved one?**
>
> _____
>
> _____
>
> **What did he like to do?**
>
> _____
>
> _____
>
> **Include special moments you have had with that person.**
>
> _____
>
> _____

USING YOUR STRENGTHS

Something I like to focus on with my clients is that they can develop their capabilities or strengths, because we all have them. Something I also want to do through this book is to remind you of the possibilities that you have, and how going and developing them, and applying them to your process. This will help you increase your self-concept and your confidence that you can do it.

Many times, when clients come to see me, they tell me about everything they have not done and what they have not accomplished. Then, I pause and ask them what they have actually accomplished; I ask them to tell me what they have done during the week, and suddenly, they share with me things they have managed to accomplish. I invite them to pause and reflect. They realize that they are indeed taking steps, albeit small ones, but they are moving forward.

I suggest that you keep a notebook where you write down all the actions you are doing, document them, and, at the end of the week or month, review them; then, you will realize how you have been making use of your capabilities. Sometimes, we do not realize how capable we are. It is important to document it and then pat yourself on the shoulder or, better yet, give yourself a hug.

Music as a mood regulator

Music influences our mood automatically. It may be that listening to a song that reminds you of that person you lost generates nostalgia, as happened to me with the song "Después de ti," performed by Raul Di Blassio and Cristian Castro, as I mentioned earlier. On the other hand, you can choose to listen to joyful music that lifts your spirits. It can also bring back beautiful memories without making you melancholic. Music is part of the arts, and we call it "music therapy." I remember that when I went out for a walk, I would choose to listen to podcasts instead of music. The first time I wanted to listen to music, the song that came out was "Agradecido" (Grateful) by José Luis Rodríguez, el Puma, where he gives thanks for so many things after recovering from a double lung surgery. It touched my soul because it has an upbeat tone, and at the same time, the lyrics are like a hymn. It struck me, and I thought it had a meaning that I had heard it. What my heart felt was the need to be grateful for the great love I felt for my mother, and how she guided me on my journey. I was thankful at that moment for so many memories I had with her.

Self-Care

> To survive a crisis, you must focus on your recovery.
>
> JIM MOORHEAD

Self-care is about doing everything we can to be responsible for our well-being in a holistic way: body, mind, and spirit. Unfortunately, losing our loved one was not in our control. However, taking care of ourselves and, in so doing, honoring their memory is something we can control. In my 11 Principles of Transformation® system, principle VI is precisely: *Take Care of Yourself.*

By taking care of every aspect of our lives, we will manage to heal this great wound, and, in this way, we will not remain stuck in pain. We must always keep in mind that what we want to avoid is to leave this wound open for the rest of our lives. Upon feeling the wound of our grief open, we may think: "I do not feel the slightest desire to take care of myself because all I want is just to lie on a couch and cry." This can happen. However, in order for our wound to heal and close, it is important that we make an effort in the process. As Silvia, a dear friend who passed away, used to say (she lost her daughter and shared her story with me in my book *Transform Your Loss. Your Guide to Strength and Hope)*: "The wound of grief is never forgotten because it leaves a scar." Yes, when we lose a loved one, we do not forget because the scar is there. However, as we process our grief and take care of ourselves, we give the wound a chance to heal little by little.

What is self-care?

> Taking care of oneself is an expression of self-love.
>
> Ligia M. Houben

Self-care includes all aspects of our being because I believe in a holistic approach; it is about taking care of our body, mind, and spirit.

Taking care of your physical dimension

Physically, take time to rest as grief drains. If possible, take naps, even if they are short, for fifteen to twenty minutes. You will feel recharged.

Eat well to nourish your body. Unfortunately, you cannot control the loss; however, you can control what you eat.

Exercise because it helps you change your emotional state by elevating endorphins, which are chemicals that help promote a sense of well-being[1].

As for your spirit, connect with your inner self and give yourself moments of inner peace. Be patient with yourself; you are going through grief, and that can affect your emotions. Apply self-compassion (check the section where I talk about this topic).

---

1 Taken from MD.com

Keep a record of your daily activities

Today's date: _____ Sleeping hours: _____ Working hours: _____
Hours on the computer or cell phone: _____
Meal times
Breakfast: _____ Lunch: _____ Dinner: _____ Snacks: _____
Do you participate in any physical activity? ___ Which one? ___
How many times a week? _____
By yourself or with someone? _____
How do you structure your day? _____
What activities improve your well-being? _____
What activities are not healthy? _____
How does physical wellness support your transformation from the inside out? _____
What kind of physical activities improve your well-being, honor your body and support you in this process? _____
_____

Note:

Take a piece of paper and write on the top: "What are my needs?" Then, examine each one and realize if you are paying attention to all of them.

How you can take care of your mind

Our mind is powerful, and sometimes, we do not take care of it in the best way. Read books that help you grow personally, pay attention to your thoughts, and develop your capacity of choice; in the same way, train it. Just as you train your body in the gym to develop your muscles or do aerobic exercises to help your cardiovascular fitness, likewise, train your mind to keep it sharp and retain your memory. My mother was an expert on this subject because, when she reached the age of 100, she was still able to do the times tables and play dominoes. Among the activities that kept her mentally active during the last years of her life were doing crossword puzzles, studying English, and learning skills, such as making necklaces, counting, and playing dominoes.

Another activity that is excellent for maintaining mental agility is putting together puzzles. Choose the activity you enjoy the most and integrate it into your routine. Besides distracting you in a positive way, it will help you have a sharp mind. Remember that when grieving, we can suffer from a lack of concentration, and we commonly forget certain things. These activities can help you be more alert.

NOTE:
Choose an activity that helps your mind and dedicate time to it every day.

PROCESSING YOUR GRIEF

What does it mean to you to take care of yourself?

_____
_____

How would your life change if you took better care of yourself?

_____
_____

> **What are you doing right now to take care of yourself physically, emotionally and spiritually?**
>
> _____
> _____

NOTE:

Make a list of five activities that you enjoy doing and that give you a sense of well-being. Choose to do one at least weekly. If you can do it every day, even better.

1. _____
2. _____
3. _____
4. _____
5. _____

THE VALUE OF RITUALS IN THE GRIEVING PROCESS

In sharing with you the 11 Principles of my methodology, you may have noticed that the seventh principle consists of using rituals when facing a loss. In this section, we will explain what they are and how they can help you.

RITUALS TO MAINTAIN THE ETERNAL CONNECTION

> Ritual is defined as highly symbolic acts that confer transcendental significance and meaning on certain life events or experiences.
>
> Kenneth J. Doka

Creating rituals has been one of the fundamental elements in my healing process. Recreating the rituals I had with my mother when she was alive has greatly filled my spiritual space. We prayed together every day, "Conversation with Jesus of Mercy," a prayer given to me by a very dear client in the form of a bookmark. And what happened? I still continue with that ritual. Additionally, I possess a treasure as I have a video of my mother praying the Lord's Prayer, which was her favorite prayer. She prayed it all the time, and I prayed it with her. All these different aspects of grief processing on a spiritual level have been of great value, of great importance.

A ritual that had great significance was the one I elaborated on when her birthday arrived on August 8, two months after her death. On that occasion, I made a video with many photos of her to honor her memory. I posted it on YouTube[2] and shared it with family and friends and on Facebook, where she always kept a beautiful place. We also had a birthday ritual for her, my older sister, my niece, and me at my house, as I mentioned before.

We gathered to pray, share stories, and sing Happy Birthday to her with a carrot cake, her favorite dessert. I bought her a card and read it to her in a very emotional way. It was a loving and bonding moment as we commemorated her memory and honored her life.

Little by little, I found a beautiful way to process my grief: playing the piano. As soon as I played the first note, I went back to my memories because, as a child, I had begun

---

2   https://www.youtube.com/watch?v=4ttZqkcrtng&t=40s

to learn to play piano shortly before my father passed away. My teacher's name was Julio Max Blanco. Due to the rigid mourning we lived at home, we did not listen to music, so I did not continue with my lessons. I then started note by note, and playing each one was like a balm for my soul. I felt I would honor my mother's memory by doing so, as she loved the piano.

As I mentioned before, I adopted that ritual for the first few months and then put it aside when I dedicated myself to writing the book to celebrate her life. That book became my purpose since it was a very special way of connection. I can tell you that this process has been what has given me the most meaning after her death and it became, in itself, a ritual. I was very eager to sit down in front of the computer and write about her, look for photos, and write about her life. Moreover, writing this book became another ritual to continue giving meaning to my loss.

Ritual for Thanksgiving Day

For Thanksgiving, something I have done and suggested others do is a family Thanksgiving ritual, being that this is precisely the day to give thanks.

The idea is for family members to place a small box or chest at the entrance of the house. Place some 4x6 cm white cards next to it, and each person writes something that makes them feel grateful for having had their loved one in their lives. After dinner, gather in the living room, bring the box, and share the different comments. This is a very special moment since, even though our loved one is not physically with us, they will still be present in our minds and hearts as we celebrate Thanksgiving. This ritual is a way to make the memory of our loved one part of the celebration. It is very beautiful and touching to be thankful for all the things a person gave you while he/she was alive and that you now remember with gratitude.

THE GRIEF DRAWER

It has been shown that it is important to set aside time to dedicate to processing our grief because, in daily life, we are so full of obligations and responsibilities that processing it can end up being the last priority. Sometimes, we have such a busy schedule that we do not even leave time for grieving. What is more, friends and family members, with the best of intentions, may tell you, "The best thing you can do is to stay busy," and you may go out of your way to not even give yourself time to think.

However, I remind you how essential it is to visit your grief and give yourself space. What you want is to connect with it in a way that helps you make it a ritual-a ritual that I have recommended to many clients and have done myself with my mother. You can start by setting up a drawer in the room where you put objects that belonged to your loved one. This will help you enter into that grieving space and process what you feel in your heart. Instead of putting it aside, give yourself some time each day or week to be intimate with your grief. You can do this by looking at mementos of your loved one, such as photographs you can look at, clothes you can smell, letters or cards you can read, objects that belonged to them that you can touch. All this connects us in a very special way because the idea is not to avoid the memories but, by performing rituals like the one with the drawer, you process your grief. You can even use an alarm to dedicate a specific time to this activity.

CREATE YOUR OWN RITUAL

A ritual can be something simple but deeply meaningful to you. For example, Marisol told me that having coffee together every morning and reading the newspaper is something she misses about her husband because it was a ritual for them. Now, what she does is have coffee on the terrace, where she can look at the orchids he used to grow. It is her new ritual.

GRIEF TRAINING RITUAL

When we conducted the training on how to facilitate bereavement support groups in churches, Dale and I would end the workshop by doing a ritual to honor our loved ones. We would place a tall white candle on a table on a beautiful candlestick. We would give each participant a ribbon where they could write the name of their deceased loved one. We also did the same. Then, each person would pin the ribbon to the candle. As they did so, and if they wished, they would say something about that person aloud.

> **PROCESSING YOUR GRIEF**
>
> Have you ever created rituals for your loved one?
>
> _____
> _____
>
> What type?
>
> _____
> _____
>
> What have they meant to you?
>
> _____
> _____

THE FUNERAL AS A THERAPEUTIC RITUAL

> As a rite of passage, the funeral assists you in recognizing the passing of your loved one, supporting" you as you start your life without the deceased, and reintegrating you back into the social group as a person whose loved one is no longer alive.
>
> THERESE A. RANDO

When we lose a loved one, one of the first things we have to do is to plan the funeral since it is a way to share with others the end of a life that was special to us and to say our last goodbye. This ritual in itself has great therapeutic value that provides us with multiple benefits, as Rando (1984) pointed out in Doka's book (2002, p. 136). Some of these benefits are:

- Confirm the reality of death.
- Assist in the expression of grief while simultaneously offering a structure that contains grief.
- Stimulate recollections of the deceased, both individually and collectively.
- Allow grievers to "do something" offering structuring activities at an otherwise disorganized time.
- Provide social support to the bereaved, reaffirming their new identity and reincorporating them into the larger community.
- Offer possible meaning for the loss, allowing mourners to understand the death within the context of their beliefs.
- Reaffirm the social order, reminding people of both the reality of death and the continuance of the community.

The Relationship Does Not End, It Transforms: Continuous Bonds

> Death ends a life, not a relationship.
>
> MORRIE SCHWARTZ

> Continuing bonds acknowledges that grief is ongoing.
>
> ELEANOR HALEY

We talk a lot about the continuous bonds that exist when we have lost our loved one. As grievers, we need that validation because our loved ones simply did not disappear from our lives, and as grievers, we choose to rebuild that relationship. That relationship can be based on love, giving you peace and feeling connected to them and allowing them to be light on your path, an inspiration. I like to say "transforming that relationship" since it is feeling the essence of that person by our side, their presence, either through rituals, writing them a letter, or writing in our journal.

Something that also helps us is to maintain the legacy through their story. Telling the story of their life, whether among family or friends, not just on social media. If we pay attention, we realize that people are doing it because they have probably realized the therapeutic value it has for them.

For me, it has been an important step in my grieving process and in my eternal connection. In fact, I did it with my father, and now I am doing it with my mother.

As a griever, it is comforting when we feel a strong connection with our loved ones after they have died. Moreover, Bonanno comments that many times, the griever behaves as if they are "communicating from an alternative reality" (Bonanno, 2019, p. 11). However, he also points out that for these continuing bonds to be healthy, one needs to see if the experiences of connection with that person are excessive or happen too often.

When we lose a loved one, it seems that, in our grieving process, they becomes our constant companion. I say this based on my experience and that of so many clients who, over the years, have shared with me that they feel this constant companionship. Additionally, John Bowlby (1982), in his book *Loss: Sadness and Depression*[1], talks about the constant attachment of widows and widowers to their deceased husbands and how they feel them as companions, something he does not consider unusual or unhelpful, but on the contrary, as he mentions a study carried out by Gilk *et al.* (1974) in which a case is presented of a widow who had inner conversations with her deceased husband and how this helped her to act independently (p. 98). I have observed the therapeutic value of these exchanges with my client, María de los Ángeles, who has established a series of conversations with her deceased husband. That has helped her gradually enter a space of healing.

---

1   *Loss: Sadness and Depression.*

We carry our loved ones in our minds and hearts; they are there, and we talk to them and feel them as a constant companion. In the section where I talk about the love story, I mention Viktor Frankl and how he had conversations with his wife, who was the source of his love.

It is up to you whether that company is a source of love, a source of smiles, or a source of peace. If you have managed to transform your suffering into something elevated that gives you meaning, or if, on the contrary, the constant relationship you have with your loved one is one of suffering, of complaints, of questions without answers because no one has them, you will not find them just by asking. If you find yourself in this space, it will prevent you from leaving the valley of pain. If you want to change this type of communication, take paper and pencil and ask yourself the following questions:

PROCESSING YOUR GRIEF

What kind of communication do I have with my loved one on a regular basis?

_____

_____

What kind of connection would I like to have?

_____

_____

What story of my loved one can I turn into a legacy?

_____

_____

LINKING OBJECTS

The term "Linking Objects" was introduced in 1972 by psychiatrist Vamik D. Volkan (1972), and the purpose of these objects is to connect us with our loved ones. These objects are usually things that belonged to them. It can be a photo, a note, or something they used. On the other hand, they can also be created to feel a connection with them. We have noticed a change in what is considered healthy in bereavement in relation to continuing bonds with this person. It used to be expected that these would not continue; now, on the contrary, it is even considered potentially healthy (Doka and Davidson, 2014, p. 226). Thus, maintaining these continuing bonds has been found to help in the grieving process because of their great significance.

I am a big believer in these objects, and they have been part of my connection to my parents. What links me to my father is a keychain that carries his motto: "Success is hard work disguised as good luck." The linking object that ties me to my mother is the heart magnet I mentioned to you when I told you my story, which is the one I wear on my clothes. I used to wear it when I traveled, and when she wore it too, it represented the fact that, despite the distance, we were united "heart to heart." By wearing it, I maintain that eternal bond, as it symbolizes the connection with my mom that will last forever.

CREATING LINKING OBJECTS

You can do several things to feel close to your loved one by creating linking objects. For example, there are some blankets on which you can put a photo or make a *collage* with several of their photos, making photo montages, like Luz María, who made some beautiful photo montages of her son in the sky, surrounded by clouds. This is something very spiritual, that fills her soul. You can also wear ashes on your necklace if your loved one was cremated to keep always them close to your heart.

Something beautiful that a dear client did was to make a butterfly garden. Marlem lost her daughter, and in her honor, she made a butterfly garden in her house. This is also mentioned in the *Transform Your Grief* workbook, as it is a beautiful thing. Butterflies are symbols of our loved ones. In telling us the story of her son, I remember how María Gough told us that as she was leaving the cemetery, a butterfly landed on her shoulder and went with her in the car. Speaking of linking objects, we have seen that they can range from things that symbolize our loved one to objects we can create ourselves. However, the greatest bond we can have is the great love that connects us to that person because love is eternal.

PROCESSING YOUR GRIEF

What kind of bonding objects do you own that make you feel connected to your loved one?

_____
_____

What kind of bonding objects can you create to feel the connection?

_____
_____

> **What items do you have from your loved one?**
>
> _____
> _____
>
> **What is the significance?**
>
> _____
> _____
>
> **What do they represent for you?**
>
> _____
> _____

ETERNAL CONNECTION. LIFE AFTER DEATH INVISIBLE TIES AFTER THIS DIMENSION.

When our loved one dies, we ask ourselves countless questions. Many times we want to understand what happened, why they had to die at that moment, or what we could have done. Another type of question we may also ask ourselves is what happens after they die. I have heard both types of questions from many clients, and I have asked some of them myself. The next set of questions I took from a book written by Tom Zuba, who lost his wife and two of his children. A story that both touches our souls and inspires us, as he has dedicated himself, through his books and talks, to helping the bereaved in their own grief:

> And do we still exist after we die, in some form or another? And is there a heaven? If there is, what is it and where is it? And does everyone go there or just some people? And are they still aware of us here on earth? And if they are, can they communicate with us? And we with them? (2015, p. 8).

As you can see, there are many questions we can ask ourselves, and generally, they have to do with our beliefs. Maybe, in your case, believing that you will be united with your loved one fills your soul with peace and hope, or receiving signs helps you maintain a bond with them and gives you meaning. Next, I will tell you about an experience I had a week after my mother passed away.

THE PEACOCK WITH THREE PEACHICKS

A week after my mother passed away, I was on my way to mass. I was absorbed in my grief when suddenly, in front of my car, a peacock with three peachicks crossed my path. Tears ran down my cheeks from the great emotion that overwhelmed me because, for me, that vision represented my mother with us, her three daughters. I reduced the car's speed to a minimum and stared at her. For me, that was a sign, what we call, in my field of thanatology, "After Death Communication (ADC)." Anyone could also say that it was "magical thinking," as we mentioned earlier. However, I did not feel that way. When these experiences happen to my clients, and they ask me if I think they are signs, I reply that what matters most is the meaning they give to them.

Seeing peacocks is a fairly frequent experience, as they are abundant in my neighborhood. However, one occasion when I felt, deep in my heart, that it was also a sign was a year and three months after my mother passed away. I was talking on the phone with my friend Lucrecia, and I was telling her how much I had missed my mother the night before, that I had an unexpected episode of "grief pang," and that it had been very strong. At that moment, I turned around to look out the living room window facing the street and saw a peacock standing right in the front yard of my house. I looked at it first with amazement and then with great emotion because I felt it was a manifestation of my mother.

For these signs, there is no such thing as time or space. We must always remember that what gives value to these experiences is the symbolism, the meaning we give them. Well, actually, it was not surprising because that day, I attended the funeral mass of a very close relative, and the experience in the church and the music filled my soul with memories. These are the triggers I have referred to earlier, which can lead us into a space of recurring grief. It is up to us whether we stay there or focus on eternal love and feel our loved one alive in our hearts.

PROCESSING YOUR GRIEF

How have your beliefs helped you cope with your loss?

_____

_____

What is your belief?

_____

_____

What do you think happens after one dies?

_____

_____

What is your concept of the afterlife?

_____

_____

Do you feel that your loved one accompanies you or is he/she in another dimension?
_____
_____

Do you think you will see your loved one again?
_____
_____

What brings you comfort?
_____
_____

Do signs exist for you?
_____
_____

Have you felt a sign from your loved one?
If so, describe it and, above all, reflect on what it has meant to you.
_____
_____
_____
_____

Healing, Honoring, and Transforming

> Accepting the spiritually, and transformative
> potential in suffering is one of
> your many choices in grief
>
> SAMET M. KUMAR

Here is a well-known phrase: "Pain is inevitable; suffering is a choice," and we can ask ourselves: is there a difference? When is it pain, and when is it suffering? This makes sense if we take into account that there are different reasons and causes for pain.

If you can find ways to ease your grief and show your spiritual strength, you can find meaning. There are different ways to do this; it all depends on us and what we want to choose.

I wish with all my soul that you would be inspired to see what you can do with your life to honor your loved one. Ask yourself the following questions: "What meaning can I find in my life? What can I do?"

You can make the decision to stay in that kind of grief, which, yes, you have the right to feel because you lost someone very important to you.

Still, with all my love, I remind you that you have the ability to choose to stay there for the rest of your life or to open your heart and mind to something great that is inspired precisely by that memory, by that love, by that life that lives in you and will always live. It is up to you to allow the flame of your loved one's eternal love to continue to live in your heart. Instead of being a cause of suffering, let it be a cause of inspiration. In the darkest moments, may that light shine even brighter and help you live your life with your loved one as your guide.

Do you experience pain or suffering?

> Pain is inevitable.
> Suffering is optional.
>
> Buddha

When we lose someone very close to us, we experience pain because the absence is tangible. It hurts us not to have them by our sides. The pain we feel in our soul can be very intense and makes us aware of our limitations and vulnerability as people. Sometimes, it is through pain that we realize how much we need to connect with others. Pain also gives us the opportunity to be present to both our needs and our lives. Now, if, in addition to feeling that pain, we find it hard to accept what has happened and we resist, we can turn it into suffering. What we do not realize is that the more we resist the pain, it becomes more present and more pronounced. That is when it turns into suffering, and instead of being in the present, we live in the past or worry about the future. Suffering can isolate us and leave us trapped in a very dark place, from which we would like to get out, but sometimes we do not know how.

Here are some suggestions that may help you to get out of suffering:

Pay attention to situations, people, or comments that can make you suffer, and avoid what is under your control. I am referring to people who, instead of holding space for you to share how you feel, try to pull you out of pain and give you ideas and suggestions. That can bring you suffering as it does not make you feel validated. Help yourself.

Observe what makes you feel better, whether peaceful or uplifting, and make an effort to carry it out whenever the possibility of falling into suffering increases. I suggest you do what I did with my grief: observe it as if you were in a laboratory and immediately recognize what could be your sources of suffering. I want to always remind you that you can handle that situation and move from suffering to peace or tranquility.

Suffering also arises when we keep thinking about how our lives changed, how we changed, and this also has to do with acceptance because it is not only not being able to accept that our loved one has died, but sometimes we also resist the changes that this absence has brought with it. Again, it is important that you recognize to what extent this resistance increases your pain because you may think that everything has lost meaning for you.

Crossing the desert of pain does not have to imply crossing the desert of permanent suffering. It is in this space where it is necessary to understand that when we connect with our inner self, even though our loved one is no longer on this plane, they continue within us as that immortal light that merges with our inner light. Only then will we be able to cross the desert to reach a permanent oasis.

If this situation is making you suffer, look at the resources you have and ask yourself if they can become an inspiration to be a better person and accomplish goals in your life that you may have never thought you could achieve. It is important that we see all the possibilities that unfold in terms of our growth, both personal and spiritual. We are constantly evolving, and things happen. As Buddha said, "Life is suffering," and if we look at Jesus's life as a human being, we will see how he also went through suffering.

We may ask ourselves: What does this imply? What is this about finding meaning? We can find meaning in the suffering we are experiencing. If you are able to stop the suffering, do it; trust in your ability. If it is impossible for some reason or situation, see how to find meaning in it by becoming a better person and seeing yourself differently in the future. If you have lost a loved one, you can find meaning in thinking about the loving moments you shared and knowing that it hurts so much because of the great love you have had, have, and will continue to have for them. If you enter that space, you will find meaning and strength. Give yourself the space; give yourself the opportunity. Life is something precious. To see the result, the meaning of certain situations that happen to us depends on how we handle them.

Understanding the importance of living through grief, you may ask yourself: what is the difference between living it and suffering from my loss? To live it is to feel and process it, to be aware of how you express it. Suffering means staying in the space of pain, amplified by the type of thoughts you allow to take over you. Although it may seem impossible, if we wish, we can choose not to fall into suffering, as Oralí Flores, who lost her beloved twenty-two-year-old daughter Albalicia in a car accident, tells us. She is co-founder of PUDE[1], a bereavement support group in my homeland, Nicaragua, and is certified in my 11 Principles of Transformation® training. She shares with us how she opened her heart to the experience of grief:

LIVING THE GRIEF, NOT SUFFERING IT
In this journey of grief, with the group of mothers, we found another angel in our lives, our good friend Ligia Houben, psychologist, thanatologist, grief counselor, and creator of the "11 Principles to Transform your Loss." With Ligia, I understood and lived grief, and its rituals, the stages, and the process of grief, guided by the 11 Principles, and at my own pace, as everyone has their own hourglass and their own time. It is a moment to open up to emotions and embrace them. It was the time to live my grief, to recognize and identify the resources that were in me to live one day at a time; to fall, and to know that I could get back up again. From my faith, I know that the Lord's promises are faithful and that we walk hand in hand with Him, in the darkest moments of our lives and, under that promise I know that He is the Light, the Truth, and the Life. He is a bastion that allows believers to lighten the pain.

WHAT DOES SUFFERING CONSIST OF AND HOW CAN WE PREVENT IT FROM BECOMING PERMANENT?
Suffering occurs when we hit bottom in the grieving process and when we go into deeper levels and get stuck

---

1 People United in Pain and Hope.

there. Many times, we choose suffering instead of simply experiencing the pain. The more you think about your loss, the more it hurts. How can you turn that into suffering? When your thoughts keep leading you into deeper levels of pain. One of the questions that can cause us to experience suffering is: "Why? The more you think about it, the deeper it hurts.

When we ask ourselves, "Why did you leave?" "Why did this happen?" or "Why are not you with me?" when we are in that deep place, we can run the risk of staying in that space. That is suffering. As we can see, there is an important difference between living grief and suffering.

When we lose our loved one, grief is there, and if one cannot face it directly, one cannot process it. However, one thing is to live it, and another is to enter the suffering and stay there. It is natural to enter that space; however, whether you stay there is your choice. I ask you, do you feel it will help you in your grief journey? Sometimes, people may say yes.

This reminds me of something a client told me when she went to the cemetery. She saw a father who was visiting his young son. And he thought that the only way to be close to his son was through suffering. Many grievers feel that the only way to feel close to their loved one is through suffering, which is what Rodriguez told her psychiatrist in reference to her son: "Sometimes I feel that pain is the only thing I have left of him, maybe that is why I do not want to stop feeling it" (148).

Although suffering can be our companion, it is not always the case. Talking to Marta after losing her partner, we were exploring the difference between remembering with love or suffering, to which she replied, "I only remember with love, not with suffering. There are many cases in which, as grievers, we remember in this way; however, at other times, suffering seems to be just around the corner.

Has this happened to you? This is where we want to reflect and see ways to transform our suffering into honor.

How can we do it?

FROM SUFFERING TO HONORING

> We can choose to suffer,
> or we can choose hope.
>
> ALEX, BEREAVED FATHER

Do you want to get out of that place of suffering and honor your loved one? It largely depends on us whether we keep ruminating, reliving the painful moments over and over again. If we remain stuck in the endless, unanswered questions.

that all contributes to suffering. Feeling alone and not understood also increases it; however, I think that what can help us most is to open our hearts to our own grief and navigate it with the intention of reaching the other shore. Every positive action we take to move from suffering to honoring will make a difference.

You may be wondering: how can I honor my loved one? In the next section, we will explore that possibility by talking about its meaning. Now, you can focus on something as simple as taking care of yourself, the sixth principle, which we covered in previous chapters. If you wish, review it again to see what actions you can take to take care of yourself. Getting out of suffering also includes forgiving yourself and letting go of guilt and recriminations. If you have not yet done the work of forgiveness mindfully, review the section dedicated to that topic to review the different suggestions.

Expressions that lead to suffering

Below, I share with you a series of phrases or expressions that validate our feelings. However, let us avoid making them permanent, as they make our pain more intense and turn into suffering. These phrases come from our soul, and we say them with anguish, pain, and sometimes even desperation. I have said all these phrases...

- *How can I continue functioning?*
- *Another day without you!*
- *How can I live without you?*
- *How hard it is to live without you!*
- *How hard it is to know that I will not see you anymore!*
- *I need your hug so much!*

You may have said the following:
- *I cannot accept that you left.*
- *I cannot accept that I will never see you again.*
- *Why did this happen to me?*

These are expressions we say when we are overwhelmed by great pain, and that make it even more intense. Let us not ignore them. When we say them, let us validate them and process what we are feeling. On the other hand, something that helps us to feel better is to give thanks for having had that person in our lives and to be grateful for our capacity to love. If we miss them so much and feel so much pain, it is precisely because of our possibilities to feel so much love. Grief and love are equivalent.

Give thanks for the beautiful memory you have. If you need to be in that painful moment, live it, do not repress it; however, that is where you have the ability to decide whether you choose intense grief to be eternal or eternal love to be the answer. Great devotion to your loved one can be your inspiration.

Throughout these months, on many occasions, I asked myself: "How is this possible? "How can I function in spite of this great pain?" And what was the answer I always gave myself? "Because I want to function. Because I decided to do it." Just like that talk I give at workshops titled "Happiness is a Choice," in the same way, I decided to function and welcome joy into my heart.

Because there is no doubt that we feel that great pain; however, within us lies the option to be happy again. There is the possibility to function in our life, to continue living with meaning. It is up to us if we choose to do so. Once we choose that, it is the beginning of our transformation, and it is the beginning of our healing. Something that will help you in your process is to be aware of your thoughts because they are responsible for how you feel.

I want to share with you what happened to me during one of those Sundays when I went to mass at Epiphany, the church where I used to go with my mother. I sat on a chair that had been placed on the side because, being still in COVID-19 times, the caution around physical distancing was still present.

From the chair where I was sitting, I could see perfectly, at an angle, the first bench, the one where I had sat Sunday after Sunday with my mother. It was surreal because I could imagine her in her wheelchair next to the bench. My mind went to the next thought:

"How I miss you, Mom!" I thought about it with such emphasis on the sorrow that I immediately felt my chest tighten with pain. I validated that pain, for it was real, and then I immediately changed that thought to the following: "What beautiful moments I lived with my mom in this church," and immediately, a sense of joy came over me. By changing the type of thought, I immediately changed the emotion. Both showed love for my mom. The first was sorrowful; the second was filled with gratitude for the times I had with her. This is what I mean when I say to you that we can avoid suffering and move toward honoring, toward eternal love.

In the questionnaire that my clients fill out the first day they come to see me, there is a list of reasons why they seek my help. One of them says, "I want to be happy." When the client chooses this possibility among others—even when they come because they have lost a loved one—I tell them that they have already walked 50% of the path. Remember that all of this depends greatly on us and our willingness.

Healing From the Inside Out

> It sometimes takes a concerted effort to shift your mind to allow yourself to heal.
>
> CAROLINE MYSS

After losing our loved one, healing will come at our own pace, as there is no set time. What will have a great influence in your healing is the desire you have to achieve it; you just need to decide it. Keep in mind that the relationship with your loved one will be a light that will always live in you.

Maintaining hope in our healing process is what helps us look toward the future inspired by love rather than suffering.

DIFFERENCE BETWEEN HEALING AND CURING

We hear a lot the adage: "Time heals everything." When we are sick, we take a medicine to *cure* us, or we undertake different actions that help to eradicate the illness. With the topic of grief, I believe that we take actions that *heal* our souls.

Time has an ambivalent effect. Sometimes, time "does not heal everything." On the contrary, it reaffirms that the absence is not temporary but definitive and unveils the loss and its lack of assimilation.

Healing vs. getting stuck

Remember: it is always a choice what you do about it. Either you choose to stay in a state of guilt, blaming yourself, telling yourself everything you did not do or say, staying in that space, or you choose to remember the beautiful things you got to do or say, as well as the moments of happiness. That will change the perspective of how you experience your grief. The first can leave you stuck, while the second will guide through the healing process.

Does time heal us?

> Time is certainly an important factor when it comes to healing. Although it may take away some of the pain, sorrow or other negative emotions associated with an experience, time on its own is not a healer.
>
> Morgan Mandriota

"I have heard that as time goes by, the months, the years, I will feel better, but that has not happened to me. On the contrary, now I need him more. Is there something wrong with me?" This is a question that some of my clients have asked me. When months go by, people tell you: "As time goes by, you will feel better," and yes, time, on the one hand, can lessen the pain; however, this is ambivalent because, on the other hand, it reaffirms the permanence of the absence. It is necessary to be aware that, with time, the absence also becomes more present because we realize that it is forever. A client said to me: "During the first months, it seemed to me that he was on a trip, but now it is the reality. He is no longer here."

At first, when we suffer the loss of a loved one, the pain is very strong, and we realize that we are sometimes in *shock* or numb; it is as if we have not assimilated the loss, as if we have not digested what happened.

The thing is, as Christine A. Adams tells us, we do not heal losses with the passage of time alone; much depends on what we do with that time. She reminds us that:

> It is not helpful to run away from ourselves on the hopes that when we stop the grief-related feelings will disappear. You cannot remain passive and expect things to automatically get better (2003, p. 142).

What can prevent us from healing?

- *Remain in denial*
- *Resorting to alcohol or drugs to cope with grief*
- *Dwelling in guilt*
- *Being unable to forgive*
- *Ruminate about what happened*
- *Thinking that time heals everything (without taking action)*

What if you are having a hard time healing your soul?

Nancy Stout notes that there are situations in which the person is trapped in a space because the inner healing has not happened as expected and because he/she feels that he/she cannot get out of that deep hole of pain. Do you identify with that situation?

She invites us to follow these steps[1]:

---

1 Adapted from the booklet *When Healing Is not Happening*, from CareNotes.

- *Confront our fears and identify the obstacles that prevent us from healing.*
- *Adjust our expectations and notice our attitude.*
- *Let go of anger and embrace acceptance.*
- *Spiritual healing.*
- *Be patient.*

We will elaborate on each of these by integrating them into our narrative of healing and meaning.

What can help you to heal your grief?

In the midst of pain, it is important to find tasks or activities that can help you feel better. Remember that you want to take care of yourself and do things that even bring you comfort.

You can engage in enjoyable activities, such as getting a massage, going to the movies, or eating your favorite food. Give yourself permission. I remember John, who shared with me that, upon learning that his family member had passed away, felt so beaten up that he stayed at home all day watching series on Netflix for endless hours, eating ice cream for comfort. These are ways to pamper ourselves when we are in a lot of pain.

Say statements such as:
- *Today, I decide to be at peace.*
- *Today, I let go of guilt and anger.*
- *Today, I transform my pain into honor.*
- *I can control my thoughts.*
- *I want to be happy again.*

I would like to share with you a beautiful statement by Louise L. Hay (1991).

Say it with your hand on your heart, feeling each word:
- *I love you and set you free. You are free, and I am free.*

PROCESSING YOUR GRIEF

What have you done at times when you feel a lot of pain?

_____

_____

Have you allowed yourself to feel it?

_____

_____

Have you done anything that brings you comfort and makes you feel better?

_____

_____

What has been the biggest challenge in healing your soul?

_____

_____

How can you transform your suffering into honoring your loved one?

_____

_____

Finding Meaning and Embracing Growth

> The meaning of your life is to help others
> find the meaning of theirs
>
> Viktor Frankl

When I read that sentence, my heart leaped because I identified completely. My purpose in writing this book, aside from giving you the opportunity to validate and process your grief, has been to help you find meaning in your loss. This has been a way for me to make sense of the death of my beloved mother. I wish to inspire you to find it, too, for if you open your soul to that possibility, you can make it a reality. I have always been fascinated by the word "meaning"; probably because of that, I named my company My Meaningful Life, LLC, as I believe that every life has meaning, and that is what I want every person to feel. In fact, my original slogan, which I had printed on my first business card, was: "Finding Meaning in Life's Transitions." This has been my philosophy in the face of life's hardships.

One way to find meaning is to create a legacy. You can do this in different ways, whether inspired by the loss of your loved one or by having their life be an inspiration to others and become their legacy. I find this very beautiful because, in this way, they become immortal.

Finding Meaning in Losing Our Loved One

> Grieving is the act of affirming or rebuilding a personal world of meaning that has been challenged by loss... It requires us to reconstruct a world that again "makes sense"... that restores a semblance of meaning and direction and entertaining the probability that your life is forever transformed.
>
> ROBERT NEIMEYER

> Meaning comes through finding a way to sustain your love for the person after their death while your are moving forward. with your life.
>
> DAVID KESSLER

You may think when you read that sentence about finding meaning that it is easier said than done. I share with you that Kessler lost his youngest son, David, tragically, and it was after experiencing that great loss that he wrote the book on finding meaning. These are his words, the words of a bereaved parent "In exploring the search for meaning in the devastation of loss, I have discovered that meaning is possible and necessary" (2019, p. 10).

The renowned psychologist Robert A. Neimeyer, PhD (2007) talks about the importance of rebuilding the sense of our personal world after it has been shaken by the loss we have experienced. He has specialized in conducting thorough research on the role that rebuilding meaning plays in the grieving process.

Now, it may be that not having your loved one by your side, you feel that life has no meaning. You may ask yourself, "What can I do now?" However, I ask you: what is the alternative: to live in pain and hopelessness and let life pass you by? I am not going to tell you, as many people probably tell you, that your loved one would not like to see you like this. Instead, I want to ask if you are honoring their memory by feeling that way. How can their love, which is a gift, inspire you to make sense of your existence? It is natural that when we lose our loved one, especially if they were the center of our life, we may feel that our lives has lost meaning, for the void is immense. However, we can fill that void in a way that uplifts us.

So, you may ask, how do you find meaning in the loss of a loved one? This may be a challenge for you because you may think it is as much as finding meaning in death. We speak of meaning from another point of view: that of feeling that our suffering can impel us to move forward with greater purpose, that this loss can help you live with greater meaning. It is also not about claiming that we need to face a loss in order to be better but that we can choose to be better because of the loss. Herein lies the finding of that meaning referred to by psychiatrist Viktor Frankl, author of *Man's Search for Meaning* (1984). Frankl was a prisoner in Nazi concentration camps. Because he noticed the difference between prisoners who endured the atrocities and survived versus others who perished, he conducted a study based on observation of the behavior and feelings of those prisoners. The conclusion he came to was that, in order to go on living, one must find meaning in what has happened. This was the basis for developing the theory of meaning, known as "logotherapy." Many times, it is our suffering, as Frankl said, that inspires us to find that meaning. Furthermore, Frankl shares in his book what his greatest discovery was in the midst of so much pain.

Viktor E. Frankl's Definition of Love

In the midst of that horror that serves as the framework for his book, Frankl realizes that love is what prevails and motivates us in the face of suffering and absence:

> For the first time in my life I saw the truth as it is set into song by so many poets, proclaimed as the final wisdom by so many thinkers. The truth-that love is the ultimate and the highest goal to which man can aspire. Then I grasped the meaning of the greatest secret that human poetry and human thought and belief have to impart: *The salvation of man is through love and in love.* I understood how a man who has nothing left in this world still may know bliss, be it only for a brief moment, in the contemplation of his beloved (1984, p. 57).

Additionally, his desire for connection with his source of love, his wife, is so powerful, that he describes how he imagined conversations with her to resist suffering:

> I resumed talk with my loved one: I asked her questions, and she answered; she asked me in return, and I answered…My mind still clung to the image of my wife. A thought crossed my mind: I did not even know if she were still alive. I only knew one thing - which I have learned well by now: Love goes very far beyond the physical person of the beloved. It finds its deepest meaning in his spiritual being, his inner self.

Whether or not he is actually present, whether or not he is still alive at all, ceases somehow to be of importance. I did not know whether my wife was alive... There was no need for me to know; nothing could touch the strength of my love (pp. 57-58).

Elaborating your love story

I hope with all my heart that this book has served you as a guide to process your own pain and develop the ability of empowerment and inner growth. My intention has been to share as much as possible about my experience so that, in that way, you can feel accompanied in yours. Since we have focused on the loss of a loved one, I wanted to include Viktor Frankl's example of his love story with his wife.

Each of us has a love story with the person who is no longer with us. I had mine with my mother, what is yours? How will you find meaning in that unique and special story?

PROCESSING YOUR GRIEF

In this space write your love story.

_____

_____

How have you found meaning in that love?

_____

How do you define that bond?

_____

> **How do you conceive it?**
>
> _____
>
> **Where do you see it present?**
>
> _____
>
> **How is the strength of your feeling?**
>
> _____
>
> **How does the love of your loved one live in you?**
>
> _____

When we allow love to reign in our hearts and be the light that illuminates our path, we realize our capacity. Despite the great suffering we may feel, we perform small actions that help us move through that depth and even honor our loved ones. This is something I have recommended for years to my clients: when they lose their loved one, they do something to honor them, and then they find meaning.

Maggie, having lost her daughter, who suffered from Lyme disease, by helping others with Lyme disease, honors her daughter's memory.

> I just became an ambassador for the Global Lyme Alliance. In 2022, I will start to promote them by going to different schools and informing the school nurses about the detri-

mental impact a tick bite may have on a child's life if not treated immediately.

Some have written books. Maggie also plans to write one with her daughter's writings: "I have started scanning and reviewing her writings. I hope to be able to do what she would have done: publish her book."

Others write poetry, make photo *collages*, create Facebook pages, continue their studies, and even create organizations to honor their loved ones.

An example of this is PUDE[2], the bereavement support group in my homeland, Nicaragua, which I mentioned to you earlier. Another example of a support group that is a way to honor the memory of her child is the one created by María Gough in her church. There are many ways to do it. The important thing is that you feel it in your soul because only you know your story. The possibility to transform suffering into honor resides within us. Take the memory of your loved one as an inspiration and think of something you can do in their memory. Find a new *what for*, for meaning can be found in different ways, even by adopting something of their personality that made them special and loved by others.

Carolina, who lost her husband, remembers how giving he was and how he loved to help. Inspired by that memory, she makes sure to continue to be a source of support in her family, just as he was.

---

[2] Personas unidas en el dolor y la esperanza (People United in Pain and Hope).

In this section, I wish to share with you the meaning that different grievers have found when experiencing the loss of their loved ones.

The meaning I have found in my loss has been the realization that life is precious and that you must strive to live it to the fullest every day..

ALFREDO, bereaved son

The meaning I have found in my loss has been the realization that love, kindness, and understanding must be given on a daily basis because you never know when suddenly you will not be able to do it when you want it most.

ARMANDO, bereaved son

After processing my grief, I found meaning in my life and resolved to honor my daughter's memory by helping others in their process through the organization PUDE (Personas Unidas en el Dolor y la Esperanza), of which I am a founding member, a project of love in memory of our children.

ORALÍ, bereaved mother

The meaning that I found in the loss of my boys is that every day is a gift, and tomorrow is not guaranteed. Live and love each day as if it were your last. Never go to bed having differences with others. We walk much lighter when we do not overload our spirit with the lack of harmony in this world. Don't get too attached to the things of this world. They are temporary and fleeting. Appreciate the spiritual values in people more than eloquent speech. God searches the heart. We must look beyond vanity and look into the soul to see God's creation.

Alex, bereaved father

The meaning I have found in my grief has been the lesson that we, as human beings, must live in an eternal here and now.

Esther, bereaved wife

I will never be able to find meaning in my father's death, but there is meaning in the way I have responded to his death and how it has changed me...I have a different appreciation for life because I know how temporary it really is. I am trying to focus more on the moments lived with my loved ones and living one day at a time.

Mío, bereaved daughter

The only meaning I have found is that life is gone in an instant and that I am not afraid of the transition to death, because I hope to meet my loved ones.

JWM, bereaved mother

What has helped me the most has been working with others who have gone through the same thing since I have found meaning in my life, for which I am very grateful to God. Feeling their empathy and reaching their hearts with my testimony is a very healing and rewarding experience.

I have also found meaning in the loss of my son by allowing me to develop his life legacy through a project of love and service to others, promoting and implementing the mutual support groups in my country, Nicaragua, in order to provide accompaniment to others who have suffered a loss like mine.

Mayra Elena, bereaved mother

The meaning I have found has been to accept that God has other beautiful paths for me, which I will walk alone, with faith that I will live other beautiful experiences.

Zuleika, bereaved wife

Finding meaning can also be seen as a door that we can open and that leads to another level of consciousness, spirituality, and human elevation. It is precisely this that can help us to find meaning, and once we do so, it is conducive to our personal and spiritual growth.

Now we enter the final part, in which we analyze what this growth entails. Are you willing to open that door? It may bring something wonderful, something unsuspected, something you never even imagined you could embrace. This can help you, from your pain, to find and live that light, to find meaning, and to grow on every level.

Tenth Principle: Rebuild your world

When I was delivering seminars for mental health professionals with PESI—as I mentioned at the beginning—when we reached the tenth principle, which is: *Rebuild Your World*, we delved deeply into the topic of finding meaning, and it was like building that new world, block by block, after the loss.

When I do the workshops on the 11 Principles of Transformation®, the activity of the tenth principle is precisely to build something with Lego blocks. There are many ways to find meaning after the death of our loved one, and among them is finding purpose. In the workbook I wrote, based on the seminar offered for PESI[3], I mention the following list, which I think may be useful for you to find ideas about how you can find that purpose that will be so close to your heart:

1. Seeking transcendence.
2. Leaving a legacy: how do you want to be remembered?
3. Embracing more love into your life: giving more love and opening your heart to receive more love from others.
4. Contributing to the world.
5. Practicing compassion: with others and with yourself.
6. Being an agent of service.

When we speak of service, we refer to how we can be present to others in times of need. This has been a source of meaning for Beatriz, who tells us:

The meaning I have found in my loss is at this time to help people who have just lost someone.

Mayra Elena has found purpose in helping others:

I have found a purpose in life by working in an organized way in an institution that provides bereavement support to others who have suffered a significant loss in their lives.

---

[3] 2016, p. 221.

Mio, likewise, has found purpose in helping others:

> I am very compassionate in assisting others who are living through some loss. I have found purpose in working with patients and families at end of life and guiding them through the process.

For Chip, the word "service" is part of his essence:

> I will let you in on a little fact about me. What has helped me the most to get out of myself and my own pain is Service. The ability to help others, to work with others has taken me to levels of happiness I never thought possible after my daughter's death. Do not give up your passions. Over time, use them. If you do not have any, then find some. My passions are fishing and playing music and singing. This was almost impossible to do in the beginning but over time has been a giant source of pleasure.

IN WHAT OTHER WAY DO YOU THINK YOU CAN FIND THIS MEANING?

There are different ways in which we can find it. I want to share with you these four sources that I found very special and are given to cancer patients in the Individual Meaning-Centered Psychotherapy for Patients with Advanced Cancer program (2014) to help them find meaning at the end of their lives. When analyzing each source of possible meaning, I felt we could also apply it to the experience of losing a loved one.

1. **Historical Sources of Meaning:** This refers to our lives story and finding meaning in the legacy we may leave behind. In the case of our loved ones, we can also find

meaning by focusing on what they left behind. As I told you at the beginning of this book, that is what I did in writing my mother's biography. Now, with heartfelt emotion I share with you how else I will carry on her legacy. My mother being a very positive and cheerful person, her favorite phrase was, "¡Arriba Corazones!" (Hearts Up!) She would say it when there was any pain or challenge to give encouragement and lift the spirit. In the hope that her message will be immortal, I will make T-shirts with her maxim as a trademark. I hope her message can help others lift their spirits!

2. **Attitudinal Sources of Meaning:** You may ask yourself what this means, and it has to do, essentially, with our attitude toward any challenge we may encounter in a life transition, such as losing a loved one. It is through our attitude that we can find meaning by transforming grief into an opportunity to become better people, to grow on a personal level.

3. **Creative Sources of Meaning:** Finding meaning in these sources is related to working on a cause, carrying out artistic activities or even in work. It consists of being involved with life.

4. **Experiential Sources of Meaning:** This last source has to do with relationships, with the connection to ourselves and to others. We can achieve this through art, nature, and by experiencing the world in its entirety. I would also add the possibility of finding meaning through love, which I consider to be the most powerful emotion; love for ourselves and others[4].

---

4 Braitbart and Poppito, 2014.

At the ADEC conference held in Indianapolis, I had the opportunity to listen to a presentation of great value, developed by the renowned psychologists Richard G. Tedeschi and Lawrence G. Calhoun, the creators of the Post-Traumatic Growth (PTG) theory, which we will explore later.

They called this presentation "Strange Blessings," which are those that can arise after a trauma or a very painful event, such as the loss of a loved one. Let us pay attention to these strange blessings, and we will realize that we can find meaning if we allow some of them to become a reality in our lives:

1. Changes within oneself, such as living a more meaningful life.
2. Changes in relationships, forgiving someone and letting go of resentment.
3. Changes in life philosophy, to appreciate every moment and think of life as a gift.

How resilient are we in the face of losing a loved one?

> Resilience is the process of adapting well in the face of adversity, trauma, tragedy, threats or significant sources of stress... Resilience is not a trait that people either have or do not have. It involves behaviors, thoughts and actions that can be learned and developed in anyone .
>
> Mía Roldán

According to psychologist and researcher George A. Bonanno, most of us are resilient when losing a loved one. He has conducted extensive studies and found that, basically, when losing a loved one, we experience three trajectories. One is chronic grief, which is characterized by the constant feeling of grief that can last for years. The other trajectory is recovery, in which we grieve after the loss, but little by little, the person recovers and continues with their life. The last, and according to Bonanno, the most common, is the resilience trajectory, in which, despite experiencing deep grief, we are able to continue with our lives after accommodating the loss. Still, Bonanno is careful to clarify that resilience does not imply that the loss is resolved or that the chapter is closed. He points out that even when we are resilient, we still feel sadness; however, this does not prevent us from being able to embrace life again and love the persons who are still present with us in this plane of life (p. 10).

Developing resilience

We are human beings with an incredible capacity for resilience. Let us keep in mind that the outcome of our lives will depend on our attitude, our desire to embrace life, and giving ourselves the opportunity to continue growing and learning. That is why, instead of focusing your energy on having all the answers—something that is impossible—spend time developing resilience, something that, according to Mía Roldán, can be learned through the type of thoughts we have and the actions we take. Elena is a good example of how you can apply a strategy to feel better. She told me that when she wants to cry, she does not hold back her tears; she is present in her grief. However, she does not stay in that space for a long time. She then thinks of something that helps her feel better, even something to be grateful for. This teaches us that, even though we cannot control what happened to us, we can control how we handle what happened to us. That is what we call "resilience."

As you can see, the theme of thoughts is key in our grieving and growth process. This is something that, once we learn it, we can develop, and it will make a significant difference in how we live our lives after facing a loss.

You can embrace hope and find your north

> After the initial months of early grief we become survivors. Then, as survivors, we have a choice. We can make the decision to just go through life day by day, or we can learn to renew our commitment to life.
>
> Christine A. Adams

> When we are no longer able to change a situation - we are challenged to change ourselves.
>
> Viktor Frankl

Pause in your journey and look back; observe the path you have taken in your grief. Where are you now? Did you think you would find yourself in this space? What can you accomplish today that seemed impossible six months ago? Have you thought about what could inspire you to turn it into your purpose? What will be your guiding star? In what ways do you want to change for the better?

The path of grief often leads us to establish a deep inner connection and sometimes even to detach ourselves from our surroundings, especially if we find them superficial. Although these times of solitude are necessary, it is also important to keep in mind that we can open our hearts to inner peace, to the cultivation of our resilience, to our personal development, to our inner growth. It is in these moments of solitude that we make the decision to remain submerged in pain or to process it and lift our gaze toward the light that penetrates through the window, toward hope.

POST-TRAUMATIC GROWTH

> [Post Traumatic Growth is defined as] positive psychological changes that the individual experiences as a result of the struggle with trauma or highly challenging situations.
>
> RICHARD G. TEDESCHI AND LAWRENCE G. CALHOUN

We often hear about people who face trauma and, despite all the adversities, become an inspiration to others. Sometimes, it is through a very painful loss that they manage to become better people. This often surprises us, and because of this, I want to share with you the theory I mentioned before, Post-Traumatic Growth (PTG), developed by Tedeschi and Calhoun—whom I spoke to you about earlier— which shows us how capable we can be when facing trauma or a great loss. In fact, the authors specify that the possibility of something significant resulting after enormous suffering is not a new concept. What they have done by introducing and conducting extensive research on this concept, is to give us guidelines for the positive outcomes in our lives resulting from this growth.

When I asked—in the PESI seminars based on the 11 Principles of Transformation®—what PTG (Post-Traumatic Growth) meant, since it is a fundamental element in my system, the majority of mental health professionals thought of PTSD (Post-Traumatic Stress Disorder). This was due to their training, as we are used to focusing on what is problematic. However, the notion of Post-Traumatic Growth shifts the focus more toward our capacity for growth, even after experiencing a great trauma. This does not mean that growth only occurs when we experience trauma or that we need to suffer it to elevate our humanity. What happens is that the person can develop in different aspects of their life. To determine if a person has experienced this growth, the mentioned psychologists developed an inventory to evaluate their responses in the following areas, with the expectation that they will respond positively in each one of them[5].

This instrument consists of twenty-one questions, which include topics such as how we relate to others, whether we appreciate life, if we find new possibilities, whether we possess personal strength, or if there have been changes in the spiritual dimension[6].

It is worth mentioning that this theory does not deny that one can experience distress when going through difficult situations, such as the loss of a loved one. However, evidence shows that *many people have this unique capacity to grow and learn from extreme adversity*[7]. I wanted to share this theory

---

5   Collier, 2016.
6   Tedeschi and Calhoun, 1996.
7   Tedeschi *et al*, 2018, p. VII.

with you, and I invite you to reflect and ask yourself if you belong to this type of people. You may not have realized it until you read these lines. It can give us hope to recognize that many people can grow through grief since we can take it as an inspiration.

Your own growth

> *There is life after death on both sides of the equation after a significant loss; not only can we survive, we can thrive. We need not replace our loved one who died in our family, but we can embrace their spirit by living with the loss as a part of our daily life.*
>
> Mitch Carmody

> Every great loss demands that we choose life again.
>
> Rachel Naomi Remen

The most desirable outcome of a healthy grieving process would be to find some benefit from the loss, as Gil-Juliá, Bellver and Ballester put it: "The grief experience can give this special gift of conviction-that our lives is a time to be lived fully" (p.163),

It will depends on us whether we choose to continue living meaningfully, growing in the process and becoming even better versions of ourselves. We can take our grieving experience as an opportunity to renew ourselves as people. We can create something in our lives that would not have happened if we had not experienced this loss. I specialized in grief due to the death of my father; if he had not passed away,

I would likely have studied business administration. Now I am writing this book due to the passing of my mother—my two great losses. I have no parents, and technically, I am an orphan. However, I do not consider myself one as my parents live in my heart. Their advice, their examples, and, above all, their love live within me and inspire me to continue helping others through grief. If I told you that it is easy, I would be lying to you, and I prefer to like to be authentic. It takes effort and, above all, the desire to achieve it. It is up to us to decide whether we want to stay in that place, living through intense grief and becoming paralyzed, or whether we want to transform suffering into honor and inspiration. Only we can make that decision.

When I speak of growth, I refer to changes in your life that strengthen you and help you improve. Perhaps now you find yourself being more compassionate toward others or more appreciative of people and things you previously took for granted. Maybe you have discovered aspects of yourself that you were not even aware existed. I remember when my father died and my mother had to take over the automobile business. She was surprised by the change that occurred within her. Amidst the pain, she grew personally and gave herself the opportunity to become an entrepreneur. I am sure that this example of how we can transform our loss had a great influence on me.

Remember that children are always watching, so we must pay attention to the message we are giving them about how to handle grief and misfortune. Keep in mind that, when facing a loss, you can choose how you want to grow as a result of your experience. Decide how you can become a better person today as a result of your time in the valley. We can use the internal tools we possess to deal with emotions and make a conscious decision about how we want to continue living.

What happens is that when people—with good intentions—tell us that we can grow, we do not like it; we reject it. It is something that has to come from within. How many times I have found myself saying, "Thank you, Mom," for things as simple as keeping my house tidy because she loved decorating and making sure everything looked nice. It is because of her that I continue to grow in this and other aspects. These may seem like small details; however, they make a difference. The beautiful thing is feeling in our soul that every positive change that occurs is inspired by our loved one. Let us know that within us, there is the possibility of achieving it. I leave you with these inspirational messages:

When we experience grief, we can look at what happens to us in two ways. You can focus on the obvious negative, the loss, the loneliness, and the pain, or you can focus on how lucky you were for the opportunity to share the time you had, the gratitude for that opportunity, and the wonderful memories. It is the same event seen from two perspectives. If you focus on the negative, you are giving up and even dishonoring the person you lost. If you focus on gratitude, you honor everyone, and that empowers you to learn and continue living.

ALFREDO, bereaved son

What I suggest to people who have lost a loved one is to love themselves and be patient, considerate, and compassionate with themselves, to forgive themselves for everything, and to forgive everyone for everything, not demand too much of each other, live each second at a time, breathe, and remember the beautiful things, the smiles, the love... that will never cease to exist.

María, bereaved mother

PROCESSING YOUR GRIEF

What new strengths have you developed after your loss?

_____

_____

In what ways do you feel you have grown?

_____

_____

How will you move forward in your life by honoring your loved one?

_____

_____

NOTE: ASK YOURSELF THESE QUESTIONS INTROSPECTIVELY

Have I changed my priorities?

What are the values I live by now because of this loss? Am I able to accept what is impossible for me to change?

What effect does it have on my life?

THE POWER OF ALCHEMY IN OUR GRIEF

> We crush coals with our bare hands
> and sometimes we manage to make
> them look like diamonds.
>
> ROSA MONTERO

You may wonder how alchemy relates to grief because we usually think of it as the transformation of metals into gold. However, the emotional alchemical power is within all of us, and we can apply it to transform our grief into personal growth.

Do you know the book *The Alchemist. A fable to follow your dreams*, by Pablo Coelho? There is a passage that always struck me, and I shared it at the end of the seminar on grief transformation for mental health professionals. It is a question that a child asks the old man:

> "What is the world's greatest lie?" asked the surprised boy.
> "It is this: that at a certain point in our lives, we lose control of what is happening to us, and our lives become controlled by fate. That is the world's greatest lie."

PROCESSING YOUR GRIEF

How can you regain control of your life with greater purpose?

_____

_____

> **What do you want your existence to be like from now on?**
>
> _____
> _____
>
> **Who do you want to be after your loss?**
>
> _____
> _____
>
> **Do you think you can see your growth as a door opening to a new dimension in your life?**
>
> _____
> _____

> Loss is an inevitable part of being human. And our choice is either to remain in pain and bitterness or to learn how to use this experience to grow into a richer, more fulfilling life.
>
> JOHN E. WELSHONS

When we lose a loved one, we can make the decision to expand another dimension of our lives and fill that void in a different way because the void of their physical absence exists; however, it depends on us what we will do with that void. If we see it as a door we can open that can take us to another level—we can call it a level of consciousness, of spirituality, of human elevation—there is where we will find our personal growth.

This type of growth develops when we open that door, which can bring something wonderful, something unexpected, something you never even imagined you could embrace. It can help you find and live that light from your pain; it can help you find meaning and grow as a human being.

If you choose, you can heal your heart and grow as a person through your loss, leaving behind the space where you feel heartbroken and entering one where you feel hopeful.

Stories from the Soul

The type of loss I am experiencing is that of my husband. I have expressed my grief by crying during the most painful moments; other days, I express it through exercise. The biggest challenge I have encountered with my grief has been being able to concentrate, managing the household, taking care of everything for my daughters, and the inability to physically see my husband. Expressing my grief helps me, as does sharing in bereavement groups. Some family members and friends have understood me. Others simply do not comprehend the pain one goes through. What I have missed most in my process has been information about what I might be feeling as a young woman and widow; I have had to do a lot of research on this topic. Maybe I missed finding groups of young women in this situation. What has helped me the most is prayer and being present in my grief. The most difficult aspect of my grief is the physical absence of my husband. To bereaved people, I suggest that they live as they can and that nothing is right or wrong. To seek help so they can feel empathy. The meaning

I have found in my loss is, at this moment, helping people who have recently lost someone.

Beatriz Briceños, bereaved wife

I am experiencing the loss of my husband, who passed away on July 16, 2016. He suffered a heart attack, recovered, and, on the third day, passed away suddenly from a ruptured heart. I have expressed my grief with deep pain and sadness, and the biggest challenge has been accepting that my husband will never again be physically in our family. In sharing my grief with others, I have received love and support most of the time. I have not always felt understood. In the kind of consumer society we live in, grieving is not accepted. It is not acceptable to be temporarily absent from our lifestyle. This situation is unfair to a person who is going through great pain that represents the loss of loved ones or emotional and psychological situations that may arise in the course of our lives. We are authentic, unique, and genuine beings, and we need to go through the dark night of our own soul to later, already transformed, return to a new life with new feelings from a unique experience of its kind in order to be able to follow the path of our own existence. What I have lacked the most is my lack of reality about the process of death, and what has helped me the most is the responsibility of being a mother and the need my children have for my support. The most difficult aspect of my grief has been the loneliness I feel in not being able to share our lives, neither my children or I, with my husband. I would suggest to someone who is grieving that they seek the help of a licensed grief counselor and, furthermore, that they do not put time into their grieving process. The meaning I have found in my grief has been the lesson that we, as human beings, must live in an eternal here and now, and we must do what corresponds to us in the now.

Esther P., bereaved wife

I feel that losing my mother is not the cause of my pain. She was ninety-five years old and, due to a fall, required a very intense surgical procedure. After surgery, she required medical care for the next eight months until her death. In her last month, she was still alert and oriented, but she was becoming very depressed due to seeing herself as helpless and feeling like a burden to me, her only son.

Since death is a natural part of life for all of us, logically, given her unfortunate condition, I feel that she is in a better place in heaven and, if there is no such thing, then she is now free of her suffering.

In my case, since my mother rarely asked for anything, I should have been more attentive and provided her with the necessities, assistance, and companionship that I now realize she needed since she lived alone until late in life.

My pain does not stem from her death but from not having done enough for her or from making the wrong decisions during her last days. At that moment, I believed she would get better as she used to do in other medical situations.

I am not aware that I express my pain, except when it comes to mind while I am with others and tears come to my eyes. I go through periods when I find it hard to sleep, thinking about what I could and should have done differently. I cry in solitude.

The biggest challenge in my grief has been accepting that there is no way I can correct what I did wrong or failed to do. It hurts me to not be able to express my love or my affection or not being able to let her know how much I value all the sacrifices she went through in her life to help her family. It also hurts me not to have the opportunity to be kind and gentle or to ask her forgiveness for wrongdoings.

Friends empathize with me and try to make me feel better by reminding me how often I visited her, how much I helped her, and how many times she told me I was an excellent son. My daughter tells me that I did a lot for her, much more than she needed. My spouse agrees with me that I should have been better, kinder, and more generous with her. I have been understood in my grief.

Going to her grave when I feel very sad and talking to her out loud as if she is listening to me sometimes relieves me, but sometimes not so much.

The hardest part of my grief has been realizing that it is now too late to do everything she deserved and that I should have done for her.

To a person who is grieving, I would say to realize that, in general, we all tend to think that we could have done better. Although I secretly still think to myself that, in my case, I should have been a better son.

The meaning I have found in my loss has been the realization that love, kindness, and understanding must be given on a daily basis because you never know when suddenly you will not be able to do it when you want it most.

ARMANDO V., bereaved son

I've experienced many losses in my life. My father, at 13 years of age, started a chain of events that led to years of active addiction. In 1999, my mother passed away, and six months later, my oldest brother did as well. As hard as those losses were to grieve, nothing could prepare me for the tragic loss of my Son, Andrew, in 2009 and his older brother, Alex, in 2015. The dark despair that followed the death of my 15-year-old son, Andrew, led to months of depression that I battled through by exercising, sharing my feelings often with close friends and support groups, shedding many tears frequently, and journaling daily.

The greatest challenge has been staying vigilant with my recovery routine. Being disciplined and putting in the footwork pays off when the darkest moments are upon us. The long period of time that the grief process takes can be daunting and feel never-ending. In those darkest hours, I found it helpful to fall on my knees and allow those feelings to flow naturally through me. I found it to be relieving, and in the quiet moments that followed those hard tears, the peace that overcame me was nothing short of God's unceasing grace. In these peaceful moments, I felt as though I could feel my son's presence closer than ever.

When sharing my grief with others, it can be uncomfortable because most people don't know how to act or what to say, and still, others would rather just have a shallow conversation about nothing at all. The subject of grief is a hard one for most people, and those who are uncomfortable with the subject tend to shy away from me. While others are truly interested in what I have to say and want to connect with me at the spiritual level. They are emotionally strong and spiritually enlightened enough to know that the subject of grief is not about death but about finding the hope that exists beyond the flesh. A hope so profound you can almost touch it once you are able to see beyond the grave. Hebrews 11:1 says, "Now faith is the substance of things hoped for, the evidence of things not seen."

The grace beyond the grief is seeing for the first time things we thought were invisible. Things beyond this world that are opened to us when our suffering is deep and our tears are sincere. God's grace is released, and we are privileged to see things that are not meant for this world. God cries with us because he is a God of compassion, but our suffering gives us the opportunity to have a deep and unique relationship with God. Your darkest moments can become the deepest moments of enlightenment you will ever experience. In our brokenness, He gets to put us back together in life-changing ways.

Grief is a feeling that must be felt for us to know how much we loved the ones we lost, but it is not a cross that we must bear as a cost of love. Rather, it is a divine nature that fills us with peace after the tears have poured forth and the spirit of the lost comes near to us.

Regarding others, I have felt understood in my grief. I have rarely felt rejected or judged.

What I miss the most is the connection that I had with each moment in the early days of my son's passing. My connection with God was extraordinary. I have never felt his presence again like I felt in the first year following Andrew's passing and the months that followed Alex's passing. I feel that what has unquestionably helped me the most has been my relationship with God. He affirmed and reconfirmed his love for me more than at any other time in my life following the death of both my sons.

The hardest aspect of my grief has been when I see my son's death through human eyes that have no hope, and, in those times, I can only see the grave. I see nothing beyond it. But in the moments that follow, I can hear my God say to me time and again, "Why do you seek the living among the dead." That is when my spirit takes hold, and the peace that surpasses all understanding reminds me of the hope that is to come and the gift that awaits those who believe. I was asked how I was feeling so many times following my son's passing that it became an annoyance to me, but I knew that people were only asking out of concern. That is when I came up with the response that made all the sense in the world. When people asked me how I was doing, I would say, "I'm having good days and bad moments." I realized that saying that I am having good days and bad days would be unfair to myself because every day brings something good with it. So, saying, "I'm having good days and bad moments," brings the truth of every day to light.

If you are grieving, don't deny your feelings. Cry as often as you'd like. Stay close to the people who love you and will let you express yourself as much as you need to. Know that God is there for you now more than ever. Know that he is not only there but carrying you through the hardest moments. Journal daily. These difficult times will bring about a connection with your feelings like you've never had before. The pen is a healing instrument. It will sow together your heart if you take the time and do it daily. You will write in ways you never thought you could write. Your spirit will express itself in ways you could never understand.

The meaning that I found in the loss of my boys is that every day is a gift, and tomorrow is not guaranteed. Live and love each day as if it were your last. Never go to bed having differences with others. We walk much lighter when we do not overload our spirit with the lack of harmony in this world. Don't get too attached to the things of this world. They are temporary and fleeting. Appreciate the spiritual values in people more than eloquent speech. God searches the heart. We must look beyond vanity and look into the soul to see God's creation.

What meaning did I find in my son's death? What am I supposed to get from losing the very people that we would die to protect, the very people that make up your life? When the unthinkable happens, what is left to do? We can crawl up into a ball of depression, resentment, anger, and despise everything about life, or we can choose, and our choice it is to make, to look beyond the obvious flesh in the ground and see a world where there is no more pain, no more tears and no more suffering. We can choose to believe beyond what our mind is meant to believe and live a life lifted in expectation of a life to come that will have no end. We can choose to suffer, or we can choose hope. It is our choice to choose.

ALEX FUNDORA, bereaved father

I experienced two deaths; the first was my husband's, on June 15th, 2019. The second was my mother's, on December

14th, 2019. I have expressed my grief mainly through crying, especially in the case of my husband. I also set up a shrine for him on my night table in our bedroom. The shrine consists of a beautiful 8" x 10" photo of him in a beautiful, silver-plated frame, a small Yahrzeit candle (this is a special Jewish mourning candle) in a small black candle holder with Jewish writing on it, the right of the photo. This honors my husband's Jewish heritage, although he was not religious in his everyday life.

There's also an angel statuette to the right of the candle and a glass of water, with a small plate underneath, to the left of the photo. I included this because I read on the Internet that water conducts spiritual energy. My regular bedside lamp is in the upper right corner of the nightstand.

Additionally, the front of the display features a copy of the complete Jewish Messianic **Bible**—both the Old and New Testaments.

Another way I've expressed my grief for my husband is by wearing only black clothes for an entire year.

As for my mom, I feel guilty about the fact that most of my crying has been for my husband. That's because I was much closer to him than my mother. He was actually the center of my world. Furthermore, my mom and I had a difficult relationship at times. However, I was wearing black for her, as well, until the pandemic started. I stopped **going** anywhere except downstairs to get the mail and to the second-floor garbage chute to throw the garbage out.

However, I always wear black pants anyway, indoors and out, which I combine with several T-shirts I own. Most of these tend to be black, but others aren't.

There is another way in which I am honoring my mother, and that is through praying the Rosary, something I'm trying to do every day. I'm doing this not only to honor her, since she prayed it every day for a very long time, but also because I feel closer to her every time I pray it.

I would love to have a shrine for my parents, too, but I don't have any really nice pictures of them to blow up to 8" x 10". Most of the nice photos of them are at their house, where my two sisters still live. Due to the pandemic, I'm not going anywhere by car or Uber, and I certainly wouldn't ask my sisters to send me any photos by mail, as these could easily get lost. The only solution would be to send them by certified mail, but my sisters would have to go to a post office to pay for that. They're not **going** anywhere, either. Also, I would have to go to Walgreens to get them enlarged.

In addition to all of the above, I have been reading books about grief, near-death experiences, the afterlife, mediumship, and afterlife contact, all by different authors. I have consulted several mediums and attempted to contact Daniel on my own. These activities are, I know, forbidden in the Bible. However, my desperation to connect with my husband was, and still is, so great that I have felt the overwhelming need to engage in these activities. I have even written him text messages, to which he has "replied." How? I would send him a text, wait a few seconds, and words would just pop into my head. Then, I would type them out. I usually sent the initial text from my own phone and then **replied to** it on his phone, which I have not disconnected. In fact, this is the precise reason I have not done so. Needless to say, I have not shared my involvement in these activities with my Christian grief **support group.** I've simply **done** them on my **own.**

The greatest challenge with my grief has been my relationship with God. At the beginning, right after my husband passed, I was very angry with Him. I was close to becoming an atheist; my faith became a struggle. I would hate God one minute, asking Him repeatedly WHY He had taken my husband so soon, and WHY, if He was truly a loving God, He had not healed Daniel, despite all my prayers, as well as the prayers of my family and Daniel's family. The next minute, I would be asking God to help me to get through this **HORRIBLE** pain, to take it away from me.

This ambivalence toward God began, if I remember correctly, about 5 to 6 months after Daniel's passing. Before that, I really **HATED** Him.

At this point, I feel that I would like to get closer to Him, but there's still some resentment toward Him inside of me. I can't really say that I HATE Him now; however, what I'm feeling is disappointment with Him. I also feel betrayed by Him because a human father who truly loved and cared about his child wouldn't allow that child to suffer or go through a **HORRIBLE** emotional experience, at least not if it was within his power to prevent it. If God is our heavenly Father, and if He loves and cares about us, He **DEFINITELY** has the power to prevent bad or sad things from happening to us. If a human father doesn't want his children to suffer, how much more should God, our Father in heaven, not want such things to happen to us? But it seems to me that, in this type of scenario, the human father is MUCH superior to the Divine Father!

Interestingly, whenever I've stated that I hated God, it was the God of the Old Testament, Jehovah, that I had in mind. I forget that Jesus is part of God. But I just can't even think of hating Jesus. It's Jehovah whom I have felt hatred for - the wrathful Father God.

Regarding how I felt when sharing my grief with others, during my first therapy session with Ligia Houben, my grief therapist, it was hard to share my feelings with her without bursting into tears, so, as far as I can recall, I spent most of that session crying. But Ligia, who had been recommended to me by one of my sisters after seeing her Facebook page, was very compassionate, empathetic, and understanding.

She also spoke to me in a very gentle, soothing tone. Even when I told her how I felt about God, she never judged me, in spite of her own firm religious beliefs. Furthermore, she told me her own story of loss and grief. She explained how she herself reacted upon being told, at the young age of twelve, that her father had suddenly passed•••She, too, described her own anger at God.

I've been having therapy with Ligia for more than a year now, and she has helped me TREMENDOUSLY. I can always count on her to listen, to empathize, to feel compassion for me. I have always felt understood by her. She has helped and is helping me to grow as a person. Even before my relationship with God improves, I know I can thank Him for bringing her into my life.

When I started participating in GriefShare, a Christian-based grief support group, Hilda, the kind, caring group leader, perfectly understood how I felt. I was reluctant to share my experience of grief during my first group session, but then, in the second or third one (I don't remember which one), I did say a few things about what happened to Daniel. One of the first things I said was that I HATED God. Hilda replied that I was very brave to say that in a Christian church. But then she smiled. She was trying to make a little joke because the name of the church where these meetings were being held (this was before the pandemic) happens to be "Brave Church." I didn't know that at the time, though, so I immediately thought she was scolding me and started feeling bad. But then she smiled and went on to say that she totally understood my anger at God. She felt the very same way after her father's passing, and it took her FIVE years to get over her own anger. She added that she felt this anger in spite of the fact that she was a committed Christian when her father passed away. She was even a church volunteer. Ironically, as well as coincidentally, her dad had the same disease Daniel had - stage 4 pancreatic cancer. So Hilda was totally supportive of my feelings, which was very comforting to me at the time, and still is. She has never judged me, and has even encouraged me to go through the GriefShare program as many times as I want. In fact, all of the members are encouraged to repeat the program at least once and are welcome to continue repeating it as many times as they want, as well.

I also have to thank God for Hilda and GriefShare.

Whenever I have shared my feelings with Jaime, one of my brothers-in-law, he has agreed with me that Daniel's situation did not make any sense. He's basically an agnostic shading into an atheist, so he has told me, during our conversations throughout all this time, that the only logical conclusion I can come to is that either there's no God, or there is, but we don't know anything about Him. At the same time, though, he keeps encouraging me to continue attending GriefShare, which he knows is Christian-based.

This might sound like paradoxical advice, but he's also aware that I **WANT** to believe in God, that somehow, I'm not able to completely let go of belief in His existence. Jaime also encourages me to continue attending the group because, whenever I've read some questions out of the GriefShare **workbook to** him, he has commented that the program also incorporates psychological principles, which he thinks is great. I guess he also thinks that the inclusion of such principles somehow "makes up for" the fact that the group is based on Christian beliefs.

I had a **TERRIBLE** experience with a former student of mine, whom I had befriended after she had left my ESOL tutoring group due to her work schedule. We became friends on WhatsApp and would send each other frequent messages and cute memes. Well, one day, shortly after Daniel's · passing (perhaps less than a month or so), I was feeling very, very depressed. I was crying a lot. So, since we were friends, I called her, seeking some comfort.

At first, her tone of voice did sound comforting. Then, all of a sudden, she started trying to convince me to donate all of Daniel's clothes. "Think of all those poor, elderly men in Venezuela", she said. (Although she's Colombian, she feels very bad about the situation in Venezuela.) She kept on insisting, too, even when I told her, through my tears, that I just could not do that.

I also told her that I was very angry at God. When she heard that, she said I should not be feeling that way toward God, adding that we human beings have to accept the **good** and the bad from Him, as well as to thank Him for everything that happens to us in life. Then, to emphasize this point, she told me that I had to THANK God for Daniel's passing!!! She even said the words, "Thank you, Lord, for my husband's death." I was SO shocked when she said all this to me that I even stopped crying and began feeling angry. **But** I really couldn't express my anger directly to her. She was my **FRIEND.** Or so I thought...So, I started shaking my head, mumbling, "**No,** no, no, no ...." I finally told her I couldn't thank God for my husband's death. Unbelievably, she then insulted me to injury by telling me that, since I could not do it, SHE would do it for me!! I was speechless for a few seconds, and then I simply hung up. Of course, this phone conversation made me feel even **WORSE.** I burst into tears as I walked into the bedroom, throwing myself on the bed. And I cried and cried and cried...

For me, that was the end of our friendship. I have not called or contacted her since that day, nor do I intend to do so in the future. I've even wondered whether she actually acted that way on purpose so I wouldn't call her again in tears. So what the HECK are friends for, then? Aren't they supposed to be supportive? I considered her a good friend, too, and felt very comfortable talking to her...until that **TERRIBLE** day. She caught me totally by surprise, too.

I don't think I will EVER forgive this woman. EVER. And if I do, I will still not attempt to renew the friendship. The worst part of the whole thing is that she herself is married. I wonder how SHE would feel if, after losing her own husband, she called a "friend", and got the same treatment SHE gave **ME**.

Oh, my gosh, as I'm writing all this down, the anger is surging inside of me...and I'm getting a headache right now...I have to take some Advil. I'm feeling as if the anger I still feel at this woman is going to consume me...I feel betrayed and disappointed at her behavior. She had always been very nice and sweet toward me when she was my student, and afterward, too. I had even begun to call her "Laurita".

At this point in time, I can see things more objectively. That's due to proper medication, ongoing, excellent therapy, and regular involvement in the grief support group. Of course, I have put in some work, as well, not only by following my doctors' instructions but also by attending as many of my grief counseling and grief support group sessions as I could and doing all assigned written work at home. All of these things have thus made me stronger, and so, my pain has greatly lessened, although I sometimes still do have crying spells.

This all means that I can now see that I was totally unprepared for some people's reactions to the news of my husband's passing and my subsequent bereavement. Well, of course, no one is ever prepared for such things. What I'm trying to say is that I never thought that "Laurita", would react the way she did when I called her in tears that day.

Now I'm recalling that another "friend", whose name is Isis, and who lives in my apartment complex, also reacted unexpectedly. She just **DISAPPEARED.** That was back in the middle of May 2019. I guess she saw that things were going from bad to worse, so she decided she just wasn't going to deal with the situation. I saw her one day at the building's mailboxes and told her that Daniel had passed. "Yeah, you told me," she replied. I honestly didn't remember doing so. I then asked her why she hadn't called me in so long, and she gave the typical excuse: she had been "very busy with work". She then promised to call me that very night.

Needless to say, she didn't. A few days later, I saw her go into the elevator, just after I had picked up my mail. She **CHEERFULLY** asked, **"Going up?" And** I very emphatically replied, in an angry tone, **"NOPE!"** Since that day, we have avoided each other. If she sees me coming her way, she'd turn around and go another way, and I do the same. Another so-called "friendship" ended...

To go back to the question, have I felt understood? Obviously, not by these two "friends". And I'm still feeling very bitter and disappointed about these two incidents......

I have felt understood by Ligia and Hilda, though. They are two of the kindest, sweetest people I have ever met! They have listened without judgment. They have hugged me. They have given me comfort, and again, I must thank God for them!

Some of the other group members have also been very understanding, but I would have to say that Hilda has been the kindest to me. She even invited me over to her house for Thanksgiving dinner last November!

As for Jaime, my brother-in-law, it's been a mixed bag. It's true that he has given me some emotional support by being there for me when I was having a crying episode. Also, he has helped me **TREMENDOUSLY** with practical things that had to be done, especially in the early days of my grief, when I could barely do anything except cry and sleep. He took care of everything. However, on certain occasions, we've gotten into heated arguments, on and off the phone. Still, I do appreciate the help he's given me thus far, and besides, I have firmly made him aware of the fact that I do not enjoy being yelled at or lectured as if he were my father. So, I have set some boundaries with him, and our relationship has improved because of it.

What I have missed the most in my process is Daniel, my husband. I have missed him so desperately, so despairingly... God has taken from me the other half of my soul, and I have not quite forgiven Him for that...

I have also missed having strong family and friend support, especially in the case of Daniel. My sisters and I are not very close, and they did not give me much emotional support in the weeks and months following Daniel's passing.

What has helped me the most is everything I've chosen to engage in - the therapy, the support group, the medications, the books I have read on my own, and the afterlife-related activities I have participated in. Praying the Rosary has also helped. Every time I prayed it, I felt a deep peace. Something is pulling me toward the Rosary. I recently began to feel inexplicably drawn to it, and I am very aware that I need to pray for it every day. When I don't, I feel something very important has been missing from my day.

The hardest aspect of my grief has been missing Daniel... In the early days, I would feel as if he had gone out somewhere on an errand and would soon be coming back. Sometimes, I've had the feeling that, as I was reading or watching TV in the living room, he was lying in bed watching YouTube videos.

One afternoon, I started daydreaming and just let my imagination **go**...Suddenly, I heard someone knocking on my door. When I opened it, there stood Daniel in his usual clothes - a dark shirt, khaki-colored shorts, socks, and sneakers. And then he said to me, "C'mon, Maria, what are you doing in there all by yourself? Let's go have some fun!" If only it had been true...

As for my Mom, sometimes I do get flashes of her lying in a casket when my sisters and I attend her wake...At other times, I see her as she looked when she was a newlywed. These images come from photos at my parents' house. Emotionally, however, the impact of Daniel's passing has been the worst. When you live with someone and share the same routines with them, and then they're suddenly gone, it leaves a HUGE void in your life...

What I would suggest to someone who is grieving, is to deal with their grief in whatever ways are comfortable and meaningful for them. Everyone is different, so each individual grieves differently. I would never try to impose on any bereaved person the things that have helped me during my own bereavement. For example, not everyone loves to read as much as I do. Therefore, Reading about grief and the afterlife might not be helpful to others who never pick up a book.

I would also never impose my own religious beliefs on another grieving person. This is a very personal, private thing. Nor would I ever tell anyone else to forget about praying to God, either, simply because I'm going through my own crisis of faith.

The most important advice I would give another grieving person, and this is universally applicable, is to tell them that there are no timelines when it comes to grief. This is a process, and no one has the right to tell anyone else to "hurry up and get over it." That's extremely insensitive.

During the grieving process, people need the most to go through it at their own pace, in their own way, and to be supported and understood. If some people fail to do these things, then the bereaved person needs to distance themselves from such people and find others who do understand and who will comfort instead of criticize.

MARÍA DE LOS ÁNGELES B., bereaved wife

My greatest loss has been the suicide of my only son, age twenty-two, in 2016.

Throughout these almost six years, I have expressed my grief in multiple ways: I have cried, I have screamed, I have laughed, I have isolated myself, I have expressed myself in the way my being has needed, and along the way, I have learned not to judge myself for it; I have learned that no form of expression is "good or bad," it is simply what is necessary at that moment and all must be given a place, they must be given their space; of course, without attacking others. It has been a roller coaster of emotions, but there is something I cannot deny: my being-soul-spirit-heart has grown.

There are many challenges that I have faced and continue to face after my son's suicide. The biggest of all has been the feeling that, in multiple ways, I paved the way for my beloved son to make that decision: that I did not spend enough time with him, that I did not dedicate enough time to him, that I did not understand him enough, that I did not support him enough, that I should have foreseen that he was going to die by suicide, that he was having a hard time... that I should have known... even though we did not live in the same country... and a long list of "that I did not...," "if I had..." and "I should have..."

Parents are supposed to take care of their children so that nothing bad happens to them and so that they do not suffer and a long list of precepts that are simply impossible to fulfill because they are independent beings from us who have their own mission and, like us, have free will. It is also assumed that parents die before their children, but I understood that this assumption is also incorrect: we die when it is our turn, when our soul decides it is so, and suicide is no exception.

Another great challenge has been my own sense of abandonment, of being "orphaned of a child," of feeling that I am alone in the world, no matter how much love surrounds me. Whenever something happens that hurts me, wounds me, or brings my mood down, even if it has nothing to do with my son, I feel alone and abandoned, and the feeling is very strong. I feel lost... empty... I recognize that, over time, this feeling has been diminishing and has been transformed into acceptance, understanding, and love for myself.

At first, I shared my grief openly, feeling that doing so was part of my process. But after receiving two very unpleasant, out-of-place, and unsolicited comments, I decided to be more reserved about it. Now, when I am asked if I have children, I say yes—because in reality, I do have a son... who lives with God, in my heart—and only with some people, and in some situations, I talk openly about his death. I understood that not talking about it openly is not hiding it or denying it; it is just sharing it with those who deserve it.

I would say that the first year and a half was the most difficult: understanding, accepting, forgiving others, forgiving myself, getting out of bed, doing daily activities, continuing to work, continuing to be a wife, daughter, sister, friend... continuing to breathe, eating... But from the first moment, I understood that I had only two options: to deprive myself and lie in bed to die while still alive—and make life miserable for those who love me—or to continue living, forgiving, learning, and growing as a human being. I was constantly feeling a pain in my chest that would not allow me to breathe. I felt an emptiness, as if my heart had been ripped out. But I understood that there is no one outside of me who can heal my pain. Only myself, hand in hand with God, can heal my wounds and my pain and transform everything into love, into light, into understanding, into gratitude, into forgiveness. I also understood deep in my heart that forgiving is only a conscious act that frees us all and that only with the firm intention to forgive—even without feeling it in our heart—little by little, that intention becomes a beautiful truth that fills us with love and light.

At the end of the first year, I tried going to a support group for people who had a family member or friend who had died by suicide. It was a shock to me to realize that people who were more than four years into their loss were still in the same place they were at the beginning. Ultimately,

I did not want to be there. I felt that they were making me feel worse, that they were sinking me in their own pain, and that they were not letting me move forward in my process. After four sessions, I decided to leave the group. However, in the last session in which I participated, the testimony of a father who felt bad because he no longer cried for his son—who had died five years ago—and the fear of forgetting him stayed with me... to which the facilitator told him that this was normal, not to worry, that this was part of a healthy process. That testimony was engraved in my heart and has helped me a lot, especially during the last two years.

Right now, I am definitely not the same as I was at the beginning, but I miss my son. Sometimes, I feel sad, with a sadness that I know is there, that has never left me, that is subliminal, which is now part of my being... and which I did not have before.

There has been a lot of inner work that I have had to do and that I continue to do. I know that my son's absence is something that is part of my life that will never change, no matter how much I cry or feel bad. It is something I have learned to live with.

Have I felt understood? Yes and no—no, especially at the beginning. Most of the time, I have felt very understood and supported, especially by my family and friends. Before, when I felt bad, I expected them to sense it without me saying anything, but obviously, that did not happen, so after a while, I understood, and now, when I feel bad, I tell them that I am in one of those "difficult moments" when I cannot even stand myself, and I ask them to please be patient with me. This has helped me to be patient with myself as well.

Thank God, those moments have become less frequent over time, and now they only happen to me at specific times: his birthday, Mother's Day, Christmas, and other sporadic moments.

At other times, I feel bad because people feel bad for not being able to understand or know how I feel or feel the same as I do because they do not know how to treat me—this happened a lot in the beginning—but little by little, we have all learned not to feel bad and to say and ask from a place of love.

Although it may seem paradoxical, what I have missed the most in my process is my son... hugging him, looking him in the eyes, talking to him, telling him how I feel, listening to what he thinks... However, from the beginning, he has been a very important part of my process, and it has helped me a lot to understand and heal his loss. I have also been greatly helped by the love of my loved ones and the acceptance of God's love. Reading, writing, meditating, praying, and giving myself time and space. Knowing that I have the freedom to express myself, to feel sad, to feel happy, to feel whatever my heart desires to feel.

The most difficult aspect of my grief has been to accept that my son is no longer physically present to understand that it is normal for me to feel alone in the world—even though I am surrounded by people who love me. It has been difficult to understand and accept that it is not temporary, that it will never pass, that just as my son lives within me, so too does the loneliness as a mother, the impossibility of giving and receiving a hug, a kiss, seeing his eyes and his beautiful smile, listening to his stories and his crazy ideas.

I also understood that I was crying for myself, for my new situation, for that feeling of orphanhood I mentioned before.

What I suggest to people who have lost a loved one is to love themselves and be patient, considerate, and compassionate with themselves, to forgive themselves for everything, and to forgive everyone for everything, not demand too much of each other, live each second at a time, breathe, and remember the beautiful things, the smiles, the love... that will never cease to exist. That each death is unique, each reason is unique, each person is unique, and each day of grieving is different. That their story is written moment by moment. That grief is full of cycles that differ in length and intensity. That it is okay to laugh and cry, to dance and be happy, to fall down and get up. That the concept of happiness changes, that it can be a melancholic happiness. That everything we feel is appropriate, even to shout, to get angry, to laugh, and to enjoy life. That we are free to feel what we feel when we feel it. That there are no guidelines, rules, good or bad things, adequate or inadequate, opportune or inopportune. And the most important thing is not to take the suicide of a loved one as something personal... Although it is difficult to understand, suicide has nothing to do with anyone but the person who did it; it is no one's responsibility, it is no one's fault, it is not related to the actions of others; it is a personal decision of the person who does it, it is part of the path he/she must follow... Yes, I know it is not easy to understand or accept, but it is the pure truth.

The meaning I found in my loss is that I found God. I found Him sincerely. And that saddens me sometimes very much because it is another "if I had" that I add to my long list: "If I had truly had God with me, within me, and if I had taught my son about Him... maybe none of this would have happened..."

I would say that ACCEPTANCE is the key to healthy grieving: acceptance of what happened and acceptance of what is felt. Acceptance and forgiveness... especially forgiveness, especially of oneself. Knowing that I AM LOVE, I AM LIGHT, I AM FORGIVENESS, I AM GRATITUDE, I AM COMPASSION, I AM UNDERSTANDING.

From the depths of my heart, I wish that some of these words may light a spark in the soul of whoever reads them and help them to heal in their own process or help them understand those who are going through it.

MARÍA, bereaved mother

My grief experience

Throughout my life, there have been many losses of loved ones that I have experienced, but there is one in particular that led me into the grieving process and to be able to understand for myself and then share with others how to live and transform a loss.

Today, the world, and particularly Nicaragua, is immersed in deep suffering due to the pandemic, and the pain that grips so many hearts is heartbreaking as they lose not one loved one but several family members and friends day by day. This leads me to share with you, readers, my experience and the steps I followed in the grief of my daughter Albalicia Duarte Flores, whose death took place twelve years and eleven months ago, on June 21, 2007, in a sudden car accident, without a farewell.

With the utmost reverence and empathy, aware that grief is unique and that, therefore, everyone can process it differently, I share with you the steps I followed in that moment of deep anguish and pain.

Faith as support in the face of pain: I recognized that the experience of that moment was too much for me and that I would not be able to get through such a tragic situation on my own, a situation that affected my husband, my daughter, my family, and me. I realized I needed someone to help me understand what was happening and live through it. Drawing on the faith I have embraced since childhood, cultivated in my family, I decided to seek support from a spiritual guide, particularly a priest, who guided me for a year on the path to healing my wound.

Sharing: Knowing that I was not alone in those moments and that many people were also living my reality made me look for other mothers who, like me, had lost loved ones. And through angels, Our Lord made us get together four mothers, willing to open our hearts, to give voice to our pain, but above all to open ourselves to hope to find a purpose that would give meaning to our lives.

Psychological support: I also sought psychological help, and, as I had to continue with my work responsibilities, I found a good and faithful friend and also a co-worker who was ready to listen to me at that moment. That is all I needed: someone who would listen to me without judging, without giving prescriptions, just listening. At that moment, that was what I needed the most, and that is what she became: a Cyrenian for my cross, which was too heavy.

Living the grief, not suffering it: In this journey of grief, with the group of mothers, we found another angel in our lives, our good friend Ligia Houben, psychologist, thanatologist, grief counselor, and creator of the 11 Principles to Transform your Loss. With Ligia, I understood and lived grief and its rituals, the stages, and the process of grief, all guided by the 11 Principles and at my own pace because everyone has their own hourglass and their own time. It is a moment to open up to emotions and embrace them. It was the time to live my grief, to recognize and identify the resources that were in me to live one day at a time, to fall, and to know that I could get back up again. From my faith, I know that the Lord's promises are faithful and that we walk hand in hand with Him in the darkest moments of our lives, and under that promise, I know that He is the Light, the Truth, and the Life; He is a bastion that allows believers to lighten the pain.

No goodbyes: When there is no goodbye, as was the case with me because of the tragic nature of the accident and her almost instantaneous death, I had to resort to the advice of experts, and with the spiritual help of my guide, I accepted and learned to say goodbye to Albalicia through different means. One of them was a letter full of love, forgiveness, and everything I could have said to her in life; it was a letter just for me, allowing me to express everything my aching heart wanted. That helped me tremendously. I also learned to find her in nature, at the beach, in a beautiful sunset, or the greenery of the mountains; there, I often unloaded my emotions and imagined myself talking to her. Now, from the bottom of my heart, I know that the priest's words made sense: Albalicia's grave was always empty because Albalicia had lived the Easter of the Resurrection, and once again, the Lord's promises of dwelling in eternal life in the Heavenly Jerusalem validate our faith and the hope of Christians.

To continue living: After processing my grief, I found meaning in my life and resolved to honor my daughter's memory by helping others in their process through the organization PUDE (*Personas Unidas en el Dolor y la Esperanza*), of which I am a founding member, a project of love in memory of our children.

The process is long, and we must be patient with ourselves and those around us. They also have to be patient with us, and we must understand when the family is affected. Everyone processes it differently; therefore, respect and understanding are fundamental during the process.

It has been a long time; however, time is relative. For my part, I have realized that my daughter lives through love, which is eternal.

ORALÍ FLORES ALTAMIRANO, bereaved mother,
founding member of PUDE

I lost my seventy-nine-year-old father. I have not done much about my grief. It is an internal process. I have mentioned to a few people close to me that I miss my father. For the most part, people do not care about your grief, so it is something you have to overcome alone. My father's illness lasted seven years, and the last two were quite intense, with treatments, surgeries, recoveries, therapies, etc. I was focused on providing him with comfort and solutions while also understanding that the end was inevitable and near. It may be that, due to the length of the illness, it gave me a chance to process the inevitable with time. Finally, the time came when all I wanted was for my father to stop suffering. Although I wish he had lived a longer and healthier life, I feel that I did everything I could without any regret. Perhaps that has helped me not need to express my pain.

My biggest challenge has been trying to understand why he died and how he died. Because I tend to be pragmatic, I find it difficult to express a particular feeling when sharing my grief. However, I have felt understood. What has helped me the most has been to know, to believe that I was a good son and that I did everything I could to help. It also helps me to know that I was a source of tranquility for him.

The most difficult part of my grief has been trying to understand why. My father was a special person. He was one of the purest human beings I have ever known. He was an intellectual, professional, intuitive, and humane doctor, almost revered by his patients. He was a believer and studious follower of his Christian faith. He was an exceptional husband and father. He was a complete man whose life's work was to help others. Why he died and why he had to suffer is hard for me to understand.

When we experience grief, we can look at what happens to us in two ways. You can focus on the obvious negative, the loss, the loneliness, and the pain, or you can focus on how lucky you were for the opportunity to share the time you had, the gratitude for that opportunity, and the wonderful memories. It is the same event seen from two perspectives.

If you focus on the negative, you are giving up and even dishonoring the person you lost. If you focus on gratitude, you honor everyone, and that empowers you to learn and continue living.

The meaning I have found in my loss has been the realization that life is precious and that you must strive to live it to the fullest every day. You never know when you will have a diagnosis, an accident, or simply what your last day will be.

ALFREDO D., bereaved son

I experienced my husband's death. The way I have expressed my grief has been by writing, crying, and even blaming him. Not for his departure, for leaving me alone.

The biggest challenge I have found with my grief has been learning to do the things he did; it has also been learning to deal with silence and loneliness. What helps you most in grief is sharing with others, talking, crying, talking, and continuing to cry. Just to be heard, even if the story is repetitive.

I have felt understood and, at the same time, not understood. I did not feel understood by my immediate family, but I did by someone I would never have expected, who ended up being there for me 100%.

What I have missed the most in my process has been company and a hug. When I said goodbye to 2021, I was alone, and it was a bit sad, but without tears, I just said to myself: "Congratulations, Zuleika."

What has helped me most has been writing—writing and the company, during these seven months, of Jesus, Mary, and Joseph.

The most difficult aspect of my grief has been to go out alone and accept that my husband's time has come, that, despite his absence, he did not abandon me and was faithful to me for thirty-four years. That he loved me and did not leave me for another woman. Now, I accept it; before, I blamed him for his departure. What I would say to someone who is grieving would be that time keeps its promise and heals all wounds.

The meaning I have found has been to accept that God has other beautiful paths for me, which I will travel alone, with the faith that I will live other beautiful experiences. I have the satisfaction of having fulfilled with him 100% with excellent care; it was a sad journey, but I did not know what else to do for his health and comfort. I pleased all his cravings, and I even got him to accept God as his savior. During his last breath of life, I held his hand and even dared to tell him, almost as if giving an order, to go in peace, that I would be conformed with his departure. As you may know, it was the hardest thing I have ever said in my life. That is why I say with tears and deep sorrow: Zuleika, mission accomplished.

Zuleika M., bereaved wife

I experienced the loss of my son Yasser Hernan in a traffic accident in a sad November 2006. He was twenty-three years old and had a promising future.

And I want to share with others that, from that date on, I have expressed and lived my grief within the faith as my first spiritual resource. Then, since 2008, together with other mothers in similar grief, I have found a purpose in life by working in an organized way in an institution that provides bereavement support to others who have suffered a significant loss in their lives.

Personally, the most difficult aspect of my grief has been learning to live without my son and struggling with this terrible reality that I have had to live with. The biggest challenge I have faced has been finding a way to feel him close, even though he will never be in our lives again and is sorely missed; living with the crushing reality, which is not at all what we wish for, and trying to make sense of life without him.

A second emotional resource for processing grief has been to promote, in an organized manner, the practice of Mutual Support to contribute to our experience in the journey of helping others to transform their grief into hope and to learn ourselves in that same effort by promoting personal confidence and awareness of our emotions and needs, as well as the ability to be resilient as a mechanism to heal our wounds and take control of our lives. In this journey, I have not been alone; on the contrary, I have met many people and specialists in the subject who have provided me with tools that have allowed me to come to light with my own resources. I would like to highlight, in a special way, for her valuable guidance, the exceptional Ligia M. Houben and her 11 Principles for Transforming Your Loss, that wonderful system of strength and hope that changed the course of my grief and my life.

I have had the opportunity to discover that one of the ways, because there is no perfect way to process grief, is to share with others what we are feeling and thinking as we walk blindly, trying to find light in the dark. Well, that is grief. Also, to be aware that we are not alone in this journey is a hopeful encouragement: to be able to break the silence and eradicate loneliness from our lives, to seek and find light to get out of the abyss of shadows to which we are subjected by our own choice.

When processing my grief, I have felt relieved and understood when exchanging experiences with others who are going through the same thing, and it happens that we can perfectly understand that person who, just like us, is going through the pain of losing a loved one. We understand that we are not the only ones, and this gives us a wonderful sense of hope that things can be different for us and our families.

In this process of healing using the resource of mutual help, I have been able to identify that others, despite their grief, showed compassion and solidarity with me, that we felt each other's pain in a very strong bond. That learning and the shared experiences allowed our group to develop self-help tools that could be replicated with other groups to give accompaniment in their grieving process to more and more people suffering the loss of their loved ones. I feel that I belong to a very select group of human beings who have survived the loss of a loved one because of the understanding and empathy that characterizes us in the new reality that we have had to live.

What I have missed the most in my grief has been to learn more about why the family and others fail to understand the need and importance of processing their grief and why they fail to engage in activities that are so transformative and healing for the pain they suffer. I continue in this search until I can find some characteristics that will allow me to identify why this type of behavior occurs.

On the other hand, what has helped me the most has been working with others who have gone through the same thing since I have found meaning in my life, for which I am very grateful to God. Feeling their empathy and reaching their hearts with my testimony is a very healing and rewarding experience.

I have also found meaning in the loss of my son by allowing me to develop his legacy of life through a project of love and service to others, promoting and implementing the mutual support groups in my country, Nicaragua, in order to provide accompaniment to others who have suffered a loss like mine. The most important thing for me was to discover that what I needed to learn to do was something I already had among my qualities. God, our Lord, miraculously revealed it to me. He showed me that this talent that I did not know I had was hidden in me since my birth and that I only had to polish it by fulfilling His will and, with His mercy, filling me day by day and step by step to achieve it.

It is also worth saying that the loss of my beloved son has taught me a great lesson because it has taught me a lot about life and death. It is the least one expects, after so much suffering, to learn something, but I did. Learning to accept that what happens to a person when they lose a loved one, like a child, is a part of life that not everyone has to live. Knowing and accepting that our grandparents, parents, siblings, friends, and even ourselves will depart at a certain moment is what we have become accustomed to; it is even said to be something natural. But to accept that a child that one expects to carry our remains to our final resting place is not going to do that, but rather the opposite, that we are the ones who carry their young remains and have to say goodbye to them before their time is not something rational that we can accept. Much less understand it to be natural, and it cannot be accepted as naturally as can be expected; it does not fit into our culture or our traditions. Nevertheless, the lesson learned is that we did it; we had to learn how to face the challenge of transforming the loss into something valuable for others.

We can feel that we have contributed our experience of grief to lessen the pain of another… and it will have been worth it. It is a terrible thing to live it actively as a slow process; it is an indescribable experience that becomes a legacy of love that our departed loved ones leave to us because it is their way of telling us that they are still with us in our hearts with love stronger than ever, so strong that it gives us the power to pour it out freely to many more who may need it.

At this time, I would like to tell someone who is going through grief that once you are aware of the passing of your loved one, set out on the path of processing your grief and transforming that harsh reality, which has changed because of the loss you have suffered.

MAYRA ELENA VIVAS, bereaved mother

I experienced the loss of my 41 year old son from a drug overdose. The way I have expressed my grief has been by talking about it with people with a similar loss and with therapist. Reading, writing and lots of crying. The greatest challenge I find is that I feel most people do not associate an overdose death as a death from a disease. There is so much social stigma about the person he was…"after all he was a drug addict." "Friends" and even close "family" don't call, text or write, they just ask to how you are. I find it hard to talk to most people because I find that losing a child leaves you speechless. Most people will compare it with losing a parent, a friend, or going through situations like divorce or losing a spouse. Thankfully, no one in my circle has lost a child. Thank God!! I do believe most people mean well…it is a situation where most are left speechless. When sharing my grief with others I feel almost guilty…don't want to make anyone feel pain because of the pain I feel especially my daughters and people who loved him. I have felt understood by those who have gone through the same situation, yes. By others, maybe.

In my process, what I have missed the most is speaking in person to those who can relate. What I have found to help me the most is staying busy, being active even though it has been difficult; my daughters, my friends, my faith, and seeing and giving thanks for Jackie, his daughter whom he left us. For her not to have him makes me very sad, he was a wonderful loving father. The hardest aspect of my grief has been trying to live.

I suggest someone who is grieving to seek help. I haven't really found meaning in my loss. I hope one day I do, not yet. I think in my case it's too recent.

Luly FONNEGRA, bereaved mother

I lost my daughter Katie at the young age of 31 to a drug overdose. She went into the hospital on September 13, 2015, and remained there until she took her last breath in my arms. I felt the life go out of her body, and I will never forget that feeling. Every year around this time of the year, I relive each day spent by her side with friends, loved ones, doctors, nurses, and family. Katie was vibrant and full of life. She had just graduated from Law School and was getting ready to take the law boards. She worked out daily at her CrossFit Gym and had tons of loving friends. Katie was in recovery and seemed to be on the right track. She started up with her using behavior, and before long, I realized she was in a bad way. I offered treatment, but she declined, and at that point, I told her she had to leave the house. That was the last time I saw her. She was coming down from last night's high and was angry with me. She left, and that night, she overdosed.

The questions I play over and over in my head are, «Why didn›t you just hold onto her?» Why this and why that? One hundred things roll through my mind, and there are NO answers for any of them. So now, today, five years ago, is the time that the doctors told me Katie wasn›t coming back, and if she did, she would never be the same. Most of the top part of her brain was dead. I had to make the decision to take her off life support and let her go. This process took another eight days, and she died October 2 around 10 am in my arms, just me and her.

This is a difficult time for me as I relive all the days she was in the hospital. The faces of her friends crying and holding onto her. The ones laughing and telling "Katie" stories. The nurses who were so overwhelmingly kind and supportive, I see all of it!!

The way I have expressed my grief has been feeling anger, Depression, Tears, and Isolation, self-blame, all passed through me for a long time at any given time like a roller coaster titled FEAR. I would get pissed off at someone trying to console me, saying, "God must have needed an Angel," "I lost my Grand Mother recently," or "How are you feeling? Any better"? Depression and tears would come late at night when my mind was up and racing. "If only I had done this or that, she would be here". Isolation would come, and it felt so UNnatural as I am a huge people person. I would not express myself to my loved ones at all. Stuff, Stuff, Stuff.

I have been able to help myself move on and learned to put one foot in front of the other by starting grief therapy with Ligia. She gave me some tools to use, and through utilizing her program of sorts, I have been able to turn and make this pain count in helping others. So, for me, Prayer and Service are huge in keeping me focused and reducing the negative feelings. I have two passions that I would not let go of through this difficult time: fishing and music. I know I have to put one foot in front of the other and make my life count. This is a slow process and takes time.

The greatest challenge is the everyday struggle to keep looking toward life and its purpose. The greatest challenge is to not isolate myself from my loved ones and close friends. I need to share what's going on with me but tend to stuff as I think people don't want to hear any sad news. Lisa, my girlfriend of 15 years, has seen this mostly as well as my son. I have to work hard at communicating from the most simple level to the deepest of levels. I have been asked to journal many times, but I have been resistant to this. I want to avoid "looking" at my feelings at any cost. I try not to show sadness to my son, but he knows better. I need him not to dwell on this tragedy, but in reality, I am powerless over him and his feelings.

All of this «challenge» of sorts boils down to finding the ability to begin transforming my sadness into an awareness of the preciousness of life and what it offers. I am slowly learning to accept the good as well as the bad and use them both. I mean after all, NOTHING could be that painful, so as I work through this choice to live, I use this pain to help others in any area of life.

When sharing with others about my grief is strange, and I will tell you why. Every time I told someone about Katie overdosing, especially those who didn't know her, I HAD to clarify the fact that she went to a private school, went to the University of Miami Law School, and taught Crossfit. I couldn't leave it that she overdosed without pointing out the good things. She was such an enigma.

In the beginning, I couldn't share my grief with anyone without giant tears. I would get choked up just mentioning her. Today, five years to the day on October 2, I am able to talk about her somewhat without tearing up as much.

Honestly, I judged others› grief on my own and did not like this aspect of me. Another person might say, well, I just lost my grandpa, so I know how you feel, or I don›t have kids, but I have Dogs, and they are like my children. On and on, I would hear comparisons that would infuriate me inside, and I would want to walk away. It took so much time to have some compassion and understand that grief is grief. Who am I to pass judgment?

Many times, I will not share about my grief as I feel people don›t want to hear it again, over and over. They expect you to move on and such. This is something I will never «move on» from but will grow from and try to share in a positive and helpful way to others.

I have most definitely felt understood because I feel that anyone with a beating heart can and will understand your situation of losing a child.

In my process, what I have missed the most is everything about her, especially her laugh. Her laugh could light up a dark night. I miss her hugs. I miss her ability to argue until you throw your hands up in defeat. I miss her nonstop energy and her inappropriate language. I mean, how do you get used to the sudden "stop" from one day to the next of your vivacious 31-year-old daughter taken away? I miss holidays with Katie, cooking and baking, and I miss all her friends coming by, which keeps me feeling younger than I am. Mostly, I miss our family, torn and damaged from this sadness, trying as individuals to cope as best as they can.

What helped me the most in the beginning was going to grief therapy with Ligia, who was instrumental in the process of learning to put one foot in front of the other. A good therapist can get you talking, writing, and problem solving over time to start towards a new beginning.

Prayer was another huge staple towards stability and hope. At first, I was so angry because I would pray for God to help Katie with her addiction, never in a million years thinking He would take her. I have come to the realization that God didn't do this; in fact, Katie made this choice to use. Prayer was and is so essential to living a healthy and productive life. I need God in my life every day so He can take my pain, give me purpose, but mostly help me be of Service. I don't have any of the answers.

I think the hardest aspect of my grief has been watching what Katie's passing has done to the lives of her brother, Mother, friends, and loved ones. Watching families grow and prosper without Katie in their lives is so hard. The daily grind of missing her. I mean, I am coming up on 5 years, and not a day passes that I don't think of her. This is not something you learn to grow out of. This is not something that passes, as her death is as real as it gets. What changes is how I use her death to keep purpose in my life…

Grieving takes so much time, and there is no ending time for this. Give yourself time to process. Grief is like a roller coaster as it rises to an unbearable level one day, only to subside somewhat the next. Find a grief therapist you can talk with. Take baby steps towards opening up. Hold on close to your loved ones. Lean on them as they want to help. Journal over time about your feelings. Find a higher Power that you can pray to. Do it. Try to start anything positive over time, such as meditation, exercise, or whatever you can to keep from staying in that sadness. It will always be there; it doesn't leave. Don't blame or judge yourself for wanting to do something fun. Don't tell yourself *how I can do this when my loved one is gone*. Over time, come out of your isolation and find like-minded people you can open up to.

I will let you in on a little fact for me. What has helped me the most to get out of myself and my own pain is Service. The ability to help others, to work with others has taken me to levels of happiness I never thought possible after my daughter's death. Do not give up your passions. Over time, use them. If you don't have any, then find some. My passions are fishing, playing music, and singing. This was almost impossible to do in the beginning, but over time has been a giant source of pleasure.

So, what is the meaning of a loss? How can I find this? I would give up everything in an instant to have my daughter back in my life, but that's not going to happen. She is gone, and I am left here to sort and pick up the pieces. What have I learned? What kind of meaning can I attribute to her death?

Life is short!! Life flies by, and Katie's death has shown me this. She is not here, but her friends' new babies are. I LOVE being around the kids. They give me unconditional love and hope. I have found so much meaning in the young and have been blessed by their love.

I have and want to help others as often as I can, the service word again. This takes me out of myself and helps me to realize there are so many people needing help.

I want to be honest and live my best life whatever that entails for the rest of my days. One foot in front of the other, giving thanks for God's world surrounded by family and loved ones. Yes, I have found meaning in her loss, and I'm grateful for the time we had and the time left.

CHIP CORLETT, bereaved father

I lost my only daughter August 27, 2019. She was thirty-three years old. For the first three months, I was overwhelmed with grief and unable to function. The simplest of tasks became impossible to accomplish.

I cried day and night. As time went on, and with the help of professionals, I was able to start functioning again. I found refuge with my son and his family. My mom was still alive and not doing great. I never told her that her granddaughter had passed away. She knew and could sense my loneliness. She passed away seven months after my daughter.

I realized that it is exceedingly difficult for others to understand your pain unless they have experienced the loss of their own child. I kept my grief isolated from them. There are no words others could say that will help with your loss. I was misunderstood. I still feel isolated with my grief. Even my own husband does not understand how I feel. I do not mean that he does not feel the pain of losing his daughter, however, he does not show it or consoles me when he finds me crying.

My life will never be or feel the same. Even though it has been over two years, there are times when I am with friends or family that I withdraw from interactions.

The hardest part of my loss is knowing that I will never be able to hug or kiss her. Will never talk to her again or feel her close to me. I will never be able to have grandchildren from her. I will never hear her calling me "Mombi." She was also misunderstood.

She spent years dealing with her own pain. She suffered from chronic Lyme Disease as well as other immune disorders. I did try to help her but not having an accurate diagnosis made it more difficult to understand her pain. This is my biggest regret. I ask myself "Did I do enough?" The word ENOUGH hunts me every day, her friends and other family members would laugh and say that she was acting like an old lady. They labelled her a hypochondriac. I was always on her side. She was an amazingly simple young woman with extraordinarily little desire for materialistic things.

The only way I can continue moving forward is with a purpose. I joined a continually active real estate team with Compass. I have started to help a few clients, and this keeps me out of the house. I also started private Pilates classes twice a week.

I just became and ambassador for the Global Lyme Alliance. In 2022, I will start to promote them by going to different schools and informing the school nurses about the detrimental impact a tick bite may have on a child's life if not treated immediately.

My daughter was a prolific writer. I have started scanning and reviewing her writings. I hope to be able to do what she would have done: publish her book. Going thru her boxes I discovered that she never discarded anything she ever received from me.

As far as finding meaning in my life will be exceedingly difficult. As the years go by, I will better understand her loss. As of now, nothing has changed, and her loss is still too difficult to bear.

I would advise someone who just lost a child to find a purpose so that they may be able to move forward. You never move on!

MAGGIE SALAZAR, bereaved mother

I am experiencing the painful loss of my soulmate, my father. My father passed away suddenly from a heart attack. Initially I sought professional help as I was in severe emotional distress. I still have a difficult time expressing my emotions to others as it is very painful to talk about it. On special days, I seek the support from my family and friends.

I talk to my dad on a daily basis as if he were still here. I feel that due to my busy lifestyle I have not had the opportunity to continue seeking help to continue expressing my emotions.

The greatest challenge with my grief has been accepting my father's death and that my life will never be the same. It is very difficult for me to accept that life has to continue without him being with us. Every time there is a special occasion or a milestone in my life, or one of my daughter's lives, or one of my family member's lives, it brings me so much sadness that he is not here for those occasions. I view everything in my life as before my father's death and after my father's death.

It has been very difficult to share my grief with others. I try not to express my emotions too much around my family as I fear that it will bring them sadness and emotional pain. There are a few particular friends that I can share some of my feelings with on the days that are very hard for me. I feel that there are many people that do not understand my feelings as they have not had a similar loss or have gone through the grieving process. I believe it is difficult for people that have not experienced such a great loss to provide words or actions that can bring me true comfort.

I have definitely felt misunderstood. Everyone grieves in their own way and differently from others. Some people believe that everyone's grief journey is the same. Some people tell me that grief will get better over time and that I need to be stronger. Grief and the pain of the loss does not get better with time. The pain becomes part of you, and you have to live with it daily, but it does not lessen. I believe grief never ends.

I miss my father so much. I think about him constantly throughout the day.

He is my first thought when I wake up every day. We had an extremely close relationship, and I was very dependent on him. He was involved in everything in my life, and I used to spend time with him every day. I miss my normal life with him, our routines, our times spend together, our conversations, all of his support. He was my best friend, my confidant.

I had such a great relationship with my dad and feel so blessed that he was so amazing and special, and the rock to our family. Knowing that I had the best relationship with him while he was alive provides me with strength and comfort in my grieving process.

I feel his love and guidance in my heart and feel him still so alive within me.

I talk to him daily as he if he were still alive, and I include him in all my thoughts and prayers. I feel blessed that I have a very strong support system which includes my beautiful mother, siblings, husband, daughters, family, and friends, and my dog.

In my career as a palliative care nurse practitioner, I assist patients and families in dealing with terminal illness, symptom management, loss, and end of life. I support them in their grieving process. I believe the process that I am living with my father's death has provided me with a better understanding of their process and allows me to be more compassionate in my role. Additionally, I have learned that we have no control of life and death and has allowed me to accept more the process of end of life. Even though my father's death was very hard because it was so sudden and unexpected, I have comfort in knowing that it did not entail chronic pain and suffering.

The hardest aspect has been accepting the way his life ended so suddenly and traumatic. My father looked well and was smiling and laughing just prior to his event. I was with him when he collapsed and took his last breath and that is a painful image I have to live with daily. Even though I rarely ever thought about the possibility of my father dying, part of me imagined his end of life would have been different. I imagined a different scene where I would have had the opportunity to have had end-of-life conversations with him and held his hand and said my farewells.

It has been very difficult for me to see pictures or videos of my father. I am hoping that one day I am able to see images of him or hear his voice in videos, but as the present moment it is an extremely painful process for me.

To someone who has suffered a loss, I would suggest acknowledging the loss and allow themselves to go through the grieving process. You cannot stop or avoid the process, you have to live it, you have to feel the emotions and the pain that comes with it. I would suggest them to express their grief and find support in family and friends. To keep in mind that everyone is different and deals with loss differently.

Life is beautiful but also very painful. We will all experience different losses throughout our lives. Most of us will experience the loss of loved ones and we will have to learn new skills in building resilience. I always remind myself that my father would have wanted me to continue "living" life, to enjoy the moments that are given to me daily because life and all the moments are temporary.

I will never be able to find meaning in my father's death, but there is meaning to the way that I have responded to his death and how it has changed me. I cannot change my father's death and how it happened, but I can change how I continue to live after his death. I have a different appreciation for life because I know how temporary it really is. I am trying to focus more on moments lived with my loved ones and living one day at a time. The love and guidance my father always gave me has provided me with the necessary skills to do the same for my daughters. I am surrounding myself with love and support from others. I am very compassionate in assisting others who are living through some loss. I have found purpose in working with patients and families at end of life and guiding them through the process. I know my father would be very proud of how I have found some meaning in this painful process of us being apart.

Mio C., bereaved daughter

I have experienced different losses. The first was the separation from my parents when I was six years old. I think I am over it now, although if I write about it today it is because I feel the pain that separation caused me. My father passed away twenty years ago. The pain of his passing was immense, because he was a present, loving father, dedicated to his children. My mother, with whom I grew up until I got married, was always by my side and her joy, which is contagious, has allowed me to overcome that pain.

Another loss, the most painful, was that of my firstborn when she was almost thirty-eight years old, leaving behind an adorable five-year-old grandson. We lost our daughter suddenly. We were separated geographically from our grandson. It has been a complex grief, as it involved two losses at the same time, with some unfavorable conditions in the relationship between the two families.

Living without my daughter for the past four years has been a challenge. She filled my life and my spaces. She was very similar to me. Managing to have an existence within normalcy and trying to continue living as I did before has been difficult, but I have fought for my marriage, my three children, and my nine grandchildren. I confess that the fight has been for them more than for me. They may tell me that it is a mistake, but it is my reality!

At this moment, I am experiencing an unexpected grief, which is the loss of material possessions, and this has resulted in losing my peace. After having attained a very comfortable standard of living, with more than deserved privileges given to us by our Lord, we have received a hard blow as a result of the COVID-19, something very sad and confusing, because at the age of sixty-five years, it implies practically to start all over again.

The biggest challenge I have had in my grief as an adult—after the death of my father and daughter—has been to resume my normal life, struggling to continue with the structures and traditions of a family. For example, now that we have just gone through Christmas, I remember how difficult it was to decorate my house having lost my daughter just two months earlier. To smile as much as possible at a Christmas celebration. I always mentioned her in every blessing at the table, even though the words could barely escape my lips.

The challenges have been many: to resume my social life with responsibilities in charitable institutions, to resume the desire to feel like a couple because, at times, I felt that I could not enjoy myself if I was in deep pain. The challenges have been many...

Sharing my grief with others has been positive. I have not wanted anyone to feel pity; I have just wanted to express my feelings with the people who I know are my support and have known me for years—my childhood friends. With my mother and my older sister, I feel that I give them my soul and they understand me. I must say that my children and my husband are forces that help me to move forward. They understand my sadness, the absence of my daughter and try to fill a little bit of the void she left me. It is not vanity, I feel that when my daughter left, my world ceased to be what it was. Today I look back and I had a life full of activities, happiness, joy and I no longer feel the same. My children and especially my grandchildren are the ones that make me laugh and enjoy.

What helped me the most at a given moment was the presence of my family, prayer, nature, the people who live in my soul and the pleasant memories with my daughter. I speak more about her departure, as it has been the hardest thing I have gone through. I am aware that she is at peace and that helps me.

The most difficult aspect is the absence. With my father, it was a strange feeling because he did not make it through heart surgery, and we were not prepared. It was all very fast. With my daughter, it was the same: she went to sleep and did not wake up. How difficult, I did not have time to prepare myself to internalize that you love so much and suddenly cannot see them or touch them.

I suggest allowing yourself to cry, to think, to remember, and not letting anyone try to direct your grief. When I say "directing the grief," I am referring to people who do not have the training to help. Grief counseling with professionals is a great help. They know how to direct us, especially when they are people touched by spirituality. Grief is unique to each person, and everyone experiences it in their own way. I know a mother who lost her son in a traffic accident, and she reacted very differently from me. It was not that I thought she handled it better than I did but that she recovered much faster.

I was glad to learn that grief is unique and can only be handled by those who grieve in the way they feel is best.

The only meaning I have found is that life is gone in an instant and that I am not afraid of the transition to death because I hope to meet my loved ones.

I do not want to end without mentioning a very special grief, my aunt Mima, who was my grandmother, mother, aunt, friend. She died almost at the age of 101. I miss her every day, but her departure was full of love and joy. I could feel how such a sweet and special being said goodbye singing to the Lord because she was convinced that she was going to a very special place.

JWM, bereaved mother

Final Reflection

My mother died exactly a year and a half ago. Today is December 7, 2021, and I am reaching the end of this book. When I began writing its first pages, my mother had only been gone for a month. Then, I stopped writing for seven months because I dedicated myself to the book about her life. Once it was published, I made it a goal to review everything I had written at the start of this book, as it was written in a mix of English and Spanish. As I read it, I realized how I was feeling inside: It was like a journal where I poured out all my pain; I put all my feelings, all my thoughts, on paper without editing, simply pouring them onto the paper. Deciding what to include in the book was an intense process because there were too many thoughts written on paper and recorded on my phone. The process itself, however, was healing because by reliving those moments, I exposed myself to the pain, which, in turn, helped me to continue processing it.

Writing this book has been an incredible journey, inspired by the great love I feel for my mother and by the great desire to help all those people who, like you and me, are grieving.

It has been a unique experience because I have been in permanent contact with my inner self. Apart from living my grief, I have been able to observe it, understand it, and embrace it as a part of me, as I have learned to live with the loss of my mother. From climbing the hills to descending into the valleys, it has been a highly healing process because, in addition to helping me through my grief, I have wanted, through the development of my own grief, to accompany you in yours.

It has been a transformative process, as this book has been an offering of love. And love is eternal.

Final Words

Upon reaching the ending of this book, I wholeheartedly hope that you have felt accompanied in your grieving process, and I hold the hope that you have opened up your mind and heart to allow the light of your loved one to guide you and inspire you to live a life of meaning, peace, and love.

I also want to thank my mother because through her example of life, she taught me what love, faith, resilience, and the joy of living are.

Her love lives on in my heart, and her legacy endures with her immortal phrase: "¡Arriba Corazones[tm]!"

Bibliography

Adams, Christine A. (2003). *ABC's of Grief. A Handbook for Survivors.* New York, NY: Baywood Publishing Company, Inc.

Amen, D. G. (2021). *Your Brain Is Always Listening: Tame the Hidden Dragons That Control Your Happiness, Habits, and Hang-Ups.* Carol Stream, Il: Tyndale House Publishing.

Ariès, P. (1975). *Western Attitudes toward Death: From the Middle Ages to the Present* (The Johns Hopkins Symposia in Comparative History). Baltimore, MD: Johns Hopkins University Press.

Bowlby, J. (2005). *The Making and Breaking of Affectional Bonds.* Second edition. New York, NY: Routledge.

Bowlby, J. (1982). Loss: Sadness and Depression. Volume 3 (1982). New York, NY: Basic Books.

Breitbart, W. S., & Poppito, S. R. (2014). *Individual Meaning-Centered Psychotherapy for Patients with Advanced Cancer. A Treatment Manual.* New York, NY: Oxford University Press.

Brené, B. (2017). *Rising Strong: The Reckoning. The Rumble. The Revolution.* New York, NY: Random House.

Calhoun, L. G., & Tedeschi, R. G. (2014). *Facilitating Posttraumatic Growth: A Clinician's Guide.* 1st ed. New York, NY: Routledge.

Carmody, M. (2011). *Letters to my son. Turning Loss to Legacy.* MN: Beaver's Pond Press.

Casablanca, A. and Casablanca, G. (2020). *The Dying Art of Leadership: How Leaders Can Help Grieving Employees Excel at Work.* Pennsauken Township, NJ: Bookbaby.

Case, S. (2020). *Hardcore Grief Recovery: An Honest Guide to Getting through Grief without the Condolences, Sympathy, and Other BS* (F*ck Death; Healing Mental Health Journal for Adults After the Loss of a Loved One). Naperville, Il: Sourcebooks.

Castelblanco, H. Lopez, B. and Castelblanco, J. (2021). *The 15 tasks of grief.* Independently published.

Chaurand, A., Feixas, G. and Neimeyer, R. (2011). "The Loss History Inventory (HPI): Presentation and clinical utility". *Revista de Psicoterapia,* pp. 95-101.

Coelho, P. (2018). *The alchemist. A fable to follow your dreams.* New York, NY: HarperCollins.

Collier, L. (2016). *Growth after trauma Why are some people more resilient than others-and can it be taught?* Volume 47, N. 10. Print edition: p. 48.

Corr, C. A., Corr, D. M., & Doka, K. J. (2018). *Death and Dying, Life and Living.* 8th. Edition. Boston, MA: Cengage Learning.

Courtney, C. C. (2012). *Healing Through Illness, Living Through Dying: Guidance and Rituals for Patients, Families, and Friends.* Scottsdale, AZ: Danton Press.

Daneault, S. (2008). *The Wounded Healer: Can this idea be of use to family physicians?* Canadian family physician. Médecin de famille canadien, 54(9), 1218-1225.

Devine, M. (2017). *It is OK That You're Not OK: Meeting Grief and Loss in a Culture That Does not Understand.* Boulder, CO: Sounds True.

Didion, J. (2003). *The Year of Magical Thinking.* New York, NY: Vintage International, Vintage Books.

Doka J. K. (2002). *Disenfranchised Grief. New Directions, Challenges, and Strategies for Practice.* Champaign, IL: Research Press.

Doka, K. J., & Davidson, J. D. (2014). *Living with Grief: Who We Are, how We Grieve.* Kenneth J. New York, NY: Routledge.

Enright, R. D. *Forgiveness is a Choice: A Step-by-Step Process for Resolving Anger and Restoring Hope.* First edition. Washington, DC: APA LifeTools.

Frankl, V. (1984). *Man's Search for Meaning.* New York, NY: Washington Square Press.

Freud, S. (1989). *The interpretation of dreams.* Círculo de Lectores. Gilbert, R. B. (2014). *Finding your way after the death of a parent.* Notre Dame, IN: Ave Maria Press, Inc.

Gil-Juliá, B., Bellver, A. and Ballester, R. "Duelo: Evaluación, diagnóstico y tratamiento". *Psycho-oncology.* 2008, Volume 5, pp. 103-116.

Hay, L. L. Hay, L. *The Power is Within You* (Original title: *The Power is Within You*). Hay House Carlsbad, CA: 1991.

Heath, I. (2007). *Matters of Life and Death*. First edition. New York, NY: Routledge.

Houben, L. M. (2007). *Transform your loss. An anthology of for- tance and hope.* Sevierville, TN: Insight Publishing.

Houben, L. M. (2016). *Transforming Grief & Loss Workbook: Activities, Exercises & Skills to Coach Your Client Through Life Transitions.* Eau Claire, WI: PESI Publishing & Media.

Jeffreys, S. J. (2011). *Helping Grieving People-When tears are not enough: A Handbook for Care Providers.* New York: NY: Routledge.

Kastenbaum, R. J. (2016). *Death, Society and Human Experience.* Eleventh edition. New York, NY: Routledge.

Kastenbaum, R. J. (1969). "Death and bereavement in later life". A. H. Kuts- cher (ed.), *Death and bereavement. Springfield*, IL: Charles C. Thomas.

Kauffmann, J. (2002). *Loss of the Assumptive World: A Theory of Traumatic Loss.* First edition. NY: Routledge.

Kessler, David (2019). *Finding Meaning. The Sixth Stage of Grief.* New York, NY: Scribner.

Klass, D. Silverman, P. R. and Nickman, S. (1996). *Continuing Bonds: New Understandings of Grief* (Death Education, Aging and Health Care) First edition. Milton Park, Abingdon: Taylor & Francis.

Kumar, S. M. (2005). *Grieving Mindfully*. Oakland, CA: New Harbin- ger Publications, Inc.

Kushner, H. S. (2004). *When Bad Things Happen to Good People*. New York, NY: Anchor Books.

Lerner, M. D. (2006). *It is OK Not to Be OK... Right Now*. Melville, N.Y.: Mark Lerner Associates, Inc. Publications.

Lewis, C. S. (1961). *A Grief Observed*. New York, NY: Harper San Francisco, HarperCollins.

Miller M. D. (2012). *Complicated grief in late life*. Dialogues Clin Neurosci. June; 14(2): 195-202.

Mitsch, R. R. and Brookside, L. (1993). *Grieving the Loss of Someone You Love: Daily Meditations to Help You Through the Grieving Process*. Dublin, Republic of Ireland: Brookside Publishing House.

Myers, E. (1986). *When Parents Die. A Guide for Adults*. NY: Penguin Books.

Neimeyer, R. (2007). *Learning from loss. A guide for coping with grief*. Barcelona: Paidós Pocket.

Neimeyer, R., Hogan, N., & Laurie, A. (2009). "The measurement of grief: Psychometric considerations in the assessment of reactions to bereavement." Stroebe, M., Hansson, R., Schut, H., and Stroebe, W. (ed.), *Handbook of Bereavement Research and Practice: Advances in theory and intervention* (pp. 133-161). Washington: American Psychological Association.

Neimeyer, R. A. (2015). *Techniques of Grief Therapy (Series in Death, Dying, and Bereavement)*. 1st ed. New York, NY: Routledge.

Nowen, H. J. M. (1979). *The Wounded Healer: Ministry in Contempo- rary Society*. Australia: Doubleday Books.

Payàs, A. (2010). *The tasks of grief: Psychotherapy of grief from an integrative relational model*. Barcelona: Paidós.

Riso, W. (2020). *Más fuerte que la adversidad*. Mexico: Planeta. Rodríguez, A. (2015). *Duelo*. Caracas, Venezuela: Oscar Todtmann editores.

Roldan, M. (2021). *Navigating Grief: A Guided Journal: Prompts and Exercises for Reflection and Healing*. Emeryville, CA: Rockridge Press.

Rosenblatt, P. C. (1996). "Grief that does not end". D. Klass, P. R. Silver- man, and S. L. Nickman (eds.), *Continuing bonds: New understandings of grief* (pp. 45-58). Taylor & Francis.

Singer, M. A. (2007). *The Untethered Soul: The Journey Beyond Your Self*. First edition. Oakland, CA: New Harbinger Publications/ Noetic Books.

Smith, C. B. (2018). *Anxiety: The Missing Stage of Grief: A Revolutio- nary Approach to Understanding and Healing the Impact of Loss*. New York, NY: Da Capo Press.

Smith, H. I. (2004). *Grievers Ask*. Minneapolis, MN: Augsburg, For- tress Publisher.

Stroebe, M. and Schut, H. (2016). "Overload: A Missing Link in the Dual Process Model?". *Omega-Journal of Death and Dying*. Volume 74(1), 96-109.

Stroebe, M. (2018). "The Poetry of Grief: Beyond Scientific Portrayal." *Omega*. Volume: 78, 67-96. First published online: 8 August 2018.

Taylor, R. (1992). *When Life is Changed Forever.* Eugene, OR: Harvest House Publishers.

Tedeschi, R. G. et al (2018). *Posttraumatic Growth: Theory, Research, and Applications.* 1st ed. New York, NY: Routledge.

Tedeschi, R. G, Calhoun, L. G. (1996). *The Posttraumatic Growth Inventory: measuring the positive legacy of trauma.* J Trauma Stress. July; 9(3), 455-71.

Tedeschi R. G., and Callhoun, L. G. (2007). *PTG: Strange blessings.* ADEC keynote presentation, Indianapolis.

Welshons J. E. (2003). *Awakening from Grief.* Makawao, Maui: Inner Ocean Publishing.

Wolfelt, A. (2016). *Grief One Day at a Time: 365 Meditations to Help You Heal After Loss.* Fort Collins, CO: Companion Press.

Young, D. A. (2021). *How to take your spiritual temperature: Discover the 10 dimensions of your spirituality: from distress to joy.* Separate publication (November 10, 2021).

Zuba, T. (2015). *Permission to Mourn: A New Way to Do Grief.* Roc- kford, IL: Bish Press.

Resources. Articles in web pages

Brenness, B. December 24, 2019. The Grief Keeps Coming.

https://medium.com/swlh/the-grief-keeps-coming-3ef76174d62a

Collier, L. November 2016, Vol. 47, N. 10, Growth After Trauma.

https://www.apa.org/monitor/2016/11/growth-trauma

Dyregrov, A., Dyregrov, K. and Kristensen, P. September 9, 2014. What do we know about grief and complicated grief?

https://psykologisk.no/2014/09/ hva-vet-vi-om-sorg-og-komplisert-sorg/

Haley, E. A Grief Concept You Should Care About: Continuing Bonds.

https://whatsyourgrief.com/grief-concept-care-continuing- bonds/

Haley, E. The Utility of Laughter in Times of Grief.

https://whatsyourgrief.com/laughter-in-times-of-grief

Robson, D. July 31, 2020. The benefits of anger: the upside of doing things angrily.

https://www.bbc.com/mundo/vert-fut-53548985

Stroebe, M., Chan, C. L. W., & Chow, A. Y. M. (2014). Guilt in Bereave- ment: A Review and Conceptual Framework, Death Studies, 38:3, 165-171. https://doi.org/10.1080/07481187.2012.738770

https://grief.com/the-five-stages-of-grief/#:~:text=The%20five%20 stages%2C%20denial%2C%20anger%2C%20,some%20linear%2 0timeli- ne%20in%20in%20grief

Raymond, C. Updated July 21, 2020

https://www.verywellmind.com/decisions-to-delay-if-youre-grieving-4065127

Anxiety and Depression Association of America.

https://adaa.org/understanding-anxiety/facts-statistics

https://mygriefandloss.org/guilt-and-grief

https://www.mayoclinic.org/es -es/healthy-lifestyle/fitness/in-depth/the-real-secret-to-a-healthy-heart/art-20270834

Owchar, N. Nov. 15, 2019. Author adds a sixth stage of grief, one he is had to live

https://www.latimes.com/entertainment-arts/books/story/2019-11-15/finding-meaning-david-kessler

Kristensen, P. Dyregrov, K. and Dyregrov, A. (2021). March 16, 2022. https://tidsskriftet.no/en/2017/04/klinisk-oversikt/what- distinguishes-prolonged-grief-disorder-depression.

CARENOTES

Parrot, L. *Dealing with the Anger that Comes with Grief.*

Stout, N. *When the Healing Is not Happening.*

VIDEOS

Ward, M. Marguerite Ward Updated, February 7, 2022.

https://www.businessinsider.com/bereavement-leave-asking-time-off-work-funeral-2020-5

https://www.youtube.com/watch?v=Sl7UwUOlTLQ&t=434s Tony Robbins podcast: Breaking Patterns and Finding Inner Peace.

206 Transforming your grief. Conversation with Tito Lagos-Bassett, March 14, 2021.

https://www.youtube.com/watch?v=UrSDuysI2Ps&t=147s

https://www.youtube.com/watch?v=WcKVt8f6rq0 talking to Father Alberto

Deepak Chopra on how to cope with loss during the coronavirus pandemic https://youtu.be/LBFufOhggvM

Moloney, P. January 22, 2020. Coping with Grief and Loss with Linking Objects.

https://www.youtube.com/watch?v=Nx2VYcbV0Nw

About the Author

Ligia M. Houben, MA, FT, CPC, is a certified grief counselor, certified thanatologist, and a professional Life Transitions and Grief Coach. She is an educator at heart in the area of grief and loss transformation and life transitions. She is the founder of My Meaningful Life, LLC, as well as The Center for Transforming Lives, located in Miami, Florida. She earned a dual B.A. in Psychology and Religious Studies from the University of Miami and an M.A. in Religious Studies from Florida International University, where she also earned a graduate certification in Gerontology. She has a Masters in Positive Psychology from *La Salle Centro Universitario* in Madrid. Ligia also has a graduate certification in Loss and Healing from the University of St. Thomas. *She is an* associate m e m b e r of ADEC (the Association for Death, Education and Counseling) and the American Academy of Grief Counseling. She has taken her message from corporations to hospitals through seminars and workshops. Her seminar "Transforming Grief and Loss. Strategies to Help Your Clients Through Challenging Life

Transitions" has been presented in more than 100 cities in the United States. The seminar is based on the methodology Ligia created: "The 11 Principles of Transformation®," which includes elements of positive psychology, neuro-linguistic programming, mindfulness, and post-traumatic growth. This system was introduced in her self-help book, dedicated to the memory of her father, *Transform Your Loss. Your Guide to Strength and Hope,* and is offered as an online as well as face-to-face program.

She firmly believes that we all have a purpose and a mission in this life. Part of that purpose has been to carry on her parents' legacy. In 2017, she published her father's biography in the book *Julio Martínez. El hombre. El padre. El empresario.* In 2021, she published her mother's biography in the book, *¡Arriba Corazones! Celebrando la vida de mi madre centenaria.*

She has a great passion for life and believes that each of us, through our attitude and beliefs, has the ability to live a purposeful and meaningful existence despite any transition or loss we may face. Her specialization in gerontology was inspired precisely by the great love she professed for her centenarian mother, Alicia Gallegos de Martínez, to whom she provided loving care during the last years of her life.

Annex

ABOUT YOUR GRIEVING PROCESS.
QUESTIONNAIRE TO DEVELOP THE STORIES

- What type of loss do you experience or have you experienced?
- How have you expressed your grief?
- What has been the biggest challenge in your process?
- How have you felt about sharing your grief with others?
- Have you felt misunderstood?
- What have you missed the most in your process?
- What has helped you the most?
- What has been the most difficult aspect of your grief?
- What would you suggest to someone who is grieving?
- Have you found meaning in your loss?

SERVICES OFFERED BY LIGIA M. HOUBEN

- The 11 Principles of Transformation® methodology: Ligia M. Houben offers her system through seminars and workshops that she teaches nationally and internationally. The 11 Principles of Transformation® can be applied to other types of losses, such as divorce, loss of a loved one, loss of a loved one, loss of a spouse, loss of a family member, etc., health, work, homeland, or any other painful transition. Ligia also offers her system in virtual modality in online programs. She offers them both as self-paced and group *coaching*. Additionally, she offers her methodology as a program to certify *coaches*, group facilitators and mental health professionals.

- Consulting and *coaching* on grief and transformation: Ligia M. Houben offers consulting to organizations and companies on how to manage and transform grief, as well as individual and group *coaching*.
- In addition to consulting, *coaching* and seminars on the subjects of grief and loss, Ligia also focuses on the topic of personal growth, living life with purpose, and using our minds to be the person we want to be.

A GIFT FOR THE READER

You can access your free *Accompanying Workbook* through the following link: *ligiahouben.com/workbook*

CONTACT INFORMATION

- The Center for Transforming Lives (305) 666-9942
- Cellular (305) 299-5370
- E-mail info@ligiahouben.com
- or visit the pages:
- https://ligiahouben.com/
- https://www.ligiahoubentraining.com/

- Podcast: Transformando el duelo/Transforming Grief
- You can reach her on social media:
- Facebook https://www.facebook.com/ligiahouben
- Instagram https://www.instagram.com/ligia_houben/
- LinkedInn https://www.linkedin.com/in/ligiahouben/
- You can subscribe to her YouTube channel:
- https://www.youtube.com/@LigiaMHouben

OTHER BOOKS IN ENGLISH

Transform your Loss. Your Guide to Strength and Hope.
Counseling Hispanics through Loss, Grief, and Bereavement.
Transforming Grief and Loss. Workbook.

BOOKS IN SPANISH BY LIGIA M. HOUBEN

Transforma Tu Pérdida. Una Antología de Fortaleza y Esperanza.
La Virgen María y la Mujer Nicaragüense: Historia y Tradición.
Julio Martínez: El hombre. El padre. El empresario. (biography of her father).
¡Arriba Corazones! Celebrando la vida de mi vida centenaria. (biography of her mother).

Allow Me to Live My Grief...
and Heal From the Inside Out
by Ligia M. Houben
was published in the USA.
October 2024

www.ingramcontent.com/pod-product-compliance
Lightning Source LLC
Chambersburg PA
CBHW051933290426
44110CB00015B/1964